RAF GATE GUARDS

RAF GATE GUARDS

compiled by

Jim Simpson

and

Kev Darling

A Royal Air Force Aviation Society Project

Airlife
England

First published in the UK in 1992
by Airlife Publishing Ltd

British Library Cataloguing in Publication Data
Simpson, Jim
RAF gate guards.
1. Military aircraft
I. Title
629.133334

ISBN 1-85310-166-4

Printed by Livesey Limited, Shrewsbury

Airlife Publishing Ltd.

101 Longden Road, Shrewsbury SY3 9EB, England.

CONTENTS

FOREWORD

by Air Vice-Marshal R. M. Austin, AFC, RAF,
President of the Royal Air Force Aviation Society

As President and one of the founder members of the Royal Air Force Aviation Society, I am delighted to be invited to write this Foreword to the Society's first publication. Gate guardian aircraft have a particular fascination for the aviation enthusiast because, whilst being very public and often rather dramatic aircraft on their mountings, they are sometimes imposters which never flew in the markings they bear; indeed one or two never flew in the Royal Air Force. Such secrets are revealed herein.

To the best of our knowledge, this book is totally accurate and it reflects the very considerable research conducted by the Society members. I hope you enjoy reading it as much as we enjoyed creating it.

THE ROYAL AIR FORCE AVIATION SOCIETY

The Royal Air Force Aviation Society (RAFAS) was formed in 1985 to cater for the interests of aviation enthusiasts within the RAF. It is officially recognised in the RAF as a hobby society and is sponsored by the Hobbies and Handicrafts Board of the RAF. It admits members from all the regular services and from those in the full time employ of any part of the Ministry of Defence; it also admits honorary members.

Its principal aim is to promote a healthy interest in aviation within the RAF — this may sound odd to the lay reader who might think that all who serve in the RAF are interested in aviation but I can assure you that this is definitely not the case! It does this by means of arranging visits, lectures and competitions. To keep its far-flung members in touch, a quarterly newsletter is published which includes articles of aviation interest.

The production of this book is the first society project that has borne fruit. It has of course been principally the work of the compilers that has achieved this but many members have contributed in smaller ways. It is therefore a representation of the interests of the members of the Society.

So, if you are reading this and wear a British military uniform or work for the British Ministry of Defence or could claim some reasonably useful or close link with the aims of the Society, you are no doubt interested in aviation and you are probably eligible for membership. Why not join us?

Squadron Leader Peter Russell-Smith
Chairman RAF Aviation Society
RARDE
Fort Halstead
Sevenoaks
Kent

ACKNOWLEDGEMENTS

Listed below are many people who went out of their way to help compile this book. Unfortunately space does not allow the listing of the many RAF Public Relations Officers who answered my letters and telephone calls; to them I say thank you. If I have missed anyone out particularly those RAFAS members who wrote or rang with snippets I am truly sorry but thank you all the same.

Air Britain
Air Historical Branch
R. C. B. Ashworth
AVM R. Austin, AFC RAF
Wg Cdr P. Ayerst, RAF (Retd)
Mick Allen
Steven J. Bond
Robert A. Bell
Sqn Ldr J. Bradshaw, RAF
BAe Brough
BAe Warton
Ian G. Cave
Ralph Clucas
DAW, RAF College Cranwell
Graham Day, Air Historical Branch (RAF)
R. King, Air Historical Branch (RAF)
A. Eagle
D. Fairhead
Flt Lt C. J. Farmer, RAFVR
Fleet Air Arm Museum
Chris Hobson
Mrs J. Killick, RAE Bedford
Martin Henderson
Sqn Ldr Hands, Editor *Sealand Roundabout*
Wg Cdr M. James
John Kyte
Dave McCarthy
MAP
Flt Lt Mathison, RAF Honington
Mr J. B. Pearson, BAE Brough
RAE Bedford
RAF Museum
A. Ritson
G. Roberts
D. Ransom
Flt Lt Robertson, RAF
S. Robertson
Sqn Ldr P. Russell-Smith, RAF
R. Shaw
Cpl J. Sheehan, S.S.Stats & Enquiries MOD
Mr Solomon, BAE Brough
John Steptoe
Glen Stanley
Dave Stafford
R. C. Sturtivant
J. A. Todd
P. Wright
J. Webber

INTRODUCTION

Normally the first aircraft a visitor to a Royal Air Force Station confronts is the gate guard. Over the years they have taken many forms: mostly they have been time expired or surplus aircraft, in some cases Bloodhound missiles (RAF Wyton still has one on display), and now in the case of RAF Henlow, a large RADAR Scanner has appeared, prompting a local newspaper to class it as the world's largest speed-trap. Whatever has been used, it has nearly always either reflected the Station's particular role or commemorated a link with a past squadron, and sometimes both.

The aim of this book has been to try and identify as many as possible of those aircraft that have acted as gate guards at home and abroad, be it past or present.

Of those aircraft now acting as station gate guards or, in certain stations, squadron gate guards, we have researched and written a comprehensive history of each one. In a selected few cases, of some that have since been removed, we have researched and written a chronological calendar of events listing the major events in the aircraft's life. It would have been impossible, due to lack of space, to research each one for inclusion so these are a few from personal choice. In the case of earlier gate guards we have included station by station (many long since closed) their gate guards with the dates as far as possible when they served. We have also tried to include at least one photograph of each aircraft showing it on display and in operational service. For this aspect of the book we have acquired many previously unpublished photographs which in certain cases are very rare.

Probably the first aircraft to be used as a gate guard was Spitfire F MkVb BM597, at RAF Hednesford from 1945. This aircraft was subsequently used for nearly 45 years in a similar role (mostly at Church Fenton) before being allocated for restoration to flying condition in 1989. Many of the first gate guards began to appear from the early 1950s; usually on the initiative of a Station Commander who had managed to acquire a surplus aircraft and put it on display. In the early days this was invariably a Spitfire due to the numbers available. It comes as no surprise then to find that the most popular types used were fighters, possibly due to the ease with which they could be transported. Spitfires, Meteors, Javelins, Vampires, Hunters and Lightnings have all been common gate guards, and at the end of 1988 there were some 90 plus aircraft on display of which 16 were Spitfires. In 1989 this was to change dramatically. Of the larger aircraft employed, only the Canberra has been used in any quantity. More recently the Vulcan has been used but probably due to the cost incurred preparing them for display, many were eventually scrapped with only one now remaining on display in the UK.

These days, the whole spectrum of RAF aircraft is represented, from several examples of the diminutive Gnat T1 trainer through to predatory Lightning and the mighty Victor and Vulcan 'V-bombers'. At RAF Lossiemouth they have an ex-Royal Navy Buccaneer S1, representing both a past link when the station was a Royal Naval Air Station and its present role as the last home of the RAF Buccaneer force. At RAF Sealand they have 'Hunter F4 WT520', which is really an ex-Danish AF Hunter F51 'E-408'; following its return to the UK this aircraft has acted as the gate guard to three different RAF Stations. In the last few years more modern types have begun to appear. At RAF Bruggen, West Germany, is Prototype Jaguar S07, XW563 displayed as 'XX822'; this aircraft once appeared at Farnborough as the Jaguar International. At RAF Leuchars, the first Phantom appeared in September 1989 replacing a Lightning, and at RAF Wittering and Gutersloh both stations have an example of the unique VTOL Harrier on display. Helicopters have not been forgotten, with several ex-Search and Rescue Whirlwinds on display, although at RAF Odiham they display XR453 in the camouflage colour scheme it carried whilst operational with No.230 Squadron.

Two major events have affected the gate guard scene over the years. The first, in 1968, was the making of the *Battle of Britain* film. Many surviving Spitfires and Hurricanes were loaned to the film company (via Spitfire Productions Ltd). Unfortunately not all found their way back from whence they had come, although many did return as gate guards. The second, and by far the most dramatic, was a change of policy by the Ministry of Defence towards the historic aircraft in its care.

In June 1988 the MOD announced two important decisions: the first was the removal from gate guard duties of all Spitfires and Hurricanes. This was an effort to protect these older aircraft from further ravages by the British weather. The only exceptions would be those stations that displayed their aircraft indoors. The only station that fell into this latter category was RAF Manston, although No.1 Squadron at Wittering who own Spitfire LA255, keep it hangar-bound when weather conditions are unsuitable. For those stations who had given up either one of these types and could claim a link from the past with either type it was decided to purchase plastic replicas as replacements. Stations such as Wattisham and Abingdon who had no past link with either type would not receive a replica. By early 1990 only Biggin Hill (one of each), Coltishall (Hurricane), Benson (Spitfire), and Turnhouse (Spitfire) had received replicas. Of the real Spitfires, most were taken to RAF St Athan and put into store to await their fate. A few, namely those aircraft from Sealand, Church Fenton, Uxbridge, Northolt and Bentley Priory, were allocated to civilian ownership for restoration to flying condition. It is anticipated that the first of these rebuilds should be airworthy sometime in 1991.

The second decision by the MOD was to limit stations to only one gate guard. A number of stations kept several aircraft on display; Manston had four, Lossiemouth, Wyton and Locking three each. By the end or 1989 most of these extra gate guards had been either sold or scrapped on site. Although this second decision might seem petty, the reasoning was sound; RAF Stations are not allocated manpower to look after display aircraft, relying more often than not on volunteers working mostly in their spare time to carry out the essential maintenance to keep them in a safe and presentable condition. Some smaller stations just did not have the manpower to cope, therefore aircraft became tatty, reflecting neither the good name of the station, nor of the RAF. It is true to say that a few stations employed local ATC cadets, but this was usually just to clean the aircraft once a year.

Despite these reductions in numbers and removal of the vulnerable older types, there have been, and still are, a number of very interesting aircraft acting as gate guards and it is worth highlighting a few here. At RAF Brawdy, for instance, is Hunter FGA9 XE624. When this aircraft served with No.1 Squadron at West Raynham it was the regular mount of Flt Lt Allan Pollock. He was the pilot who flew under Tower Bridge on 6 April 1968 (although not in this aircraft); his aircraft was subsequently 'zapped' with a Tower Bridge emblem which it carried for many months. At RAF Spitalgate near Grantham (now no longer an RAF Station) was displayed Hunter F4 WV398 in the late 1960s; this is probably the only aircraft to have returned to operational flying following use as a gate guard and it still flies with the Swiss AF as J-4203.

At RAF Waddington is Vulcan B2 XM607, an aircraft that flew several 'Black Buck' missions in the Falklands conflict. At RAF Lyneham is the only Comet on display, XK699:Sagittarius. This aircraft performed the last flight of an RAF Comet C2, landing on the grass at RAF Henlow where it remained stored for many years. A number of stations have displayed the same aircraft for over 25 years. At RAF Stanmore Park they have used Javelin FAW1 XA553 as the gate guard since May 1963; likewise No.14 MU, RAF Carlisle have displayed Hunter F1 WT660 on the gate since May 1957. Finally, at RAF St Mawgan in Cornwall is Shackleton AEW2 WL795 (masquerading as a MR2). This must be one of the few aircraft of its type never to have served at this one-time Shackleton mecca.

What the future holds for the present gate guards is obviously now known, but if the past is anything to go by it will be fluid. Prior to 1989 an average of ten aircraft were changed around throughout the year as they were either replaced or swapped. At present there are approximately 70 aircraft on display (not including plastic replicas) a figure that is slowly increasing as stations who gave up Spitfires receive something else as a replacement. One encouraging sign is the increase in overseas gate guards, one of the latest being a Lightning at RAF Akrotiri in Cyprus. One hopes that this simple method of preserving the RAF's past will be retained and encouraged for future generations.

Many people have helped in the production of this book, most of whom are listed in the acknowledgements, but there are a few that we would particularly like to thank. The first is Squadron Leader Peter Russell-Smith, our Chairman, for suggesting and then encouraging the project from its very beginning in 1987, for access to his extensive photographic collection and assistance with the gate guards of yesteryear. Without his help we would not have been able to include the many operational shots that we believed were essential to the book; the same goes for Brian Pickering and the staff of MAP. Many thanks to Air Vice-Marshal Roger Austin, our President, and Squadron Leader Martin Henderson for their time proof reading. Martin, I hope they made your train journeys more bearable. And finally, thanks to all those members of the Royal Air Force Aviation Society not already mentioned, who helped in many ways.

Jim Simpson and Kev Darling
March 1990

RAF GATE GUARD AIRCRAFT 1991

These aircraft are currently known to be acting as gate guards; the list is accurate up to March 1991.

Station	Aircraft	Serial	Code	Markings
Abingdon	Hunter F5	WP185		
Akrotiri	Whirlwind HAR 10	XD184		84 Sqn
	Lightning F3	XS929	Q	56 Sqn
Bentley Priory	Hunter FGA9	XE597	F	
	Lightning F1A	XM173		56 Sqn
Boulmer	Lightning F3	XP745	H	29 Sqn
Bracknell	Hunter F6A	XG196		
Brawdy	Hunter FGA9	XE624	G	234 Sqn
Bruggen	Jaguar SO7	XX822	AA (really XW563)	14 Sqn
Carlisle	Hunter F1	WT660	C	43 Sqn
Chivenor	Hunter F6	XF509		
	Whirlwind HAR 10	XD186		22 Sqn
Coltishall	Lightning F1A	XM172:172		229OCU
Cosford	Hunter FGA9	XG225		237OCU
Cottesmore	Canberra PR7	WH791		
Cranwell	Vampire T11	XD429	(really XD542)	
	Canberra B2	WJ637	(really WH669)	ARIES II
Digby	Meteor T7	WH166	A	25 Sqn
Ely	Meteor NF14	WS774		264 Sqn
Finningley	Meteor F8	WK864	(really WL168)	616 Sqn
Gatow	Hastings T5	TG503		
Goose Bay	Vulcan B2	XL361		9 Sqn
Gutersloh	Harrier GR3	XW917	L	3/4 Sqn
Halton	Hunter F6	XF527		
Henlow	Hunter F1	WT612		
Hereford	Hunter FGA9	XG252	U	54 Sqn
Honington	Buccaneer S2	XK526		
Innsworth	Javelin FAW9	XH903		
Kemble	Meteor F8	WH364		601 Sqn
Laarbruch	Canberra B(I)8	XM264		16 Sqn
	Hunter F6A	XJ673	(really XE606)	20 Sqn
Leeming	Javelin FAW4	XA634	L	137 Sqn
Leuchars	Phantom FG1	XT864	BJ	111 Sqn
Linton on Ouse	Provost T1	XF545	O-K	1 FTS
Locking	Gnat T1	XM708	Red Arrows	
Lossiemouth	Buccaneer S1	XK532	LM:632	
Lyneham	Comet C2	XK699	'Sagittarius'	
Manston	Spitfire XVI	TB752	LZ-F	66 Sqn
	Hurricane IIcb	BN230	FT-A (really LF751)	43 Sqn
Marham	Victor K2	XH673		55/57 Sqn
Neatishead	Meteor F8	WK654		247 Sqn
Newton	Hunter F1	WT694		43 Sqn
N. Luffenham	Meteor NF14	WS776		25 Sqn
Odiham	Whirlwind HAR 10	XR453		230 Sqn
Quedgley	Meteor T7	WF784		
Scampton	Gnat T1	XR571	Red Arrows	
Sealand	Hunter F51	WT520	(really E-408)	74 Sqn
Shawbury	Whirlwind HAR 10	XP351	Z	2 (A)FTS
Stafford	Javelin FAW2	XA801	F	46 Sqn
Stanbridge	Hunter F5	WP190		
Stanmore Park	Javelin FAW1	XA553		
St Mawgan	Shackleton AEW2	WL795	T	
Swinderby	Vampire T11	XD506		

Valley	Gnat T1	XR534		4 FTS
Waddington	Vulcan B2	XM607		
Wattisham	Lightning F1A	XM192	X	111 Sqn
Watton	Meteor NF14	WS807		46 Sqn
West Drayton	Lightning F2A	XN769		92 Sqn
West Raynham	Javelin FAW8	XH980	A	85 Sqn
Wildenrath	Hunter FGA9	XF418		92 Sqn
Wittering	Harrier GR3	XV779	A	233OCU/1 Sqn
	Spitfire F21	LA255	JX-U	1 Sqn
Woodvale	Meteor T7	WA591		
Wroughton	Canberra B2	WJ676		50 Sqn
Wyton	Canberra PR9	XH170		39 Sqn

Stations currently displaying glassfibre replica aircraft as gate guards.

Station	**Type**	**Markings**	**Sqn**
Benson	Spitfire	EN343	
Bentley Priory	Spitfire	K9926:JH-C	317 Sqn
	Hurricane I	P3386:FT-A	43 Sqn
Biggin Hill	Spitfire I	N3194:GR-Z	301 Sqn
	Hurricane I	L1710	
Coltishall	Hurricane I	V7467:LE-D	242 Sqn
Church Fenton	Spitfire I	L1096:PR-O	609 Sqn
RAFM Hendon	Hurricane IIc	BE421:XP-G	174 Sqn
	Spitfire IX	MH486	
RFN Northolt	Spitfire IX	MH777:RF-N	303 Sqn
Turnhouse	Spitfire I	L1070:XT-A	603 Sqn
Swanton Morley	Spitfire	P8448:UM-D	152 Sqn
Uxbridge	Spitfire IX	BR600:SH-V	64 Sqn

Note: All Spitfires were built from a mould of a Spitfire VIII; all Hurricanes were built from a mould of a Hurricane IIc.

HAWKER HUNTER F5
WP185
RAF ABINGDON

Because of problems affecting the Rolls-Royce Avon engines installed in the Hunter F1s, mainly surging when the aircrafts' guns were fired, Armstrong Whitworth Ltd. at Baginton were contracted to build a batch of Hunters based on the Hunter F1 but fitted with a surge-free Armstrong Siddeley Sapphire engine. These aircraft were designated the Hunter F2. Unfortunately, these aircraft also suffered from another of the Mk1's problems — short duration and range. Hawkers cured this lack of endurance problem on the Hunter F4 by increasing its fuel capacity, so as a follow-on order to the F2, Armstrong Whitworth received a further order to build 105 aircraft based on the Hunter F4 but fitted with a Sapphire engine. This aircraft became the Hunter F5.

WP185 was ordered as part of Contract SP/6/6315/CB7a and following construction at Baginton made its first flight in June 1955. Following initial flight testing, which included a visit to No.5 MU at RAF Kemble for final fitting out, it joined No.1 Squadron at RAF Tangmere who coded it 'P'. At the time of its arrival 1 Sqn was not operational as it was in the process of converting from the Meteor F8 to the more powerful Hunter. The unit was eventually declared operational in the following September.

WP185 appears not to have stayed with 1 Sqn too long because shortly thereafter it was reported with another Tangmere unit, No.34 Squadron, who recoded it 'E'. It was with this squadron when in May 1956, as part of 'Operation Quickfire', 25 Hunters from Tangmere were hurriedly detached to RAF Akrotiri in Cyprus for use as top cover as part of the build up of British and French forces in the Suez Crisis 'Operation Musketeer'. On arrival in Cyprus the aircraft were painted with yellow and black stripes in a similar fashion to the D-Day invasion stripes of the Second World War and were tasked to maintain an Operational Readiness Flight, being scrambled on many occasions to investigate straying aircraft. At the end of the emergency, 34 Sqn returned to Tangmere on 24 December 1956, reverting to their more normal air defence duties in British skies. On 10 January 1958 the squadron disbanded and their now redundant aircraft were passed some five days later to No.208 Squadron, also at Tangmere, so that they could work up on surplus aircraft prior to receiving the 'big-engined' Hunter F6 before departing overseas.

On 29 August 1958, WP185 was declared surplus to requirements once again, its task with 208 Sqn complete, and delivered

WP185 in the RAF Museum at Hendon in April 1989. *(C. P. Russell-Smith)*

to RAF Henlow where it was put into store. It was issued with the maintenance serial 7583M as it was planned to use it for display purposes once a suitable venue could be found. This didn't happen until 1973 when the aircraft was taken to RAF Hendon to join the RAF Museum. It remained on display there until November 1989, when as part of a big change around in its exhibits, probably linked to the MOD's change of policy towards its historic aircraft, it was allocated to RAF Abingdon as a replacement for the station's previous gate guard, Spitfire F22 PK624, which they had had to give up as part of the same policy change.

On arrival at Abingdon the aircraft went into No.71 MU to undergo preparation for display. This was completed in early 1990, and the aircraft was put on display near the main gate shortly thereafter.

WESTLAND WHIRLWIND HAR 10
XD184
RAF AKROTIRI

The Westland Whirlwind originally began life as a licence-built version of the Sikorsky S-55, and as such became the first helicopter to be built in any numbers for the British armed forces. In its Mk1 form it first flew in August 1953, the later HAR 4 variant built with the more powerful Pratt & Whitney R-1340-57 piston engine flying in July 1954.

XD184, c/n WA27 was the sixth of ten aircraft ordered as part of Contract 6/Acft/8593, the initial production batch of Whirlwind HAR 4s. These aircraft were built at Yeovil and were delivered to the RAF between July and August 1954. On 30 August 1954, XD184 was declared ready for collection and following its initial acceptance checks was despatched by sea to the Far East to join No.155 Squadron at RAF Seletar, Singapore, on 11 November. This unit was reformed on 1 September 1954 to provide transport and casualty evacuation support for the British Army during the confrontation between the Malayan Government and Communist insurgents. It was hoped that with the introduction of the more powerful Whirlwind HAR 4, the problems of lack of power in the hot and humid conditions would be cured; unfortunately it was found that even this type was also still seriously underpowered. (It was not overcome until the introduction of the Whirlwind HAR 10 fitted with the Gnome Turboshaft.)

On 13 January 1959, having served faithfully for four years as part of the FEAF, XD184 was returned to the UK, arriving back on 1 May. It was put into storage with No.20 MU at RAF Aston Down until a decision as to its future could be made. It subsequently joined No.228 Squadron at RAF Leconfield on 18 December 1959, beginning a role that it was to remain in for most of the rest of its operational life. No.228 Squadron was reformed on 1 September 1959 (when No.275 Squadron was renumbered) to become an air-sea rescue squadron, flying a mixture of Sycamores and Whirlwinds painted in a distinctive all yellow colour scheme. XD184 remained with the unit until 13 November 1962 when, as part of an update programme, it was selected to undergo modification by Westlands at Yeovil, to HAR 10 standard.

The modifications took over a year to complete and on 31 December 1963 it was declared ready for collection. The most obvious difference was the fitting of an elongated nose fairing containing a Rolls-Royce Gnome turboshaft. XD184 was again sent overseas, this time to Cyprus, and by 27 January it was with No.103 MU at RAF Akrotiri for acceptance. Six days later it joined No.1563 Flight at Nicosia; this unit had originally been formed as the Middle East Trials Flight from No.103 Squadron to carry out a series of hot and high trials. Once these trials had been completed the unit stayed in existence and operating in parallel with No.1564 Flight at RAF El Adem, carried out search and rescue duties. This situation remained until 17 January 1972 when the decision was taken to re-form No.84 Squadron at RAF Akrotiri from the aircraft of 1563 Flt and a detachment of No.230 Squadron, who supported the United Nations forces on the island.

On 13 January 1972, XD184 was sent to RNAY Fleetlands for a major servicing and following this routine work returned to Cyprus in July, officially joining 'A Flt' of 84 Sqn on the 17th. No.84 Sqn marked their aircraft with playing card insignia and in the case of XD184 this was the 'Ace of Spades'. It also received the squadron's 'Scorpion' motif on its cargo door.

XD184 at RAF Akrotiri in 1968. *(C. P. Russell-Smith)*

For the next ten years or so XD184 mostly patrolled the coastline of Cyprus, being employed on numerous SAR missions. These were not the only duties it performed, because the squadron's 'B Flt' also had a role to support the UNICYP, flying camouflaged Whirlwinds; on two occasions, from 9 January to 12 February 1980 and 21 May to 4 June 1980 it was used in this support role, although it is not known if it was camouflaged (probably not due to the short duration of the periods of loan).

On 18 December 1981 the decision was taken to re-equip 84 Sqn with the larger Westland Wessex HC2. By 1 March 1982 the process was virtually complete and it was left to XD184 to fly the last sortie by an 84 Sqn Whirlwind. After completing 7,286 flying hours in 25 years of service it was grounded.

The aircraft was put into store at Larnaca as it was originally intended to use it as a fire trainer, but it was later decided to put it on display at the AHQ Cyprus. For this role it was issued with the maintenance serial 8787M. No.84 Sqn then heard of its fate and following discussions it was decided that it would be best employed as a gate guard at RAF Akrotiri. It was eventually moved back by road to Akrotiri and following a complete restoration for display it took up its duties in September 1984 as the station's first gate guard.

ENGLISH ELECTRIC LIGHTNING F6 XS929

RAF AKROTIRI

Without doubt the Lightning must rate as one of the most dramatic of Great Britain's post-war fighters. In F6 form this twin-engined aircraft reached its zenith, having at long last gained a higher fuel capacity, extended loiter time and longer supersonic endurance for its attack phase. Coupled with an improved 'Airpass' radar system (AI-23B) and refined avionics, the Lightning F6 became the best of its breed. The first aircraft of this mark entered service with No.5 Squadron at RAF Binbrook in December 1965, with the final deliveries joining the RAF in August 1967.

XS929 was built by the British Aircraft Corporation (BAC) (which had absorbed English Electric) at Preston as part of Contract KD/2T/0139 and was given the construction number 95262. It followed the usual pattern for aircraft built at Preston, making its first flight on 1 March 1967 in the hands of test pilot T. M. S. Ferguson to nearby Salmesbury, from where it was declared ready for collection on 27 April 1967. It didn't have long to wait to enter service because the following day it joined No.11 Squadron at RAF Leuchars.

Its career with 11 Sqn, who coded it 'E', was largely uneventful although it did undergo some Cat3 repairs by No.71 MU and a contractor's working party from BAC in October 1970. By December 1970 it was back with the squadron, soon returning to its routine air defence sorties. The aircraft remained at Leuchars until 8 August 1973 when it flew to RAF Akrotiri in Cyprus and joined No.56 Squadron five days later.

The squadron coded XS929 'L', and whilst with them it retained its overall natural metal finish, although it did carry the unit's red and white checks either side of the nose roundel, with the squadron's 'Firebird' motif on the fin.

In 1974 when Turkey invaded the northern part of Cyprus, 56 Sqn went to full combat alert status. They mounted numerous combat air patrols over the Sovereign Base Area protecting the many transport aircraft flying into and out of Akrotiri. As the situation rapidly deteriorated it was decided that to maintain the integrity, viability and safety of the many resident squadrons, the best thing to do was to return them to the UK. For 56 Sqn this meant departing Cyprus on 23 January 1975 for its new home at RAF Wattisham.

In March 1976 a new designate squadron was formed at RAF Coningby when the unit was selected to receive the Phantom. This was the beginning of the rundown of the Lightning force

By 1978 XS929 had joined 11 Sqn coded 'E'. *(M.A.P.)*

and subsequently on 28 June 1976 the Lightning element of 56 Sqn was disbanded. XS929 subsequently flew to RAF Binbrook on 1 July and was put into storage.

Following some eighteen months in store, XS929 resumed its flying career on 14 December 1977 when it rejoined 11 Sqn, now one of the last two UK-based Lightning units. It was coded 'E', replacing XS920 which had transferred to the other Lightning unit, No.5 Squadron. XS929 flew with 11 Sqn until 8 August 1979 when it again returned into store at Binbrook. The station had a policy of rotating aircraft into store in an attempt to conserve the fatigue life of the remaining airframes as no replacement was in sight at the time.

XS929 reappeared from Aircraft Storage and Servicing Flight (ASSF) on 11 February 1981 rejoining 11 Sqn again. This time it was coded 'BF' and remained with them for four years. On 21 August 1985 it moved to the Lightning Training Flight (LTF) who promptly painted it in the unit's 'Blue Bar and Lion Markings' (taken from the Binbrook station badge) and coded it 'DG'. On 26 February 1986 it was loaned to 5 Sqn with whom it remained uncoded, and returned to the LTF on 23 December. It went full circle, rejoining 11 Sqn, recoded 'BG' the following day. The aircraft now entered a period varying between flying and temporary storage. From 20 to 26 February 1987 it was back with 5 Sqn, joining 11 Sqn the following day. On 4 May 1988 it entered its final spell of store because three weeks later it made its last flight. This last flight took the aircraft back to Cyprus where on landing it was grounded, issued with the maintenance serial 8970M, and allocated to RAF Akrotiri for display.

Shortly after arrival the aircraft was put into store to await preparation for restoration. The work commenced later that year and much of the work entailed removing the aircraft coat of olive drab paint and replacing it with the markings of No.56 Squadron. The work was finished in early 1989 and on 20 May it was unveiled to the public for the first time, joining the station's other gate guard, Whirlwind HAR 10 XD184.

ENGLISH ELECTRIC LIGHTNING F Mk1A XM173

RAF BENTLEY PRIORY

This mark of Lightning only differed from its predecessor, the F1, with the addition of a UHF radio and the facility for a detachable in-flight refuelling probe — an effort to increase the type's poor endurance.

XM173 was built by the parent company at Salmesbury, Lancashire and was given the construction number 95060. It first flew from Salmesbury on 1 November 1960 with company test pilot J. K. Isherwood at the controls. Following its initial test flights it was issued to No.56 Squadron at RAF Wattisham who at the time were in the process of converting from the Hawker Hunter F6. On its arrival it was coded 'V'.

It retained this code for only two years because in April 1963 No.56 Sqn gave up some of their aircraft to No.226 OCU, and subsequently it was re-coded 'C'. It remained on the strength of 56 Sqn until early 1965 when it was replaced by the more powerful Lightning F3. It eventually found its way to RAF Coltishall where it joined the strength of No.226 OCU, in particular No.145 Squadron — one of the OCU's two shadow squadrons. It was issued with the standard OCU code, having the three numbers of its serial displayed in a large format on its fin. It remained with the OCU for the next seven years, apart from a fourteen-month visit to No.60 MU from 11 July 1965 for rebuild following a Cat 3 accident. It subsequently returned to Coltishall in September 1966.

XM173 at Leuchars in March 1972. *(C. P. Russell-Smith)*

XM173 ended its days at RAF Binbrook. This shot shows it undergoing maintenance there in 1974. *(C. P. Russell-Smith)*

The aircraft was next on the move in February 1972, this time to RAF Leuchars for use as a high-speed target with the station Target Facilities Flight (TFF). On arrival it was painted in the markings of No.11 Squadron, one of the resident units at Leuchars who occasionally loaned the aircraft as a spare. It only stayed at Leuchars for a few months because when 11 Sqn moved to RAF Binbrook in July they took it with them. On arrival at Binbrook it joined the station TFF although it retained 11 Sqn colours until the following October.

XM173 paid a second visit to No.60 MU from 15 October 1973, but this time it was for a much-needed major servicing; on completion of this work it returned to Binbrook once again. On 31 December 1974 the Binbrook TFF was disbanded and as a result XM173 was grounded. Following this grounding it was issued with the maintenance serial 8414M and became a surface decoy on Binbrook's airfield. Interestingly, as well as acting as a decoy the aircraft was also used for camouflage trials to help assess what paint schemes the then natural metal Lightnings should be painted in. It acquired a variety of schemes; medium matt grey, dark green, light blue grey and finally standard grey green. This final scheme was retained by the aircraft when in 1981 it was allocated to HQ No.11 Group RAF Bentley Priory for display.

On its arrival at Bentley Priory it was given No.74 (Tiger) Squadron colours, presumably because they were the first RAF squadron to receive the Lightning although it never saw service with them. In mid-1990 the aircraft was returned to its 56 Sqn colours by a team from RAF St Athan led by Cpls Bailey and Russ.

HAWKER HUNTER FGA Mk9
XE597
RAF BENTLEY PRIORY

The Hunter was notable as the last conventional production fighter aircraft produced by the Hawker Aircraft Company and can trace its origins back to the programme that began with the Seahawk and culminated via a series of private ventures in the prototype Hawker P1067. The design team led by Sydney Camm and under the watchful eye of Sir Tommy Sopwith had every reason to be proud of their new design. It was workmanlike in operation and followed the classic lines laid down by many of its forebears, all of which adhered to the basic principle 'if it looks right, it is right'.

XE597 was originally built as a Hunter F6 at Hawker's Kingston on Thames factory. It was ordered as part of Contract 6/Acft/9629 and was given the construction number 41h/695176, being part of the batch XE526/XE655. The aircraft first flew on 16 April 1954 with company test pilot David Lockspeiser at the controls but it wasn't declared ready for collection for another four months, instead remaining at Kingston.

On 30 August 1954 it was finally declared ready for collection and on the following day it flew to No.19 MU at RAF St Athan for its service acceptance. Following this work it went into short-term store before joining No.66 Squadron at RAF Acklington on 10 October. Its stay with its first unit was rather brief because on 7 November it joined No.63 Squadron at RAF Waterbeach. This was a more permanent arrangement because the aircraft was duly coded 'A' and painted in the squadron's black and yellow checks.

On 31 October 1958, 63 Sqn disbanded; five days later XE597 joined another Waterbeach unit, No.56 Squadron. It stayed with this squadron for only six months and it is not known if it was coded. On 6 May 1959 it returned to its builders at Kingston for conversion to FGA 9 standard. This conversion work entailed fitting an Avon 207 engine rated at 10,050 lbs s.t.; modifications to the cockpit conditioning system to enable it to be operated in hotter climates were also undertaken. Other work carried out involved increasing its oxygen capacity and the installation of a tail braking parachute. The wings were also modified, increasing their strength, and the plumbing was also installed for the carriage of 230-gallon fuel tanks. The conversion was completed on 22 February 1960 but it wasn't until 1 March that the aircraft was once again flown to No.19 MU for acceptance.

In March 1960, No.208 Squadron began to relinquish their aged Venom FB4s to re-equip with the Hunter FGA9. On 8 April,

XE597 departed the shores of Britain to undertake the long delivery flight to RAF Eastleigh, Nairobi, Kenya, where the aircraft immediately joined 208 Sqn. Its new unit coded it 'G' and it was soon in use training the unit's pilots to bring them up to operational standard on this new aircraft. Thirteen days after arrival it suffered a flying accident and was subsequently declared Cat 3. A team from No.71 MU at RAF Bicester began the task of repairing the aircraft the next day taking until 26 May to complete it. XE597 was returned to the squadron and was soon training aircrew once again.

The aircraft stayed in Kenya until October 1961 when it returned to No.19 MU arriving there on the 12th for another bout of modifications. On completion of this work it joined the Ministry of Aviation on 22 March 1962 for a series of trials. Little is known of this work but it is understood that they included a large amount of gun firing and took until early 1963 to complete.

XE597 in No.1 Sqn markings at RAF Odiham in March 1966. *(C. P. Russell-Smith)*

On 18 March 1963 the aircraft returned to its former home at Waterbeach where on arrival it joined 54 Sqn once again, now part of No.38 Group Air Support Command. This unit, together with No.1 Squadron, were the only remaining Fighter Command Hunter units and although their primary role was ground attack they did retain a secondary air defence capability. This secondary role was put to the test in July 1963 when as part of Exercise Top Hat the Hunter force were required to intercept high flying V-Bombers. This was followed in the same month by Exercise Mystic which saw the V-Force practising their low-level role with the Hunters again acting as the defenders. Unfortunately when the main part of 'Mystic' took place the weather at Waterbeach was so bad the Hunters remained grounded.

On 14 August No.54 Sqn joined No.1 Sqn at RAF West Raynham, thus combining the two Hunter squadrons at one station. Following this move further detachments took place. One such exercise began in October 1963 with the two units finding themselves at RAF El Adem in Libya for Exercise Triplex West. This was designed to test an all forces reinforcement of units in the Mediterranean. Also taking part were Hunter FR10s from No.2 Squadron in Germany and Javelins from No.23 Squadron at RAF Leuchars. The exercise was to last two months but the part played by XE597 only lasted three days because it suffered a bird strike putting the aircraft Cat 3. The aircraft was grounded at El Adem and on further investigation it was found that the aircraft was more severely damaged than at first thought. The decision was taken to send the aircraft home by sea at the end of the exercise. On 6 January 1964 the aircraft arrived at Kingston and was re-categorised Cat 4; the repairs took until 31 March 1965 to complete.

On 6 April, XE597 returned to West Raynham but this time it joined No.1 Squadron who immediately coded it 'A'. It was soon on its travels once again when the squadron was detached to RAF West Freugh for an impromptu Armament Practice Camp (APC) as part of Exercise Easter Lightning. This entailed exercising a multi-force counter insurgency plan and although the Hunters performed adequately it was found that jet aircraft at the time were hardly ideal for use against low slow-flying targets, something the US Air Force experienced in Vietnam.

In 1968 the Hunter force were modified with the Sperry Mk8s gunsight, equipment that could be used in both the air-to-air and air-to-ground modes. Also included in the mods was the ability for the aircraft to use SNEB pods and rocket projectiles. Once fully conversant with the new equipment the Hunter force were given an extra task, this time in the frozen north as part of the ACE mobile force. XE597 undertook its last detachment with 1 Sqn in March 1969 when it went to El Adem for a full APC exercising their guns, bombs and SNEB pods.

On 18 July 1969 the 1 Sqn nameplate was transferred to RAF Wittering where it was scheduled to re-form with another Hawker aircraft, the unique VTOL Harrier. The Hunters remained as temporary cover until the Harriers became fully operational but this was effectively the end of XE597's front-line service.

On 26 September it went to No.71 MU at RAF Bicester for a major servicing from where it reappeared on 30 October. It returned to West Raynham and joined the station flight. It next moved on 16 March 1970 when it joined No.229 OCU at RAF Chivenor. This was the largest user now remaining of the Hunter, training pilots in the art of ground attack and air combat, a role for which the Hunter was ideally suited. It suffered another Cat 3 accident on 17 April 1973 but was soon repaired and was back flying after about a month.

On 24 February 1975 the aircraft was sent to No.19 MU for a

series of repairs and modifications that had accumulated over the preceding months. When it returned to flying duties No.229 OCU had disbanded with its role being taken by the Tactical Weapons Unit (TWU) at RAF Brawdy. The choice of Brawdy as a training base was strange because the station had a far from ideal weather record. This problem was highlighted in 1978 when No.2 TWU was formed at RAF Lossiemouth in Scotland. XE597 joined the new unit on 9 June and remained with them until 14 April 1981.

XE597 in August 1970, when it was flown by No.229 OCU. *(C. P. Russell-Smith)*

Its next move took it back to Brawdy once again, rejoining the TWU. It was allocated to No.79 Squadron, one of the TWU's shadow squadrons, and was coded 'F'. It flew on for a further year until 25 March 1982 when it went to No.5 MU at RAF Kemble for another major servicing. Following this work it returned to Brawdy in September.

Although the Hunter was more than suited to the task, its days were numbered when the RAF began to introduce the Hawk T1 in its place. XE597 finished its flying career on 29 April 1985 when it was finally grounded. It was allocated the maintenance serial 8874M and put into short-term store at Brawdy. On 4 October it was moved by road to HQ No.11 Group, RAF Bentley Priory, taking up gate guard duties immediately.

ENGLISH ELECTRIC LIGHTNING F Mk3 XP745

RAF BOULMER

The association of RAF Boulmer with such a high performance aircraft as the English Electric Lightning may not be immediately apparent. However Boulmer has for many years provided the ground control for aircraft such as the Lightning. Therefore, to cement their link with the fighter stations of No.11 Group, the then SASO 11 Group, Air Commodore D. P. Hall, formally dedicated XP745 as gate guard on 13 December 1976.

XP745 was the twenty-sixth Mk3 built; it was given the construction number 95173 and made its first flight in the hands of Dougy de Villiers on 18 March 1964 from Salmesbury, the place of its birth. Like many other aircraft of its type, it was initially retained by the manufacturer for modifications, and it wasn't until 20 May 1965 that the aircraft reached its first operational squadron, No.56 based at RAF Wattisham, Suffolk. No.56 Sqn flew the aircraft coded 'J' and decorated with the squadron's distinctive red and white checked tail at Wattisham until 31 May 1967, when it emigrated to RAF Akrotiri, Cyprus to replace the Javelin-equipped No.29 Squadron.

XP745:H was put on display at Boulmer in 1976 to cement the station's link with No.11 Group's fighters *(M.A.P.)*

XP745 remained with No.56 Sqn until July 1969 when the aircraft was returned to No.60 MU at RAF Leconfield, Humberside. Whilst there the aircraft underwent its only major servicing which was completed by March 1970. The following month XP745 was issued to 29 Sqn, again at Wattisham; it coded the aircraft 'H'. No.29 Sqn had re-formed on 1 May 1967 at Wattisham with Lightning F3s discarded by the squadrons re-equipping with Lightning F6s. It had an uneventful career with 29 Sqn for the next four years, flying its last operational sortie on 15 November 1974.

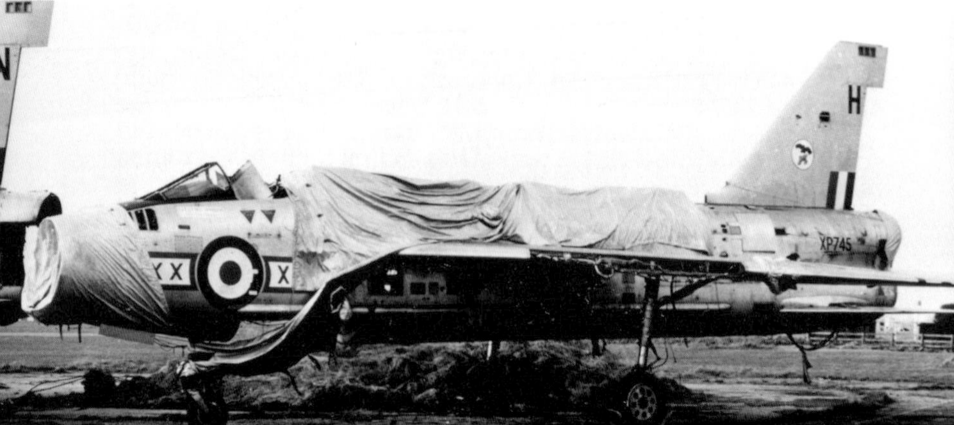

XP745 was retired to No.60 MU at RAF Leconfield in February 1975. *(M.A.P.)*

On 4 February 1975 the aircraft made one last flight to No.60 MU, RAF Leconfield for disposal, achieving a total of 1,886 hours 45 minutes flying time whilst in service. At Leconfield it was used as a source of spares and was gradually stripped of usable components over the next twelve months. Luckily it was not to suffer the fate of so many other Lightnings at the hands of the scrap merchant.

At this time the engineering staff at Boulmer were searching for a suitable aircraft to act as a gate guard and, through their close liaison with RAF Binbrook, heard that a number of F3s were surplus. Group Captain J. K. Rodgers, CO of Binbrook at the time, arranged for XP745 to go to Boulmer. The aircraft was given the maintenance serial 8453M and was taken by road to its new station.

XP745 was prepared for display by RAF engineers from Abingdon, Binbrook, Leconfield, Waddington and REME Killingworth, ably assisted by cadets from No.1000 (Blyth) Squadron ATC, and was painted in the markings of 29 Sqn with the code 'H'.

The local ATC cadets annually clean the aircraft, and in 1982 it had major maintenance work carried out on it to keep it up to display standard.

HAWKER HUNTER F6A XG196

RAF BRACKNELL

XG196 was one of 383 Hunters built for the RAF between 1955 and 1957 by Hawkers at their Kingston factory as part of Contract 10345. It first flew on 10 September 1956 and on 3 October it was delivered to No.5 MU at RAF Kemble for service preparation and acceptance. After a month at Kemble the aircraft was issued to No.19 Squadron at RAF Church Fenton on 2 November.

No.19 Sqn was the first RAF squadron to re-equip with this new mark of Hunter, taking them in exchange for their Meteor F8s. Whilst with the squadron, XG196 was coded 'U' and was painted in the standard colour scheme of dark green and grey with the blue and white chequers of the squadron markings on either side of the fuselage roundel. XG196 remained with 19 Sqn for some six years and during this time it took part in the 1958 SBAC Farnborough show as one of twelve 19 Sqn Hunters. In July 1959, it moved with the squadron to RAF Leconfield. The aircraft was obviously reliable because it reached 1,000 flying hours on 13 April 1961.

In 1960, with the introduction of the Lightning, the days of the Hunter as the premier interceptor were numbered and it was no surprise when, in mid-1962, 19 Sqn was nominated to receive the new fighter. The squadron accepted its first Lightning on 17

On display outside the RAF Staff College is Hunter FGA9 XG196. *(C. Hobson)*

December 1962 and by March 1963 it was fully equipped. XG196 was one of the last Hunters to leave and, having flown some 1,450 hours in front-line service, it was delivered to No.5 MU once again on 22 February 1963, this time for a well-earned servicing and eventual storage.

On 11 February 1964 the aircraft was transferred to No.19 MU at RAF St Athan by road for preparation for its re-entry into RAF service. It was ready for collection after a test flight on 2 September and was delivered to No.229 OCU at RAF Chivenor two days later. Coded '24' it joined No.234 Squadron, one of the OCU's shadow squadrons (the others were Nos.79 and 63). The aircraft continued its career with the OCU training new pilots and it passed 2,000 hours on 10 March 1967. It went back to St Athan for a major servicing on 29 July 1968 and returned to Chivenor on 8 October having had its code changed to '31'.

On 11 November 1970, the aircraft achieved 3,000 flying hours; another visit to St Athan for a major servicing began on 10 April 1972. In February 1973 the aircraft needed a complete mainplane change and this was carried out by a team from No.71 MU, RAF Abingdon; in August 1973 it required modifications to its intakes and this was carried out by the same unit.

On 2 September 1974, No.229 OCU was renamed the Tactical Weapons Unit (TWU) and on the next day it officially took up residence at RAF Brawdy. The TWU's role was to train pilots in the art of ground attack and low-level operations prior to conversion to the Buccaneer, Jaguar, Phantom and Harrier.

On 9 April 1975, XG196 was taken off flying duties to undergo conversion to F6A standard. This included fitting a brake parachute, modifying the flaps, and adding wing hardpoints to bring it to virtually the same standard as the Hunter FGA 9. After conversion it returned to 234 Sqn, now part of No.1 TWU, and was recoded '25'. It passed its 4,000th flying hour on 25 June 1975 and again went to St Athan for a major servicing on 5 February 1976. In September 1978 it was transferred to No.79 Squadron, still at Chivenor, and remained with this squadron for the rest of its career.

On 22 May 1980, the aircraft passed 5,000 hours but its days were numbered because the RAF was starting to introduce the Hawk T1 as a replacement for the Hunter. On 8 May 1981, XG196 made its last flight, and was finally grounded with a total of 5,125 hours 10 minutes in the air (about 213 days) having served continuously for over twenty-four years. On 6 June the aircraft was declared Cat 5 (GI) although this was later changed to Cat 2. It remained at Chivenor until 18 May 1981 when it was transferred to No.5 MU for disposal; it was declared a non-effective airframe on 8 September. On 24 November it was allocated to the RAF Staff College at Bracknell and received the Support Command maintenance serial 8702M. On 5 December it was delivered to Bracknell by No.71 MU and placed on display at the front of the College.

HAWKER HUNTER FGA Mk9 XE624

RAF BRAWDY

XE624 was built by Hawker as a P1099 Hunter F Mk6 at Kingston on Thames as part of the second production batch (totalling 100 aircraft) of Contract 6/Acft/9629. It made its first flight on 17 June 1956 in the hands of test pilot David Lockspeiser.

It followed the route of many earlier Hunters when it was flown to No.5 MU at RAF Kemble on 3 July to undergo its service acceptance prior to issue to a squadron. It was soon in action because on 27 July it joined No.263 Squadron at RAF Stradishall; it was coded 'B' and was still with this day-fighter squadron when it was renumbered No.1 Squadron on 1 July 1958.

In February 1960, XE624 went to RAF Horsham St Faith as part of the second contract placed by the RAF to convert some of its F6s to interim FGA Mk9 standard. This included fitting strengthened wings to permit carriage of extra armaments needed in the ground attack role and a brake parachute, but not the larger Rolls-Royce Avon 207 engine; this was fitted later to bring the aircraft to full FGA Mk9 standard. On completion of this work, carried out by an RAF and manufacturer's working party, it returned to 1 Sqn.

No.1 Sqn moved to RAF Waterbeach on 7 November 1961 and it was at this station that XE624 suffered a Cat 3 flying accident on 6 February 1962. Repairs were carried out by a team from No.71 MU, RAF Bicester and on 13 March it was returned to 1 Sqn. On 10 October, following major servicing at RAF St Athan, XE624 returned to 1 Sqn, which had by then moved to RAF West Raynham.

It stayed with 1 Sqn until 19 November 1969 when it moved across the airfield to join No.4 Squadron (UK Echelon), a unit which had passed its No.54 Squadron number-plate to a Phantom unit and which was waiting to convert to the Harrier GR1. On 31 March 1970, XE624 moved to RAF Wittering with the squadron, providing continuation flying for the pilots until their conversion began.

It stayed at Wittering for only a month; on 30 April it was on the move again, this time to RAF Chivenor where it joined No.229 OCU. It was allocated to No.79 Squadron, one of the OCU's three shadow squadrons, and coded 'G'. Together with Nos.63 and 234 Squadrons these formed the OCU and were responsible for all Hunter conversion training within the RAF. On 2 September 1974, No.229 OCU was renamed the Tactical Weapons Unit (still retaining the three shadow squadrons) and

XE624 awaiting its next pilot at RAF Brawdy. *(C. P. Russell-Smith)*

moved to RNAS Brawdy which became RAF Brawdy. XE624 went north to RAF Lossiemouth to join the newly formed No.2 TWU on 24 August 1978 and stayed there until 23 February 1981 when it returned to No.5 MU for another overhaul.

When it emerged on 29 June, XE624 was flown to RAF Brawdy to join 234 Sqn; it retained its 'G' code and remained with that squadron until 29 April 1985 when it was put into storage at Brawdy to await its fate. At that time, Brawdy had an ex-Danish AF, Hunter Mk51, 'E-408', on display masquerading as a No.43 Squadron Hunter F4. It was decided to replace E-408 which moved to RAF Cranwell in December 1984 with a more appropriate version of the Hunter; therefore the now surplus XE624 was allocated. After preparation for display, it was declared Cat 5 (DISP) on 4 October, issued with the maintenance serial 8875M, replacing E-408 immediately.

SEPECAT JAGUAR GR1 'XX822' (XW563)

RAF BRUGGEN

XW563 was built at Warton by the British Aircraft Corporation (BAC), who had teamed with Dassault/Breguet to form SEPECAT, and was the second of three prototypes built in Britain.

It was rolled out on 25 March 1970 and after three months of technical trials the aircraft made its first flight, of about an hour, on 4 June 1970 in the hands of test pilot Paul Millet. There then followed a career with BAC and the RAE at Boscombe Down and Farnborough as a trials and development aircraft. It was the first aircraft fitted with the Elliot Inertial Navigation System, carrying out trials in 1971 and 1972, and it was the first aircraft fitted with a modified 'wedge' nose that would contain the laser ranging equipment. In February 1971 it was loaned to the RAF for a series of maintenance trials and, under the command of Sqn Ldr Pat Miller, a team of twenty technicians spent ten days taking the aircraft apart. They then completed over 200 different engineering tasks before XW563 was returned to the manufacturer.

Following complete restoration Jaguar SO7 XW563 was put on display outside the station headquarters. *(RAF Bruggen)*

In 1972 it was fitted with the first Passive Warning Receiver fin (the small box-shaped attachment at the top) for flutter trials and, later in the year, was used for stores handling trials. It was also converted to 'Jaguar International' standard and appeared in this configuration at that year's Farnborough SBAC air display.

The 'International' standard was offered for export and three countries, Ecuador, Oman and India, bought the aircraft. The main differences between that and the RAF standard were more powerful engines and the carriage of over-wing Magic missiles. XW563 remained a weapons trials aircraft with the A&AEE at Boscombe Down for the rest of its life until 1977 when, having flown some 700 hours, it had outlived its usefulness and was delivered to RAF Bruggen and grounded. It was immediately issued with the Support Command maintenance serial 8563M and broken into two parts. The rear half became a weapons loading trainer and the front half went to No.431 MU at Bruggen for battle damage repair training.

In 1985 with the replacement of the Jaguar in the RAF Germany inventory by the Tornado, the Station Commander of Bruggen, Group Captain J. K. Sim, OBE AFC RAF, began a project to convert the battered remains of XW563 to a display airframe. Work began on 1 April when No.431 MU and the station workshops began the task of converting the aircraft to GR Mk1 standard. Parts were taken from various sources: the fin came from XX963 (the Jaguar shot down by an RAF Phantom) and the left tailplane from the crashed XX958. The team also modified the nose, cannon fairings and dive brakes to give it an authentic appearance.

On completion of the work the aircraft was painted as XX822, 'AA' of No.14 Squadron; this was the first and last Jaguar squadron to be based at RAF Bruggen and the code 'AA' was carried by the Squadron Commander. It was hoisted into its display position on 23 October 1985 and the following month was formally unveiled by the Deputy Commander of RAF Germany, Air Vice-Marshal D. T. Bryant, OBE RAF.

The real XX822 was built as part of the second production order by BAC at Warton; it was completed in mid-1975 and issued to 14 Sqn. On 2 July 1976 the aircraft crashed fifteen miles west of Ahlhorn in West Germany killing the pilot. It was the first fatal accident involving a Jaguar.

HAWKER HUNTER FMk1 WT660

RAF CARLISLE

Currently displayed in the markings of No.43 Squadron, the first RAF Squadron to fly this classic fighter, WT660 has now been displayed continuously at RAF Carlisle for over thirty years.

Built by Hawkers at Kingston on Thames as part of the Contract SP/6/5910/CB7a, it first flew on 11 November 1954 in the hands of company test pilot Frank Murphy; four days later it was ready for collection.

On 17 November it was delivered to No.5 MU at RAF Kemble where, after initial acceptance, it went into storage. On 2 February 1955 it was issued to the Day Fighter Leaders School (DFLS) at RAF West Raynham where it was used to train pilots in combat tactics.

On 31 August 1955, WT660 suffered a Cat 3 flying accident and Hawkers were called on to effect repairs; on 8 November it was returned to DFLS. The rest of its career at West Raynham appears to have been uneventful; rather surprising in view of the problems with the early Hunters. They had poor range and endurance and experienced engine surges, particularly when the guns were fired; this resulted in many accidents to the 139 FMk1s built.

WT660 was transferred to No.229 OCU at RAF Chivenor on 5 February 1957, but it stayed there for only about two months when on 5 April it returned to No.5 MU for disposal. On 11 April it was struck off charge and issued with the maintenance serial 7421M, prior to joining No.71 MU at RAF Bicester for use as an exhibition airframe. It remained in their charge for just over a month and, on 16 May, it moved north to RAF Carlisle for use as a display airframe. It has remained there to this day.

WT660 (7421M) has been on continuous display at No.14 MU since 14 May 1957. *(RAF Carlisle)*

WESTLAND WHIRLWIND HAR 10 XD186

RAF CHIVENOR

This aircraft had a similar beginning to its RAF career to XD184, currently on display at RAF Akrotiri, Cyprus, in that it was originally built as a HAR 4 and spent the early part of its life in the Far East.

XD186, like XD184, was built as part of the initial production batch of Whirlwinds ordered by the RAF, against Contract 6/Acft/8593. It was given the construction number WA29 and was completed by August 1954. After completion and air testing it was declared ready for collection on 30 August. The aircraft was immediately prepared for despatch to the Far East, and on 1 November, after a journey by sea, it joined No.155 Squadron at RAF Seletar, Singapore.

No.155 Sqn had re-formed at Seletar on 1 September 1954 with Whirlwind HC2s and HAR 4s to provide transport and casualty evacuation support for the British Army and local police in their operations against Communist guerillas in Malaya. Unfortunately, these marks of Whirlwind proved to be somewhat underpowered for the task, a problem that was not resolved until the introduction of the HAR 10 version.

XD186 remained in Singapore until 11 September 1958 when, after suffering a Cat 3 flying accident, it was returned to No.20 MU at RAF Aston Down prior to going back to Westlands at Yeovil for repair. At the same time as the repairs were being carried out the opportunity was taken to modify the aircraft to HAR 10 standard. The most obvious difference after modification was the fitting of an extended nose cone that contained a Rolls-Royce Gnome turboshaft in place of the Pratt and Whitney R-1340-57 piston engine.

On 26 November 1959 it was declared ready for collection and on 3 December it joined the Central Flying School helicopter flight at RAF South Cerney. It moved with the school to RAF Ternhill in August 1961 and was still with them on 18 January 1962 when it suffered a Cat 4 flying accident.

The aircraft was again returned to Yeovil for repair and on completion it was painted in the distinctive yellow colour scheme. On 1 January 1963 it was issued to No.228 Squadron at RAF Leconfield; this was to be the start of a long career with the RAF's Search and Rescue force. On 1 September, 228 Sqn was renumbered No.202 Squadron with XD186 officially transferring the next day.

On 3 August 1968 the aircraft flew to the RNAY at Fleetlands for a complete overhaul and following this it rejoined 202 Sqn.

During its time with the squadron it carried the codes 'C' and 'F' at various times although records do not show exactly when. On 6 April 1977 the Search and Rescue Wing (SAR Wing) was formed as part of No.18 Group, RAF Strike Command. This united Nos.22 and 202 Squadrons, the two UK-based dedicated SAR units, under one Headquarters, first at RAF St Mawgan and then at RAF Finningley.

When the last Whirlwinds retired from Chivenor in 1982, the 22 Sqn SAR Flt at Chivenor preserved XD186 outside their hangar. *(R. Clucas)*

As was policy with its aircraft SAR Wing would regularly rotate the aircraft on its strength around the various flights. XD186 is known to have served at RAF Valley, RAF Brawdy, and with the HQ Flight at Finningley. When 202 Sqn gave up their last Whirlwinds in 1980, after they had re-equipped with the Sea King HAR 3, it left only 22 Sqn flying the Whirlwind in the UK.

XD186 ended its days with 'A Flight', 22 Sqn at RAF Chivenor being finally grounded in 1981. On 10 May 1982 it was declared surplus to requirements and issued with the maintenance serial 8730M prior to going on display outside the flight's hangar at Chivenor.

HAWKER HUNTER F6 XF509

RAF CHIVENOR

Originally designed by Sydney Camm as the Hawker P1067 to Air Ministry Specification F3/48, the famous Hunter prototype first took to the air on 20 July 1951 flown by Neville Duke. The Hunter FMk6, designated P1099, was developed as the 'big-engined' Hunter using the 10,000 lb thrust Rolls-Royce Avon 203.

As was common in the 1950s, companies often sub-contracted production; because they had already been involved with earlier versions of the Hunter, an order for 100 aircraft was placed with the Sir W. G. Armstrong Whitworth Company at Baginton, Coventry. This was Contract SP/6/9818/CB7a, and XF509 was part of that order. The aircraft was ready for collection at Baginton on 30 April 1956, but it was not until 3 December that it was delivered to No.5 MU at RAF Kemble for service acceptance. On 22 January 1957, XF509 was delivered to RAF Stradishall, Suffolk, to join No.54 Squadron; on arrival it was coded 'M'.

It was customary at the time for Fighter Command to send its fighter squadrons on regular deployments to the Mediterranean for live gun-firing practice, and it was on one of these visits, to Akrotiri in Cyprus, on 3 September 1958 that XF509 suffered a Cat 3 accident. The following day it went into No.103 MU at Akrotiri for repair and was reissued to 54 Sqn, still at Akrotiri, on 11 October.

On 29 April 1959 the aircraft changed owners when it joined the Air Fighting Development Squadron (AFDS) at RAF West Raynham, Norfolk. This unit was part of the Central Fighter Establishment (CFE) and was responsible, amongst other things, for the development of combat tactics. XF509 stayed with AFDS until 22 February 1963 when it changed owners once again, this time going to Ministry of Aviation charge for use by the Royal Aircraft Establishment at Thurleigh (Bedford) as a chase and trials aircraft. One of its first tasks was to deploy to Bristol from 17 April 1963 for duties as a chase aircraft for the Fairey Delta FD2 programme. It remained with RAE until 30 September 1966 when it returned to the RAF's charge at No.19 MU, RAF St Athan. After a brief stay, it moved on 14 February 1967 to No.5 MU at RAF Kemble for refurbishment; it was then issued to No.4 FTS at RAF Valley to become a training aircraft.

It joined No.3 Training Squadron, coded '73', and was used for the advanced training of pilots before they progressed to the OCUs. Its time at Valley was not without incident because on 2 March 1976 it suffered a bird strike and the repairs were not

Hunter F6 XF509 has been the gate guard at Chivenor since May 1983. *(R. Clucas)*

completed until 2 September; it then returned to No.4 FTS and flew on for a further three years until 19 June 1979 when it once again returned to No.5 MU, this time for storage and disposal.

It was not until 31 August 1981 that the aircraft was struck off charge and, bearing its new maintenance serial 8708M, it returned by road to RAE Bedford to begin life as a ground instructional airframe and a source of spares for the RAE's other Hunters. It remained at Bedford for about eighteen months before moving to RAF Cosford to join No.2 S of TT. but it was soon put up for disposal probably because of the amount of equipment removed by its previous owners.

In early 1983 RAF Chivenor were looking for a suitable aircraft to display at their gate and, on 5 April 1983, XF509 was allocated to them. After moving there by road it was placed on display on 25 May 1983.

It was initially on display to the right of the main entrance to the station whilst rebuilding work was completed on a new station headquarters and guardroom. It was subsequently moved to a permanent location across the road.

In 1990 the aircraft underwent restoration and repainting following which it was painted in the markings of No.151 Squadron and placed in a flying position on a plinth close to its previous position.

ENGLISH ELECTRIC LIGHTNING F1A XM172

RAF COLTISHALL

Now sadly no longer in service with the Royal Air Force the English Electric Lightning will long be remembered as a truly classic fighter.

XM172 was built by the parent company at Salmesbury, Lancashire. It made its first flight on 10th October 1960 when it was delivered to the company's test airfield at Warton.

The F1A was essentially much the same as the F1 but with the inclusion of a UHF radio and a removable in-flight refuelling probe.

No.56 Squadron at RAF Wattisham was designated as the first unit to receive this particular mark and XM172 was in fact the first aircraft delivered to them on 14 December 1960. Whilst with 56 Sqn it was first coded 'P', and when in April 1963 the squadron passed some of their aircraft to No.226 OCU at RAF Coltishall, XM172 was recoded 'B'. In the 1960s 56 Sqn flew an aerobatic team called 'The Firebirds'; XM172 was one of the aircraft allocated for this display team and was seen at many airshows during this period.

In February 1965 the aircraft was transferred to RAF Coltishall to join No.226 OCU. This particular unit was divided into two shadow squadrons, Nos.65 and 145, and was the major training unit to convert pilots onto the Lightning. In its time with No.226 OCU, XM172 flew with both these squadrons. As was standard on 226 OCU aircraft, it was coded with the three numbers of its serial displayed on the nose in large black characters.

XM172 served with both 226 OCU shadow sqns, in 1971 it was flown by 65 Sqn. *(C. P. Russell-Smith).*

XM172 as part of No.56 Sqn's 'Firebirds' aerobatic team on 16 June 1963. *(C. P. Russell-Smith)*

On 11 August 1965 XM172 went to No.60 MU at RAF Leconfield for a major servicing, returning to Coltishall in September 1966, on this occasion joining No.145 Squadron. It remained at Coltishall until 15 October 1973 when again it returned to Leconfield, but this time for disposal.

Saved from the scrapman's torch in early 1974 it returned once again to Coltishall, this time to become a display aircraft. After preparation for display, which required the aircraft to be considerably lightened, XM172 was placed on display on 24 September 1974 in a dramatic flying attitude in the markings of 145 Sqn. As with all display aircraft XM172 was issued with a maintenance serial and although it was not displayed on the aircraft it became 8427M.

In April and May 1981 it underwent a total repaint having the 145 Sqn markings removed, these being replaced by those of No.226 OCU.

In March 1989, as part of the one gate guard policy, the aircraft was put up for disposal and eventually purchased by a private collector from Southampton. It was still on display in October 1990 and although its immediate future is uncertain it has been reported that its new owner has permanently loaned it back to Coltishall. Whether or not the MOD will allow this to remain the state of affairs remains to be seen because the station also display a glass fibre replica Hurricane.

HAWKER HUNTER F6A
XG225
RAF COSFORD

The Hawker P1099, Hunter F6 continued the development process that had begun with the emergence of this classic aircraft, designed by Sydney Camm. It was powered by the Rolls-Royce Avon 200 srs engine rated at 10,000 lb st with reheat (the renowned big engine), and also featured a redesigned wing, featuring leading edge extensions added to eliminate an inherent pitch up that had shown itself in earlier marks of the type. Interestingly it was originally envisaged that this Hunter variant would only act as stop gap until the introduction of the Lightning; in the end 415 were built and remained in front-line service for over twelve years.

XG225 was built by Hawkers at Kingston as part of Contract 6/Acft/10345 and was part of the batch XG225 to XG239. It first flew from Kingston on 20 October 1956 in the hands of David Lockspeiser and upon completion of routine flight testing the RAF were informed that it was ready for collection on 31 October. The following day it was delivered to No.5 MU at RAF Kemble for service acceptance.

On 26 November XG225 joined its first operational unit, No.92 (East India) Squadron at RAF Linton-on-Ouse. This was the beginning of a long association with this squadron and three days later it flew its first operational sortie with it. On 1 March 1957 the squadron moved to RAF Middleton St George. XG225 was to pursue a largely uneventful career with 92 Sqn until on 19 February 1959, it was the victim of a Cat 3 flying accident at its home base. Four days later a team from No.60 MU, RAF Leconfield began the repair work, finishing on 22 April, returning it to 92 Sqn the next day.

It was during this period of RAF history that aerobatic display teams seemed to proliferate. The most famous Hunter team was the 'Black Arrows' of No.111 Sqn, although 92 Sqn flew a small five-aircraft team. In 1961 111 Sqn gave up its Hunters in exchange for the English Electric Lightning F1, leaving a gap for a new aerobatic team. Permission was granted for 92 Sqn to form its own team which became known as the 'Blue Diamonds'. Once the team had been created the squadron's aircraft were rotated through Marshalls of Cambridge to receive a coat of royal blue paint highlighted by a white cheat line, code and serial. XG225 duly underwent the process from 9 to 30 January 1961.

In late February 1961 the squadron was sent to RAF Akrotiri in Cyprus where it began training for the forthcoming display season. Unfortunately on 3 March, XG225 suffered Cat 3 damage in a flying accident. Because the work involved to repair it was beyond the skills of RAF Akrotiri, a team from Hawkers were used instead. The aircraft was subsequently repaired and on 22 June it returned to the squadron (by now back in the UK).

Throughout 1961-2 the Hunter F6 fleet were progressively updated to F6A standard, and it became the turn of XG225 to undergo this process on 6 November. The aircraft underwent modification to bring it as near as possible to the forthcoming Hunter FGA9, featuring strengthened wings enabling it to carry greater loads. XG225 underwent the mods at No.60 MU, RAF Leconfield using kits supplied by Hawkers. The work was completed by 23 November and it returned to 92 Sqn three days

XG225 flew with 92 Sqn's 'Blue Diamonds' aerobatic team. Here seen at Wethersfield in May 1962. *(C. P. Russell-Smith)*

later. The Blue Diamonds remained the RAF's premier aerobatic team until April 1963 when the squadron began to be re-equipped with the Lightning F2; by 27 May XG225 had joined the rest of the squadron's now-redundant Hunters in storage at No.19 MU, RAF St Athan.

On 9 January 1964 it was withdrawn from storage and issued to No.229 OCU at RAF Chivenor to become a training aircraft. The aircraft had barely settled down in its new role when on 10 March it suffered another flying accident. Two days later a team arrived from Hawkers to begin the repairs. On 22 April on completion of the relevant work XG225 was officially returned to the OCU but didn't actually return to flying duties for another eight days because it was required to undergo some scheduled maintenance.

XG225 continued to provide good service until 3 February 1967 when during some routine maintenance it was found that the area around the gun blast deflectors was severely damaged. The aircraft was subsequently declared Cat 3 and because of the nature of the work involved, it was left to a team from Hawkers to carry out the repairs. Work didn't begin until 7 February and was completed ten days later, when it resumed its duties with the OCU

On 4 August 1974, 229 OCU was disbanded, although its Hunters were immediately taken on charge by the Tactical Weapons Unit at RAF Brawdy. This new unit which officially formed on 2 September combined all the previous duties performed by the OCU plus those carried out by Nos.45 and 58 Squadrons at RAF Wittering, aimed at producing pilots fully conversant with all aspects of ground attack. XG225 joined No.79 Squadron, one of the unit's two shadow squadrons, and was coded '27'. In order to extract the maximum value from the Hunter in this new role an avionics update programme was undertaken; XG225 had the work carried out between 18–31 December 1975.

The aircraft remained at Brawdy until 2 April 1980 when it made a sudden move to No.237 OCU at RAF Honington. The use of single-seat Hunters by this Buccaneer unit (they already used two-seat Hunters to teach new Buccaneer aircrew) became necessary due to the grounding of the Buccaneer fleet, some of which were found to be suffering from inner wing structural cracks. This had been discovered as the cause of a crash by a Buccaneer in the Nevada Desert. In order that Buccaneer pilots could remain current to fly, each of the Buccaneer squadrons and the OCU were issued with some Hunters.

XG225's stay with the OCU lasted five months and on 9 September 1980 it flew to No.5 MU at RAF Kemble and was put into long-term store. On 27 August 1981 it was declared non-effective stock and four days later was on its way to No.2 School of Technical Training at RAF Cosford complete with the maintenance serial 8713M to become a ground instructional airframe.

The aircraft remained in this role until 1988 when it was chosen to replace Vampire T11 XD613 on display on the parade ground at RAF Cosford. Following the relevant preparation work it took up its duties towards the end of the year, in the markings of No.237 OCU.

This shot of XG225 was taken at Honington when the aircraft was serving with 237 OCU. *(C. P. Russell-Smith)*

DE HAVILLAND VAMPIRE T11 'XD429' (XD542)

RAFC CRANWELL

The advent of the jet fighter in its single-seat form had shown the need for some sort of two-seat trainer to ease conversion to this new type of advanced aircraft. This led to private ventures by both Glosters, who produced the Meteor T7, and De Havilland, who produced the DH115 Vampire T11.

XD542, construction number 15286, was built by the company at their Broughton works near Chester, as part of Contract 8981. After being test flown it was transferred to Hawarden Airfield, also near Chester, where it was declared ready for collection on 30 June 1954.

It was initially delivered to No.10 MU at RAF Hullavington, Wiltshire, and after preparation for service issue it was delivered to the Central Gunnery School (CGS) at RAF Leconfield on 23 July 1954, where the aircraft was coded 'H'. In the following September the aircraft suffered a Category 4 flying accident, and because repairs were beyond local resources, they were carried out by No.60 MU from RAF Dishforth, who completed them by 1 November 1954, when the aircraft was reissued to the CGS. It remained with the CGS for only another two months, and on 1 January 1955 it moved to the Fighter Weapons School (FWS) also at Leconfield, who recoded it 'N'.

On 31 July 1956 it suffered another flying accident, and as this was again beyond local resources No.60 MU were called in to carry out the repairs. These took from 15 August to 25 October to carry out and on completion the aircraft returned to the FWS.

XD542 continued its flying career until 14 October 1957 when it was declared surplus and returned back to No.10 MU, this time for storage. Shortly after arrival it was given the maintenance serial 7604M. It remained in storage until 22 June 1959, when it was allocated to No.12 S of TT at RAF Melksham, Wiltshire, for use as an instructional and display airframe. It remained at Melksham until 24 July 1964 when it was transferred to the growing museum at RAF Colerne, Wiltshire. After its arrival the aircraft underwent a complete restoration to display standard, remaining on display until Colerne closed in 1975.

With the closure of Colerne, the museum aircraft were split up and dispersed, some aircraft going to other museums, and some going to other RAF stations to act as gate guards. XD542 fell into the latter category and on 30 September 1975 it was transferred by road to RAFC Cranwell.

After arrival at Cranwell it was reassembled and repainted in the incorrect markings of 'XD429:28' of the RAF College, and

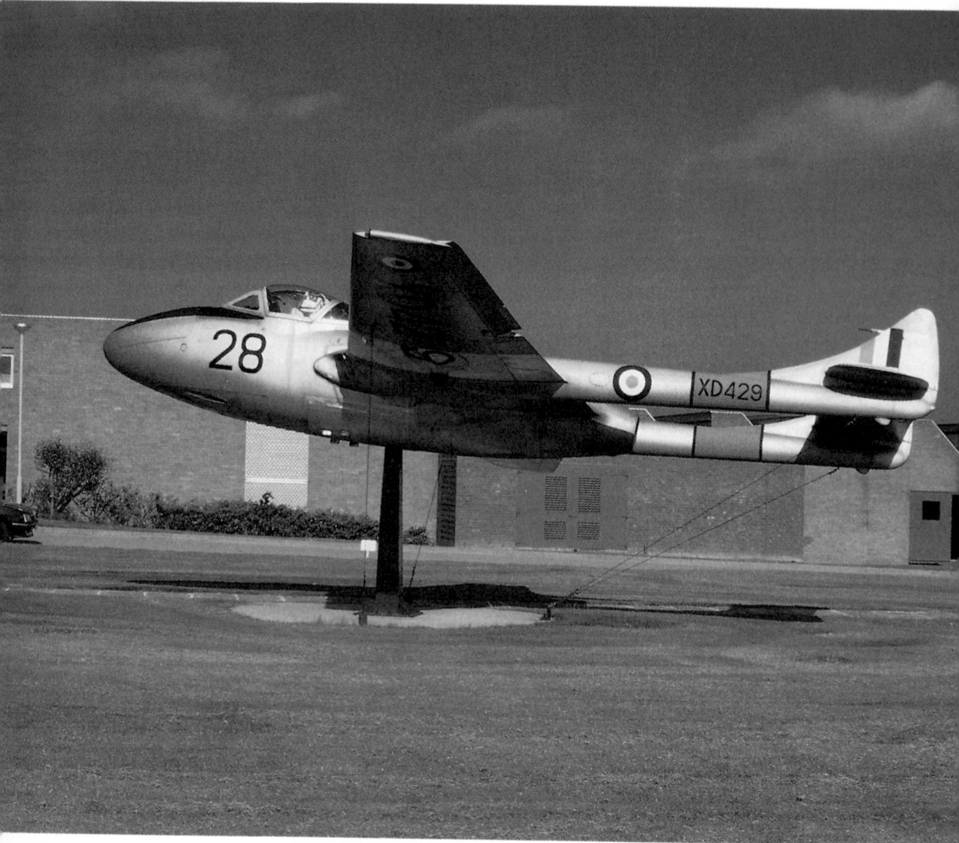

RAF Cranwell's gate guard is Vampire T11 'XD429'. Following total restoration in 1988 it was moved to a more public position by the station's main entrance. *(J. A. Simpson)*

with its undercarriage retracted was placed on a plinth outside the Flying Training School Headquarters. XD542 has had regular maintenance carried out on it over the years and it was last repainted in 1986. (As a footnote, the real XD429 [construction number 15297] served with No.7 FTS, CNCS, and RAFC Cranwell before being dumped at RAF Andover in 1964.)

On 21 June 1988 the aircraft was removed from its long-held position outside the FTS HQ for the last time. It then underwent another lengthy period of maintenance which took until December 1988 to complete. It was then put in a new display position on 13 December nearer Cranwell's main entrance where it still remains.

ENGLISH ELECTRIC CANBERRA B2(T) 'WH699' (WJ637)

RAF CRANWELL

The first production variant of the English Electric Canberra to enter service, the BMk2, began to equip the bomber squadrons of the RAF in May 1951 when No.101 Squadron replaced its elderly Avro Lincolns with the new jet. Because the piston-powered bombers had to be replaced quickly the decision was taken to get several contractors to build Canberras. This led to Contract 6/Acft/5943 being issued to Handley Page at Radlett where production ran from April 1953 to April 1955.

WJ637 was one of those aircraft and came out of the works in 1954; after acceptance checks it was delivered to No.35 Squadron at RAF Upwood. The aircraft was still with the squadron during the Suez crisis in 1956, and although 35 Sqn was placed on standby, it took no part in the hostilities as a unit although some of its aircraft and crews were sent to the war zone. WJ637 remained with 35 Sqn and was still on strength when, as the last B2 squadron, it disbanded on 16 September 1961; it later re-formed as a Vulcan squadron.

WJ637 next served with No.231 OCU, initially at RAF Bassingbourn, and when in the late 1960s they moved to RAF Cottesmore joining the Canberra-equipped Nos.98 and 360 Squadrons, the aircraft went with it. Once the OCU had settled in at their new base, they began to code their aircraft; WJ637 became 'Z'.

In 1975, with the closure of Cottesmore, the Canberras of 231 OCU moved to RAF Marham. At this time also, some B2s, WJ637 amongst them, were converted to B2(T) standard. This entailed fitting more extensive navigation equipment and an additional ejection seat in the cockpit. After modification, WJ637 was used as a trials aircraft at the A&AEE Boscombe Down for a brief time, and when it returned to Marham it was again coded 'Z'.

In 1981 the decision was taken to concentrate all Canberra operations at RAF Wyton, as Marham, much like Cottesmore previously, was required for Tornado operations; WJ637 moved with the OCU to Wyton. However, on 23 September the aircraft made its last flight. This was from Wyton to RAF College Cranwell where the aircraft was struck off charge, allocated the maintenance serial 8755M and issued to Aircraft Hall to assist in the training of junior engineering officers.

It remained in this role until early 1984 when it was 'acquired' by the Director of the Department of Air Warfare (DAW), also at Cranwell. In order to maintain a link with DAW's predecessor, the College of Air Warfare at RAF Manby, the Canberra was

WJ637 photographed at RAF Luqa, Malta, in May 1970.
(C. P. Russell-Smith).

repainted as 'WH699 Aries IV', an aircraft that had gained many aviation records in the past. In mid-1984 the aircraft was placed on display outside Trenchard Hall, all the Aries IV achievements are painted on the aircraft's nose.

ENGLISH ELECTRIC CANBERRA PRMk7 WH791

RAF COTTESMORE

RAF Cottesmore's association with the Canberra can be traced back to 1954 when a B2 Wing moved in for a short time. But more recently, from 1969 to 1976, it was the home of three Canberra units: Nos.98 and 360 Squadrons and No.231 OCU.

WH791 was built by the English Electric Co. at Salmesbury, Lancashire, and as such was the tenth Canberra PR7 built. It first flew in March 1954 and was ready for collection by the end of the month; on 31 May it was delivered to No.542 Squadron at RAF Wyton.

No.542 Sqn had re-formed on 14 May as the first PR7 squadron and spent much of its time working up on this new version of the Canberra. The squadron's life was relatively short-lived as on 1 October 1955 it was disbanded and WH791 was passed to No.82 Squadron, also based at Wyton. No.82 Sqn was re-equipping at the time, converting from the Canberra PR3, and WH791 flew with them for just under a year. However, on 1 September 1956 this squadron also disbanded, passing most of

In the markings of 81 Sqn, WH791 seen on RAF Tengah's dispersal in August 1966. *(C. P. Russell-Smith)*

its aircraft, WH791 included, to another Wyton unit, No.58 Squadron. In January 1957, after a couple of months with 58 Sqn, WH791 went to Boulton Paul's for modification before returning to the squadron in May 1957.

Whilst with 58 Sqn it seems highly likely that the aircraft went on many exotic detachments because the unit provided aircraft to go to the Far East, the Maldives, Bahrain, Aden, Somaliland and Christmas Island, the home of Britain's nuclear test programme.

This photograph of WH971 was taken in September 1973 shortly after it had been repainted. It carries the incorrect serial 'WH-717'. *(C. P. Russell-Smith)*

In April 1960, WH791 was temporarily withdrawn from service to spend the next fourteen months undergoing modification prior to service in the Far East. On 27 June 1961 it was allocated to No.81 Squadron at RAF Tengah, Singapore. No.81 Sqn was the only dedicated RAF photo-recce squadron in the Far East and was at the time converting from the Meteor PR10. The squadron's main role at first with its new Canberras was to carry out surveillance of possible trouble spots in connection with the recently finished Malayan Emergency. Later, much of its work involved photographic survey work around Malaya.

WH791 spent the next nine years going about its routine business until on 16 January 1970 the squadron disbanded. The aircraft were flown back to RAF St Athan for disposal and, following a period of storage, WH791 was struck off charge on 11 February 1972. On 13 October, instead of being broken up, it was allocated the maintenance serial 8187M and allocated to Cottesmore for display.

After delivery to its new home it was prepared for display and originally painted as 'WH717', a B2 of No.44 Squadron and one of the first Canberras to be based at Cottesmore. However, in April 1974 the aircraft was repainted and all traces of these markings were removed; it was returned to its original and correct markings retaining them to this day.

GLOSTER METEOR T7 WH166

RAF DIGBY

The origins of the Meteor T7 go back to 1947 when, without any official requirement for a trainer, Glosters went ahead and produced a tandem two-seater as a private venture. The company had been quick to realise that as more squadrons re-equipped on the Meteor, the days of putting only experienced pilots in the cockpit were over, and a more formalised approach to training was needed.

To produce a prototype, Glosters took a Meteor F4 (G-AIDC) and built a new front fuselage onto it. Re-registered G-AKPK, this aircraft first flew in its new guise on 19 March 1948.

The Air Ministry was suitably impressed and issued specification T1/47 which resulted in Contract No.6/Acft/5621 being issued. A total of 640 aircraft were eventually built for the RAF and Royal Navy.

Meteor T7 WH166 in 1984 prior to its repaint. *(J. A. Simpson)*

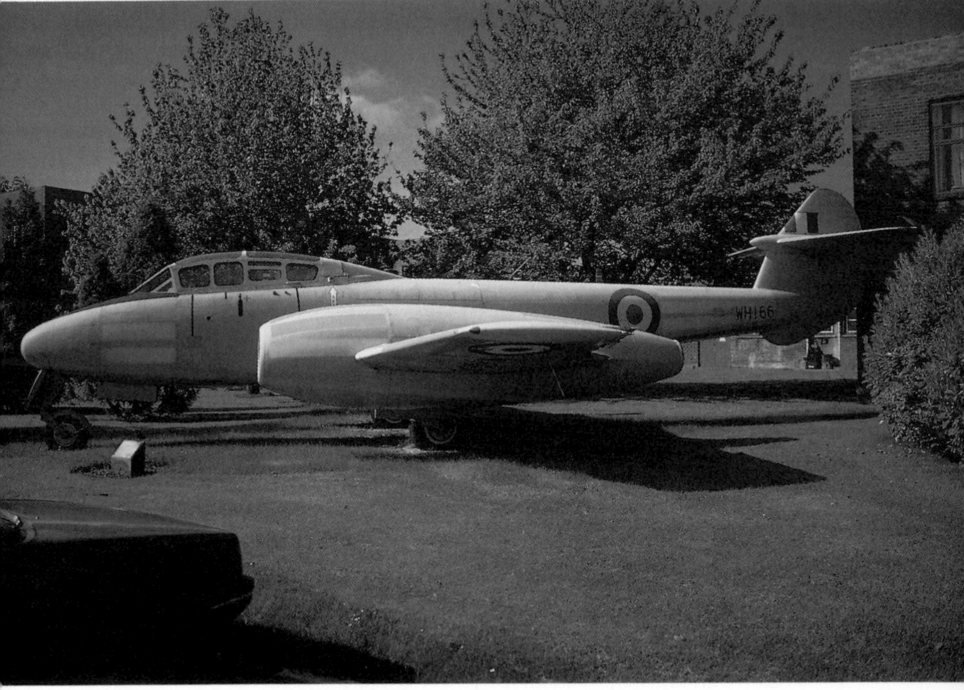

On 20 December 1951, some three years after the first prototype flew, WH166 was completed and declared ready for collection from the Gloster Aircraft Company at Hucclecote, near Gloucester. After initial air tests the aircraft remained at Hucclecote for only a short time from where it was issued to No.208 Advanced Flying School (AFS) at RAF Merryfield, Somerset on 1 January 1952.

No.208 AFS had formed within Flying Training Command (FTC) equipped with a mixture of Vampire T11s and Meteor T7s on 19 November 1951 barely a month before WH166 was completed, and aircraft assigned to this unit carried two figure codes; WH166 was allotted the code '10'.

WH166 remained with its first unit until 4 June 1953 when it was transferred to No.210 AFS at RAF Tarrant-Rushton, Dorset which had formed during the previous year. This unit also flew a mixture of Vampires and Meteors with the aircraft wearing a single letter code. No information has come to light regarding the code allotted to WH166.

On 29 October 1953 the first of several accidents to befall WH166 occurred. As Flt Lt B. C. Fitch (Instructor) and Flt Lt K. W. Simpson (Pupil) took off from Tarrant-Rushton the complete tread of the starboard tyre and the mudguard broke away from the aircraft. Forty-one minutes later the pilot carried out a wheels up landing. The damage was subsequently declared Category 3; the fault was discovered to have been due to inadequate vulcanising of the tread casing. A team from Glosters was despatched and between 3 November and 30 March 1954 WH166 underwent extensive repairs. Once completed, the aircraft was declared operational again and soon resumed flying duties with 210 AFS.

Late the following month on 29 April 1954, the aircraft was on the move once again when it was transferred to No.205 AFS at RAF Middleton St George (now Tees-side International Airport) and allotted the code '34'. Although its time with this unit was short because four weeks later on 1 June, they were re-designated No.4 Flying Training School (FTS).

The origins of this unit date back to April 1921 when it was formed at Abu Sueir in the Egyptian Canal Zone for the purpose of training pilots. The unit later moved to Habbaniya in Iraq where it disbanded in July 1941. Some six years later 4 FTS re-formed at Heeney, Southern Rhodesia and continued to operate until early 1954 when it was disbanded once again. Following the re-formation at Middleton St George, WH166 was absorbed by the new unit continuing to serve in the day fighter training role.

On 9 February 1955, WH166 was withdrawn from flying and placed into storage. It initially went to No.12 Maintenance Unit (MU) RAF Kirkbride but was transferred to No.38 MU RAF Llandow on 4 May 1955. Twelve days later the aircraft suffered its second accident and was once again declared Cat 3. As a result, No.34 MU RAF Stoke Heath sent a team to Llandow on the day of the accident to effect the repairs. Although unconfirmed, this may have been due to the fact that No.38 MU was a Receipt and Despatch unit thereby lacking the specialist equipment that was needed for the task. However by 26 June the damage was re-assessed Cat 4 and WH166 was handed back to No.38 MU pending refurbishment.

For ten months the damaged aircraft remained in storage at Llandow until on 20 April 1956 it was handed over to Avro's. This company had been given the task of refurbishing the aircraft and took it to their works five days later. The work carried on throughout the following summer and was eventually completed on 28 September 1956. The work also included replacing the original Derwent 5 engines with uprated Derwent 8s. On leaving the factory on 12 October WH166 returned into storage once again at No.12 MU. On 1 February 1957 with no immediate requirement for the aircraft, it was transferred to non-effective stock.

WH166 remained on the non-effective list until 13 March 1959 when it was moved to No.33 MU RAF Lyneham for preparation and disposal. However its stay at Lyneham proved to be a short one because on 9 June it was transferred to active flying duties once again joining the RAF Flying College (RAFFC) at RAF Manby, Lincolnshire.

Formed at Manby from the Empire Air Armament School, the college was established to give selected officers of the RAF, USAF and Commonwealth Air Forces, a practical course in flying in all weathers, navigation and the use of weapons.

By 1955 it was realised that many officers selected for the year long course were not in full current flying practice or instrument rated on jet aircraft. As a result, No.3 (Meteor) Squadron (the operators of WH166) was formed at Manby to meet this requirement flying from the nearby satellite airfield at RAF Strubby, an airfield equipped with longer and better runways than at Manby.

In addition to the Meteor F8s and T7s, the RAFFC also operated Canberra and Hunter aircraft. However, due to increasing costs, more complex and expensive aircraft, it was decided that the last Flying College course would complete training in December 1960. Despite this WH166 remained with the RAFFC continuing to fly from Strubby, but now part of the All Weather Jet Refresher Course (AWJRC).

The purpose of this unit was to bring up to current flying status pilots returning from ground tours. It also had the function of getting them instrument rated before a type/role course and subsequent flying appointment.

One such pilot was Wg Cdr J. F. Manning AFC ALCM who joined No.219 AWJRC following five years in ground posts. Already an 'A-Category' instructor on Meteors and a previous instrument rating examiner, Wg Cdr Manning took off for his first flight in WH166 on 10 April 1961 with Flt Lt Doggett as first pilot on a sector-recce. This was followed by a further flight with the same instructor on 2 May. This second sortie was general handling, one consisting of spins, aerobatics and circuit flying. Over the next six days Wg Cdr Manning flew WH166 on five separate occasions culminating in a night solo on 8 May. On completion of this refresher course the Wg Cdr went to The Central Flying School (CFS) at RAF Little Rissington to bring him up to the relevant standard for a flying instructor. He subsequently took up the appointment of Chief Instructor/Wing Commander Flying at No.5 FTS RAF Oakington.

WH166 in CFS colours at the Biggin Hill Air Fair in September 1967. *(via C. P. Russell-Smith)*

On 2 August 1961 three months after Wg Cdr Manning completed the AWJRC, WH166 was involved in another flying accident, again declared Cat 3, the aircraft was this time repaired at Manby by a team from No.60 MU RAF Leconfield. It remained grounded until 26 October 1961 when once more serviceable it resumed flying at Manby. However, late the following month on 21 November, it was once again withdrawn from active service returning to No.33 MU and put into storage.

Over the next few months WH166 also spent time at No.5 MU RAF Kemble from 31 July to 18 September before returning to Lyneham. Then, after nearly a year in storage the aircraft returned back to Manby and operational flying this time joining the College of Air Warfare (CAW) (formerly the RAFFC). Within the space of four months however, the aircraft was returned back to No.33 MU on 13 March 1963. No reason for its removal can be established but it was re-issued to the CAW on 24 June 1963 and transferred the same day to No.5 Civilian Anti-Aircraft Co-operation Unit (CAACU) at RAF Woodvale.

This unit mainly operated Meteor TT20s for target towing, but they flew WH166 for the next eighteen months before handing it over to the CFS at RAF Little Rissington on 26 January 1965 for what was to be its last flying tour. On joining the CFS fleet the aircraft was given the code '27' remaining with them until 9 September 1969 (the longest period it had spent with any one unit), when it was finally declared a non-effective airframe.

Three days later the aircraft was grounded and struck off charge, and at the same time issued to RAF Digby as primarily an instructional airframe and allotted the maintenance serial 8052M. Its role as an instructional airframe was changed on 1 December 1969 to that of a display aircraft and it soon took pride of place opposite Digby's Station Headquarters. For many years the aircraft retained its high profile day-glo markings but these have now given way to the distinctive markings of No.25 Sqn, consisting of broad silver bars edged top and bottom with black on each side of the fuselage roundel. On the tail appears a small black disc containing the letter 'A' in white. These change of markings were applied by the resident members of No.25 Sqn (then a Bloodhound Missile unit) to reflect a type once flown by the unit. Unfortunately the aircraft never flew on their strength, furthermore, no Meteors let alone WH166 were ever stationed or operated from Digby's grass runways.

By 1991 it was rumoured that the aircraft had been put up for disposal, since No.25 Sqn had become a Tornado operator at RAF Leeming.

ARMSTRONG WHITWORTH METEOR NF(T)14 WS774

RAFH ELY

WS774 was the fortieth of the mark built at Baginton, by Armstrong Whitworth, as part of Contract 6/Acft/6412/CB 5Cla. It was ready for collection by the RAF on 9 February 1954, having been test flown for the first time by Sqn Ldr J. O. Lancaster on 25 January for thirty-five minutes. The aircraft flew for a second time in the hands of the same pilot the following day, this time for twenty-five minutes. These flights took place at Bitteswell, about 12 miles east of the main factory, and following its second flight it was signed off test. After a final painting the aircraft was earmarked for conversion to a radar trainer and because of this remained with the company for conversion. The subsequent

Meteor NF(T)14 WS774 in No.264 Sqn colours. *(J. A. Simpson)*

modifications removed the Air Intercept (AI) radar installation and replaced it with REBECCA Mk4, a simple landing aid.

Now as a NF(T)14 it was collected by the RAF on 17 March and delivered to No.8 MU at RAF Little Rissington. There it stayed until 14 June 1955 when it joined the All Weather Operational Conversion Unit (AWOCU) part of No.228 OCU at RAF Leeming where it was given the code 'S'. It remained with the AWOCU until 13 March 1958 when it was delivered to No.12 MU at RAF Kirkbride for further storage.

On 11 May 1959, WS774 was issued to No.2 Air Navigation School (ANS) at RAF Thorney Island and was coded 'D'. It moved to No.1 ANS at RAF Stradishall on 17 January 1962 retaining the code 'D'. Whilst with this particular unit it suffered a flying accident on 13 May 1964 which was deemed Cat 3. The repairs were started the next day by a team from No.71 MU at RAF Bicester and were completed by 1 July; the aircraft returned to No.1 ANS the next day.

On the grass at Thorney Island in May 1960, WS774 in the 'red triangles' of No.2 ANS. *(C. P. Russell-Smith)*

WS774 was finally retired from active service on 6 January 1966 and was delivered to No.5 MU at RAF Kemble, a last flight of 30 minutes, and was put into storage. It remained there until 1967 when it was allocated to RAF Upwood for display. The aircraft was issued with the maintenance serial 7959M and was put on display on 25 July.

Its stay at Upwood lasted about two years as it was moved to RAF Ely in 1969, again for display. It was painted in the markings of No.264 Squadron (which it still retains) and put on display just inside the main gate.

GLOSTER METEOR F8
'WK864' (WL168)
RAF FINNINGLEY

The Gloster Meteor was the first jet fighter flown by the RAF, and when, only two weeks after becoming the first squadron to receive the new jet, No.616 Squadron moved to RAF Manston to begin operations against the German flying bombs (doodlebugs) on 27 July 1944, a new era began in RAF operations. This particular aircraft, which carries the markings of 616 Sqn, is really WL168 and unfortunately never flew with the squadron.

WL168 was ordered as part of Contract 6/Acft/6066/CB7(b) from the Gloster Aircraft Co. Ltd. It was built at Hucclecote and was part of the sixth, and last production batch (some 343 aircraft) of 1,090 Meteor F8s built. On 26 January 1954 the RAF were informed that it was ready for collection and on 22 February it was delivered to No.12 MU, RAF Kirkbride for service acceptance.

On 6 April it joined its first unit, No.111 Squadron, coded 'X', at RAF North Weald to be used as a standard day fighter. On 1 July 1955, 111 Sqn began to re-equip with the Hunter F4 so WL168 moved around the airfield at North Weald and joined No.604 (County of Middlesex) Squadron Royal Auxiliary Air Force (RAuxAF) and was used by them in a similar role. This remained the state of affairs until the surprise disbandment of the RAuxAF in March 1957 when, together with by now many surplus Meteors it returned to No.12 MU for storage.

Many of these surplus aircraft were scrapped, but WL168 was more fortunate because two years later, on 27 January 1959, it joined the Armament Practice School (APS) at RAF Sylt in West Germany as a target tug. It spent this part of its flying career towing targets (usually a banner) for pilots attending the school to shoot at, a somewhat hazardous existence but one that appears to have been carried out without too much difficulty. On 7 September 1961, it was flown to No.33 MU at RAF Lyneham for storage. This proved to be its last flight because on 14 November it was declared non-effective stock and finally, on 11 April 1962, was struck off charge.

Again it was fortunate, because on 10 May, instead of going for scrap it was issued with the maintenance serial 7750M and taken to No.35 MU at RAF Heywood, where it was put on display. It appears that it didn't stay very long at the MU because it was soon with the RAF Museum Regional Collection at RAF Finningley, joining a number of other aircraft that were regularly put on display at the Station's annual Battle of Britain displays. In WL168's case, following refurbishment to display standard, it

Meteor F8 WH456:L (WL168) in 616 Sqn R:AuxAF colours in the mid-1970s, when it was part of the Finningley Museum. *(via J. A. Simpson)*

was painted as WH456:L of No.616 (South Yorkshire) Sqn RAuxAF, (markings that it retained until it left Finningley early in 1977). The squadron had re-formed at Finningley on 10 May 1946 as a Mosquito NF30 night fighter unit. It stayed at the station until 5 May 1955 when it moved to nearby RAF Worksop, remaining there until disbanding in March 1957.

In 1977 with the impending Queen's Silver Jubilee display at Finningley, the Regional Collection was disbanded and dispersed. At first, many of the aircraft were taken to RAF Swinderby, WL168 (WH456) included, and then passed to other museums or stations for further display. WL168 remained at Swinderby until 1979 when it joined the RAF Museum collection at RAF St Athan. Shortly after arrival it was again refurbished, but this time it was repainted with its own serial and put back into the markings of 111 Sqn coded 'A'.

In early 1988, the MOD changed its policy towards the historic aircraft held in its charge and as a result the St Athan museum was disbanded. WL168 returned to RAF Finningley in the early part of 1988 and following yet another restoration, this time for display outside, it was again painted with an incorrect serial and colour scheme. It now carries the serial WK864 and the markings of No.616 Sqn once again. On 10 June 1988, positioned by the main gate at Finningley, it was formally dedicated as the station's first gate guard.

The real WK864 was another Hucclecote-built Meteor and entered service on 9 June 1953 with 616 Sqn at RAF Finningley. It flew with them until October 1956 when it returned to its builders for repair following a Cat 4 flying accident. Following completion of this work it spent some time in storage at Nos.33 and 20 MUs before joining the APS at Sylt in December 1958. It remained at Sylt until September 1961 when it once again returned to No.33 MU for further storage and eventual disposal. It was struck off charge on 3 December 1962 and was finally sold for scrap on 21 November 1963.

HANDLEY PAGE HASTINGS TMk5 TG503

RAF GATOW

The Hastings was RAF Transport Command's main transport aircraft throughout most of the 1950s and 1960s. It was designed in the closing years of the Second World War to Air Ministry Specification C3/44, in parallel with a less successful civil version, the Hermes.

TG503 was built at Radlett by the Handley Page Aircraft Co. and was the fifth production CMk1. It first flew in September 1947 and was initially retained by the manufacturers for a short period of trials and development work. Upon completion of these trials it was delivered to the Airborne Forces Experimental Establishment at RAF Beaulieu. This unit was responsible for the development of air dropping techniques applicable to the type. After a few weeks it was on the move again, this time to RAE Farnborough for fuel jettison trials.

In early 1948 it was decided to send TG503 on an extensive route proving flight to Australia and New Zealand. On 11 March 1948 the aircraft left RAF Lyneham, commanded by Handley Page's chief test pilot Sqn Ldr H. G. Hazelden, and after staging via Malta, Habbaniyah, Mauripur, New Delhi, Negumbo, Singapore and Darwin, it arrived in Sydney seven days later. It stayed in the Antipodes for about two months before leaving for home on 20 May, finally arriving back at Radlett two weeks later. (This tour resulted in the sale of four Hastings C3s to the RNZAF.)

As the aircraft arrived back from its trip the political climate in Germany was worsening and on 24 June, the Berlin Airlift began. TG503 is known to have taken part in the airlift,

TG503 at RAF Gatow as part of a memorial to the Berlin Airlift. *(G. Van Roye)*

'Operation Plainfare', probably on the strength of No.47 Squadron. However the aircraft was soon being used once again as a trials aircraft, this time in the meteorological role. (Twelve aircraft were later converted to Met 1 standard for use by No.202 Squadron at RAF Aldergrove.) In April 1949, TG503 went to Khartoum for tropical trials, later returning to Boscombe Down for radio trials. As part of these latter trials TG503 was given a special radio fit which it retained right up to being struck off charge.

The next few years saw TG503 still engaged on trials work, in particular on the H2S Mk9 radar with the Radar Research Establishment at Defford in 1951 and also similar trials at RAF Wyton in 1953.

In June 1956 the aircraft was delivered to RAF Lindholme for assessment by the Bomber Command Bombing School as a replacement for their ageing Lincolns. The Lincolns were fitted with a version of the H2S radar and were used to train V-Bomber crews in radar navigation and bomb aiming. After three years with the school it was decided to convert more Hastings to this role and in 1959-60 seven others were converted by Airwork Ltd. at Blackbushe with the type designation T5. Thus TG503 was the prototype Hastings T5.

In August 1960, TG503 was sent to Radlett for a much needed overhaul; this took until September 1961 when the aircraft was returned to Lindholme. Throughout the 1960s the eight Hastings T5s trained hundreds of navigators and, when the last Hastings in Air Support Command were retired in February 1968 and those of No.70 Squadron a few months later, they became the last ones in RAF service.

In August 1972 the Strike Command Bombing School, as it had become known, moved to RAF Scampton where, on 1 January 1974 it was absorbed by No.230 OCU and officially became known as the Radar Training Flight. However, it was more commonly known as 'No.1066 Squadron', a reference to the aircraft's name rather than its age.

By 1974 there were only four T5s left (TG503 included), the others having been retired. During their last few years of service, in addition to training navigators, they were often used for 'Offshore Tapestry' patrols, keeping an eye on the North Sea oil rigs and fishing fleets. The four aircraft also took part in the Icelandic 'Cod Wars' and occasionally reverted to their original role flying transport tasks.

However, in 1977 the aircraft had become uneconomic to maintain and the decision was taken to disband the flight; this took place on 30 June. TG503 was flown to RAF Gatow in Berlin, where it was issued with the maintenance serial 8555M. It had its ventral H2S radome removed and was repainted in the old Transport Command colours so that externally, at least, it looks like a Hastings C1. It was placed on display as a proud reminder of the RAF's contribution to the Berlin Airlift.

AVRO VULCAN B2
XL361
RAFSU GOOSE BAY

Arguably the most charismatic of the post-war four-engined 'V-bombers', the Vulcan in prototype form first took to the air in 1952. Evolving from the earlier B1 the Vulcan B2 (the prototype XH533 first flew on 19 August 1958) was a considerable development over the preceding variant. The first and most obvious difference was in the wings; they featured an extended span as well as a pronounced 'cranked' and drooped leading edge. Other innovations included an Airborne Auxiliary Power Pack (AAPU), a Ram Air Turbine (RAT) and an ECM tailcone. This gave the giant delta some measure of self defence plus two sources of emergency electrical power.

XL361 was built at Woodford as part of Contract 13145, and as part of the contract's third production order was declared ready for collection on 14 March 1962. It was flown to RAF Scampton the next day to join No.617 Squadron. The aircraft was painted in the standard gloss white overall finish reflecting its role as a high altitude nuclear bomber and it managed three months of accident-free operation before suffering a ground accident on 18 June. The aircraft was declared Cat 3 and returned to Woodford for repair by its builders. It remained with Avros for the next ten months although not under continuous repair because it managed to put in an appearance at the SBAC Farnborough that September. It finally returned to Scampton on 1 April 1963 and immediately rejoined 617 Sqn.

One point to note about this particular aircraft is that it was constructed to be Blue Steel compatible (as were all the B2 fleet) but lacked provision for the later intended Skybolt Air Launched Ballistic Missile (that most B2s had) that was subsequently cancelled.

On 20 August 1963 it was loaned, via the Ministry of Aviation, to Bristol Siddeley for a series of trials in conjunction with the Olympus Series 200 engines that were somewhat marginal in power. These trials lasted until 31 December 1963, after which it returned to operational duties with 617 Sqn.

On 2 April 1964 with the advent of centralised servicing the Scampton Bomber Wing was formed. As part of this change of policy aircraft lost their individual squadron identities and were pooled on a needs basis between the three resident squadrons; Nos. 27, 83 and 617 in Scampton's case. (This centralised servicing policy lasted until 1975 when semi-autonomous units were formed once again.)

On 25 March 1965, XL361 went to Woodford for a series of

modifications followed by a major servicing and repainting into the new 'V-force' livery of gloss grey and green upper surfaces with a gloss white lower surface. This new colour scheme emphasised the change of role that had been forced on the RAF by the Soviet Union's acquisition of high altitude anti-aircraft missiles capable of destroying high flying bombers. The aircraft returned to Scampton on 20 January 1966 and following the fitting of its previously removed ECM equipment it was soon back on flying duties.

Taken at the SBAC Farnborough of 1962 this photograph of XL361 shows the aircraft in 617 Sqn markings. *(C. P. Russell-Smith)*

On 13 October 1966 it flew to Bitteswell for another series of modifications, these taking until late November to complete; it was back with the Scampton Wing by 1 December. It flew on without incident until 23 February 1968, when it was the victim of another Cat 3 accident. The repairs this time were carried out by a team from Hawker Siddeley, taking some two months to complete. The aircraft eventually returned to flying duties on 29 May.

It underwent further modification work in 1969 arriving at HSA Bitteswell on 14 October and staying there until 9 December. By the time it returned to Scampton, 83 Sqn had disbanded leaving only 27 and 617 Sqns active although No.230 OCU had begun to move in from 7 December. From that date the aircraft, as with the rest of the station fleet, alternated between the three resident units, it being with 27/617 Sqn on 19 November and with the OCU by 30 November 1970. This continued to be the pattern for the next few years; it joined 27/617 on 5 April 1971, transferring to the OCU on 12 May. On 12 August it returned to Bitteswell for more mods, returning to 27/617 Sqns on 29 December. This toing and froing was rudely interrupted on 18 May 1972 when it was again Cat 3 following a ground accident.

The work this time was declared beyond local skills so a team from No.71 MU at RAF Bicester were tasked to effect the repairs. The lengthy repairs began on 13 June 1972 and were finally completed on 7 November; the aircraft rejoined the OCU the next day.

On 29 March 1972, 27 Sqn disbanded as a bomber unit although it did re-form on 1 November 1973 as a Maritime Reconnaissance Squadron based at RAF Waddington. XL361, following continued service with the OCU, was the first aircraft delivered to the newly re-formed squadron on 14 January 1974, to be used as a crew trainer until it could be replaced by a fully converted aircraft. XL361 only remained with 27 Sqn for a very short time because by 16 January it had returned to the OCU at Scampton. Between 16 January and 29 March 1973, XL361 was used by the resident Scampton units some sixteen times, and was also used by 27 Sqn on some twelve occasions. After 29 March the aircraft remained with the OCU until 16 December 1974 when it was loaned to MOD(PE) for a trial installation of the Marconi ARI18228 RWR system that eventually replaced the earlier but now obsolete 'Blue Saga' equipment.

It remained with MOD(PE) until 10 January 1975 when it again returned to the OCU, although this stay was shortlived because it joined 617 Sqn four days later. Some nine months passed before it underwent further trials with MOD(PE) involving the same equipment. These lasted two months until 3 September when it returned to 617 Sqn at Scampton. By now the Vulcan squadrons had returned to a semi-autonomous form (from 1 April 1975) so XL361 was painted with 617 Sqn's distinctive dambuster motif on its fin.

XL361 was next on the move on 3 August 1977 when it joined another Scampton unit, No.35 Squadron. This unit had returned from RAF Akrotiri, Cyprus following the Turkish invasion of the island in 1974. XL361 remained with this squadron at Scampton until the Vulcan force began to run down in 1981. On 13 April 1981 the aircraft joined what was to be its last unit, No.9 Squadron at RAF Waddington. It was to stay with them until December 1981. On 13 November 1981, whilst in transit to RAFSU Goose Bay as part of a 'Lone Ranger' training sortie, XL361 suffered a serious anti-icing failure resulting in serious damage to the airframe. After landing at Goose Bay the damaged Vulcan was immediately declared Cat 3(R) to await a more detailed inspection by a team from No.71 MU at RAF

Following a severe in-flight defect, Vulcan B2 XL361 was prepared for display retaining 9 Sqn colours. *(P. Bolland)*

Abingdon. Once the damage had been assessed the aircraft was re-categorised Cat 5 as it was deemed beyond economic repair.

On 21 December XL361 was declared Cat 5 (Spares Recovery) after which it was intended to scrap the remains. Fortunately for the aircraft, it was re-categorised Cat 5 (Ground Instructional Use/Display) in June and allocated to Goose Bay for display. Shortly after this a team from Goose Bay worked to prepare the aircraft to withstand the harsh Canadian winters and, following completion, the aircraft was put on display near the RAF Support Unit.

HAWKER SIDDELEY HARRIER GR3 XW917

RAF GUTERSLOH

Since 4 January 1977, when No.IV(AC) Squadron transferred from RAF Wildenrath, RAF Gutersloh has been the main operating base for RAF Germany of the unique Hawker Siddeley Harrier VTOL aircraft. On 1 April 1977, IV Sqn were joined by No.3(F) Squadron and these two units have remained the only RAF front line operators of this aircraft outside the UK. It therefore came as no surprise that when XW917, a surplus time-expired aircraft, became available the station had it put on display.

XW917 was built at Kingston on Thames by the parent company as a Harrier GR1, part of a twelve-aircraft order comprising of both GR1s and T4s. These aircraft were serialled XW916 to XW927 and were finally delivered to the RAF by July 1972. It was airborne for the first time on 30 June 1971 on a delivery flight to Hawker Siddeley's Dunsfold airfield where it underwent flight testing. On 23 August the aircraft joined its first unit, IV(AC) Sqn at RAF Wildenrath.

IV Sqn, which had previously been equipped with the venerable Hunter FGA9, had re-formed at Wildenrath on 1 June 1970 as the second Harrier squadron (No.1 Squadron being the first), although it was the first to form in RAFG. Interestingly, the first Harrier they received was XV779, now the gate guard at RAF Wittering. XW917's stay with this, its first unit, lasted only until 18 May 1972 when it was transferred to 3(F) Sqn also at Wildenrath. On its arrival it was coded 'L', and apart from several brief periods of loan back to IV Sqn the aircraft remained with this squadron for the rest of its operational life. Its first period of loan back to IV Sqn was later that year, from 9 to 23 October; it is not known what code if any it carried with the squadron.

On 11 June 1974 the aircraft underwent conversion to GR3 standard; this entailed incorporating several modifications, one of which was the installation of an uprated Rolls-Royce Pegasus 103 engine. The most obvious external difference was to its nose cone; this was enlarged to accommodate the laser ranging equipment. Another external difference, probably carried out at a slightly later date, was the addition of a RWR antenna on the fin. When the work was completed it rejoined 3 Sqn at the end of the month.

The aircraft was the victim of a Cat 3 flying accident (almost certainly a bird strike) on 30 October 1974; this required the skills of its builders to effect repairs, which took until 30 June

1975 to complete, when the aircraft once again rejoined 3 Sqn.

1977 saw a rationalisation of RAF Germany's ground/attack force when the Jaguar GR1 began to enter service. No.20 Squadron, the third Harrier unit, was disbanded to eventually become a Jaguar operator; this left 3 and IV Sqns which were then transferred to RAF Gutersloh in northern Germany. IV Sqn arrived first, on 4 January, followed by 3 Sqn on 1 April. This has remained the situation to this day, although both squadrons now operate the somewhat more sophisticated Harrier GR7. XW917 continued to be operated by 3 Sqn throughout the late 1970s and 1980s although by March 1984 it had been recoded 'AL' as part of the RAF's adoption of double-letter codes. It was loaned once again to IV Sqn from 29 March–2 April 1984, after which it returned to 3 Sqn.

XW917:L of 3 Sqn at the RAF Valley Open Day on 11 August 1973. *(C. P. Russell-Smith)*

XW917's final period of loan to IV Sqn was from 18–20 September 1984. It then gave another three years of uninterrupted service until by 19 November 1987 its fatigue life had expired. It was grounded, declared Cat 5(Scrap) and allocated for spares recovery. When all useful items had been removed, plans were made to turn the aircraft into a gate guard for RAF Gutersloh. The project was led by Flt Lt Hutchinson, OC Gutersloh's Visiting Aircraft Section and involved many agencies within the station's engineering wing. However, the vast majority of the preparation work was undertaken by SGTs Dyson and Elliot together with Cpl Hargreaves of the General Engineering Flt who together contributed some 1,000 Mhrs to the project. Eventually on 8 July 1988 the completed aircraft was atop a plinth in a flying attitude where it still remains.

HAWKER HUNTER F6
XF527
RAF HALTON

Since losing its last gate guard in August 1970, Spitfire XVI RW386, RAF Halton had remained unguarded. This position was reversed with the installation of Hunter F6 XF527 in June 1986.

XF527 began life at Baginton, Coventry, where it was built under licence by Armstrong Whitworth Aircraft Ltd. as part of Contract SP/6/9818/CB7(a). It was the last Hunter produced by Armstrong Whitworth, and was built without the leading edge extensions and gun blast deflectors (which were fitted later). It was initially issued to No.33 MU, RAF Lyneham on 27 July 1956, from where, after a short period of storage, it was delivered on 17 October 1956 to No.19 MU, RAF St Athan for service preparation.

XF527 first entered service on 30 October 1956 with RAF Linton-on-Ouse Station Flight; this was rather quicker than normal because, at the time, No.19 MU were busy with redundant Hunter FMk4s returning from re-equipping and disbanding squadrons. The aircraft did not stay at Linton very long and, on 18 December, it moved to join RAF Church Fenton's Station Flight.

It was on the move again on 12 February 1957, this time to join

XF527 on its home patch at RAF Valley in August 1975.
(C. P. Russell-Smith)

No.19 Squadron, also based at Church Fenton, who coded the aircraft 'J'. By May 1958 it had been recoded 'P', and in June 1959 it moved with the rest of the squadron to RAF Leconfield where it stayed until December 1959.

In early 1960, XF527 joined No.66 Squadron at RAF Acklington, who coded it 'S', and when this squadron disbanded on 30 September 1960, it went to No.111 Squadron at RAF Wattisham, coded 'F'. It remained with the 'Treble One' for only a brief period and it soon appeared on the strength of the Air Fighting Development Squadron (AFDS), which was part of the Central Fighter Establishment (CFE) based at RAF Binbrook; whilst with this unit it was coded 'T'.

On 14 March 1962 it was delivered to No.5 MU at RAF Kemble for servicing, modification and eventual storage. It did not appear again until 1967 when it appeared on the strength of No.4 FTS at RAF Valley, Anglesey. As part of No.3 Training Squadron it still wore camouflage and was coded '70'. The use of Hunters by No.4 FTS was a response to complaints from long-legged pilots about the lack of leg room in the Folland Gnat.

On 5 February 1975 it suffered Cat 3 damage and, because repairs were beyond local resources, it was transferred by road to No.5 MU, RAF Kemble. After repair it was returned to 4 FTS but this time in the new training scheme of red, white and light grey.

XF527 remained at Valley until transferred to RAF Brawdy to join No.1 TWU for use in the weapons training role. After arrival at Brawdy, it was repainted once again in camouflage and given the code '36'. It remained with No.1 TWU until 21 September 1979 when it returned to Kemble for servicing and storage.

With the grounding of the Buccaneer fleet in 1980, surplus Hunters were issued as temporary replacements to enable Buccaneer pilots to retain their flying currency. XF527 was one of the aircraft brought out of storage; it was sent to RAF Laarbruch, West Germany, where it was placed on the strength of the Station Flight. By September 1980, the Buccaneers had been returned to flying status and XF527 was returned to Kemble, once again into store.

On 2 November 1981 the aircraft was declared a non-effective airframe; it was transferred to No.1 S of TT at RAF Halton where it was given the Support Command maintenance serial 8680M. Whilst with the School it was used by the students as a hydraulic system trainer but, in 1986, with the arrival of more modern aircraft in the shape of the Jaguar, Halton began to disperse their Hunters.

At the express wish of Halton's Station Commander, Group Captain R. H. Kyle, the airframe trainees of Course AAF 151 spent two months refurbishing XF527 to display standard and, resplendent in its old training colour scheme of red, white and light grey, it was placed in the position it now holds outside RAF Halton's Station Headquarters on 26 June 1986.

HAWKER HUNTER FMk1
WT612
RAF HENLOW

The Hawker Hunter was designed in parallel with the Supermarine Swift to Air Ministry Specification F3/48 and was developed from the Hawker P1067. The first flight of the F1 (WT555) took place on 16 May 1953 and 113 were built by Hawkers at Kingston upon Thames with another batch of twenty-six being built at Blackpool.

WT612 was built at Kingston as part of Contract SP/6/5910/ CB7(a) dated 14 March 1951, and it first took to the air piloted by Hawker's test pilot Frank Bullen on 13 July 1954. Although it was destined never to see operational service, it went to No.5 MU, RAF Kemble for its acceptance checks, arriving there on 7 September 1954.

The Hunter F1 as built, was powered by the Rolls-Royce Avon 104 or 107 series engine and, in an effort to increase the aircraft's performance, WT612 became the second Hunter to be fitted with the uprated Avon RA 14 Mk115 engine. After conversion WT612 was test flown by both HSA and A&AEE pilots, not only to check on improved performance, but also to see if a modified front end could eliminate the problems associated with cannon firing at high altitude, a problem that the standard production aircraft suffered from.

The trials life of this aircraft lasted from September 1954 until 23 May 1957 when the aircraft was replaced by WT656 and was placed in storage at No.5 MU, RAF Kemble. On 16 September it was declared non-effective stock and two months later on 22 November it was transferred to No.2 Radio School, RAF Yatesbury for ground instructional purposes, where it became 7496M.

In 1963 there was a reduction in the number of training schools and Yatesbury closed. The now redundant WT612 was looking for a new home, but it did not move until 2 August 1965 when it was allocated to RAF Catterick for fire fighting training. Fortunately this move was cancelled and on 23 September it was re-allocated to RAF Hereford for display. Sometime during its transfer to RAF Hereford it was stripped of all usable components and acquired the incorrect serial WT216.

Eventually repainted with its correct serial and with maintenance serial applied, WT612 joined fellow F1 WT651 as a backdrop to the various passing-out parades that took place on the parade square. It remained at Hereford until 20 January 1983 when it moved to No.1 S of TT, RAF Halton for instructional use. After arrival the staff at Halton discovered that so much of its

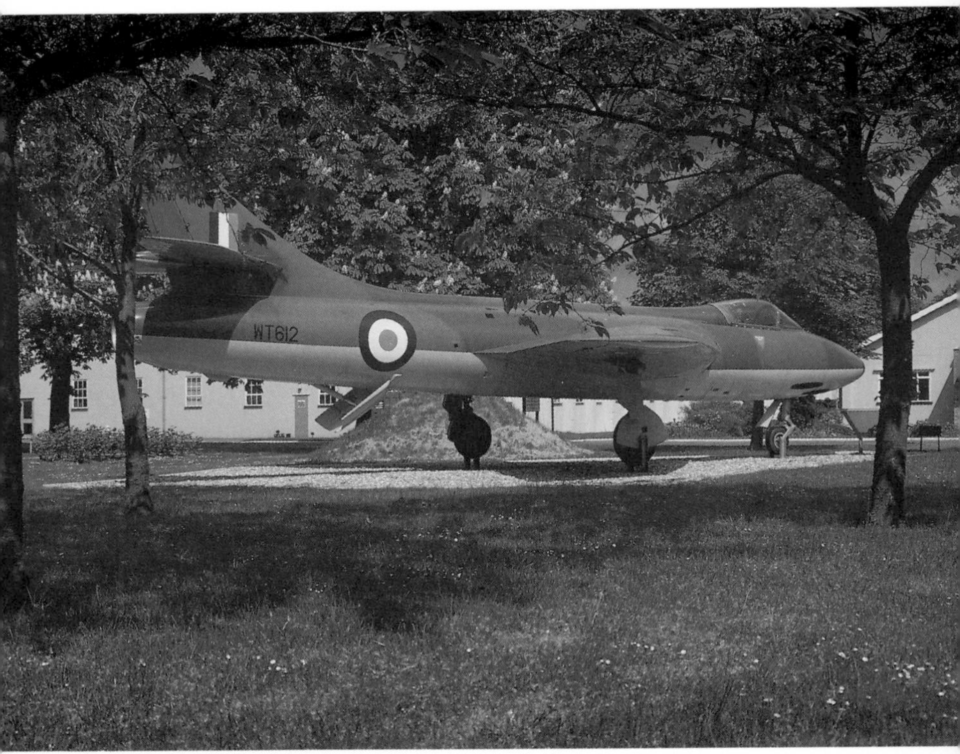

RAF Henlow have displayed this Hunter F1 WT612 since 1984.
(J. A. Simpson)

internals had been removed that it would be only of limited use as a training aid. As a result of this WT612 left Halton and moved to RAF Henlow in May 1984 where the aircraft was refurbished, given a fresh coat of paint and placed on display in the position it holds today.

HAWKER HUNTER FGA9
XG252

RAF HEREFORD

For many years RAF Hereford had on display a pair of Hunter FMk1s which were used as a backdrop to the many passing-out parades that were held on the station. In early 1982 these two aircraft were removed from the display leaving only Spitfire TE392, and even this was removed in 1984, leaving the station 'unguarded'. The station's links with the Hunter were rekindled in February 1988 when XG252 arrived from No.2 S of TT, RAF Cosford to take up duties as a gate guard.

XG252 was built by Hawkers at Kingston on Thames and emerged from the factory in October 1956 as a FMk6. This mark of Hunter was given the type designation P1099 but was more commonly known as the 'big-engined Hunter', being the first of its type to be fitted with the 10,000-lb thrust Rolls-Royce Avon 203.

On 25 October 1956, XG252 was airborne for the first time in the capable hands of company test pilot Frank Bullen and following these initial test flights the RAF were informed that the aircraft was ready for collection on 5 November. The RAF took delivery of it almost immediately, when on the following day it followed the route of many of its predecessors and was flown to No.5 MU, RAF Kemble for service acceptance.

It remained at Kemble for just one month and, on 6 December, it joined No.66 Squadron, coded 'D', at RAF Linton-on-Ouse. The squadron moved to RAF Acklington on 14 February 1957 and remained there until it disbanded in September 1960. XG252 remained with 66 Sqn right to the end and, prior to being re-allocated to another squadron, it was converted to FGA Mk9 standard. It was sent to RAF Horsham St Faith, as part of the second conversion contract, to be brought up to interim FGA9 standard by an RAF and manufacturer's working party. This included fitting a brake parachute and strengthened wings for the carriage of the various ordnance required for its new ground attack role; the more powerful Rolls-Royce Avon 207 engine was not fitted at this stage, but at a later date, bringing it up to full FGA9 standard.

Following conversion it joined No.54 Squadron at RAF Stradishall, coded 'U', although in May 1961 it was loaned briefly to the Ministry of Aviation for trials. It returned to Stradishall on 6 June 1961 and was issued to the Station Flight, with whom it remained until 1 January 1962 when it rejoined 54 Sqn at RAF Waterbeach. It went to No.5 MU for servicing on 11 December returning to the squadron on 16 May 1963, but on 25

June it suffered a Cat 3 flying accident which required a team from No.60 MU, RAF Dishforth to carry out the necessary repairs. The aircraft returned to 54 Sqn on 1 August, just in time to move with the squadron to RAF West Raynham two weeks later.

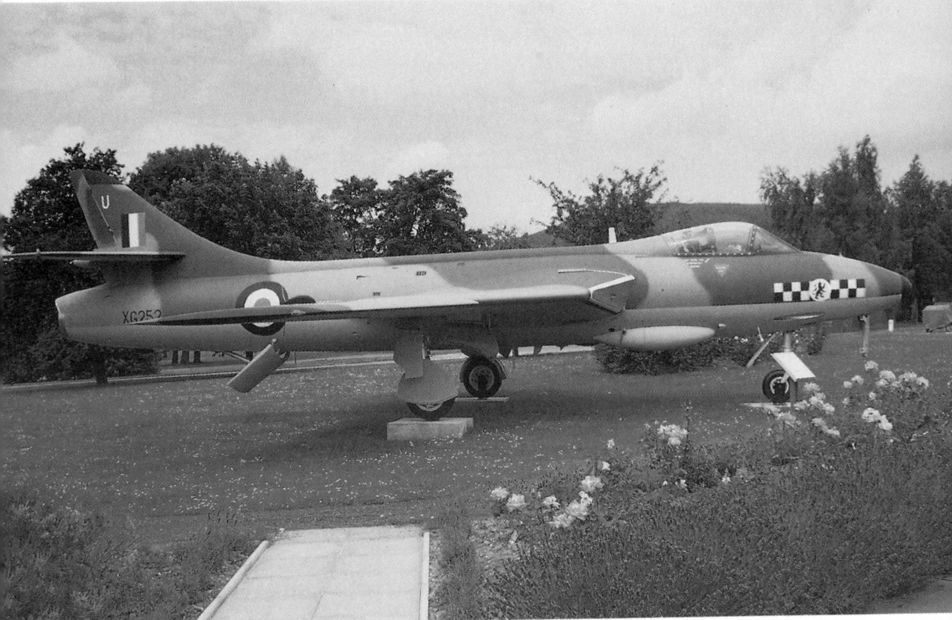

RAF Hereford were without a gate guard for a number of years, this situation was remedied in 1988 when Hunter FGA9 XG252 in 54 Sqn colours took up residence on the gate. *(J. Kyte)*

On 3 October 1963 it suffered another Cat 3 accident whilst on detachment for the squadron's annual gun-firing exercise; this time it was repaired at RAF El Adem in Libya before returning to 54 Sqn in November. It flew on with 54 Sqn for the next seven years until 16 March 1970 when it was transferred to RAF Wittering to provide continuation flying for pilots awaiting conversion to the Harrier.

On 5 June it flew to RAF St Athan for servicing and preparation for transfer to No.8 Squadron in Bahrain. It joined its new squadron on 4 February 1971 and stayed with it until September. Instead of going to Sharjah when the squadron moved stations, it returned to No.5 MU arriving there on the 30th. After a period of storage, it joined No.45 Squadron on 30 August 1972; it had re-formed on 1 August at RAF West Raynham as a ground attack training unit, skills that would be required by pilots who would go on to convert to the Harrier and Jaguar.

XG252:73 in 45 Sqn markings at its home base of Wittering in 1975. *(C. P. Russell-Smith)*

After initial work-up at West Raynham, 45 Sqn moved to RAF Wittering in September where it retained XG252 until disbandment on 4 June 1976. Following another servicing at Kemble, XG252 joined the Tactical Weapons Unit (TWU) coded '45' at RAF Brawdy on 27 July. Brawdy became No.1 TWU on 31 July 1978 when a similar unit, No.2 TWU, was formed at RAF Lossiemouth. XG252 joined No.2 TWU on 24 January 1980 and stayed with them until 1981 when it again returned to No.5 MU, this time for a major servicing.

It rejoined No.1 TWU at Brawdy on 26 October but stayed for only a year; on 25 October 1984 it flew to RAF Cosford to become a ground instructional airframe, where on landing it was declared Cat 5 (GI). It was immediately issued with the Support Command maintenance serial 8840M prior to joining No.2 S of TT for use as a training airframe by recruits learning engine, jet pipe and ejection-seat servicing techniques.

In November 1986, RAF Hereford was allocated XG252 for display purposes. It was dismantled by a team from No.71 MU, RAF Abingdon and taken by road to Hereford, arriving on 2 February 1988; after preparation, which included a respray into 54 Sqn colours coded 'U', it went on display in early 1988.

BLACKBURN BUCCANEER S2 XK526

RAF HONINGTON

XK526 began life as the tenth Blackburn NA39 Buccaneer to be built at the Brough works. As the first of four pre-production airframes, the aircraft first flew on 3 August 1960 from the company airfield at Holme-on-Spalding-Moor. Some two months later, in October, XK526 flew to A&AEE Boscombe Down for a period of pilot familiarisation, prior to CA release, and a series of engineering assessments. Early 1961 saw the aircraft involved in aircraft carrier landing trials aboard HMS *Ark Royal* during a Mediterranean cruise. By April 1961 the aircraft was back at Holme-on-Spalding-Moor in preparation for tropical trials that were to take place in Singapore. When this work was completed, the aircraft returned to Boscombe Down in June 1961, and began the Far Eastern trials some four weeks later.

To overcome the lack of power from the Gyron Junior engines fitted in the Buccaneer S1, Blackburn selected XK526 for the installation of Rolls-Royce RB168 engines, carrying out the necessary structural changes and other improvements at the same time. This work was carried out at Holme and took some sixteen months.

XK526 returned to flying status with its 'second' maiden flight on 17 May 1963, as the Spey-engined prototype, now known as the Buccaneer S2. The aircraft spent the next five years of its life flying trials from Holme, RAE Bedford and A&AEE Boscombe Down. August 1964 saw the aircraft with RAE Bedford for a series of catapult launching trials and again in 1966, for arrestor trials. In June 1967, XK526 moved to Boscombe Down for six weeks of low speed handling trials and it returned to Bedford again in March 1968 for a fortnight of jet blast deflector trials. Finally, in August 1968, the aircraft returning to the company airfield at Holme to flight test a dummy EW pod. When this work was complete, the aircraft was placed in storage at Holme from February to June 1969 following which it was returned to flying status for a prolonged drag research programme.

Having made some 552 flights as an S2, the aircraft was allocated to the MRCA (Tornado) radar development programme; it was passed from the manufacturers, now known as Hawker Siddeley, to Marshalls of Cambridge during June 1972. Marshalls had been contracted to carry out a major servicing on the aircraft and to incorporate the required changes for the MRCA project but, during its stay at Cambridge, the aircraft was taken off the programme, and was reassigned to research and development work with the Royal Radar Establishment (RRE) at

Pershore. The servicing and conversion work for this new task was completed by November 1975.

The aircraft arrived at Pershore on 26 January 1976 to take up its duties with RRE. Although little had changed externally, the aircraft was considerably modified internally. The cockpit had been configured for pilot-only operation, permitting civilian observers and equipment operators to occupy the rear seat, and Pershore technicians installed a synthetic aperture radar system. XK526 remained at Pershore until late 1977 when the facility was closed and RRE and its aircraft were relocated to RAE Bedford. There, the aircraft was withdrawn from use having flown a total of 613.45 hours; it remained at Bedford in this state until 1980.

Having finished its flying career, XK526 was allocated to the range facility at Pendine Sands in Wales and what would have been almost certain destruction. A reprieve was on hand, however; in January 1980 the aircraft was re-allocated to RAF Honington for Battle Damage Repair Training (BDRT). It was moved to Honington by road on 9–10 March 1980 and was given the Support Command maintenance serial 8648M, although this has never been carried on the aircraft.

In late 1982 the aircraft was moved from its uncovered location on the airfield, to the comparative luxury of a hangar at Honington, and preparation for its eventual display at the main gate. XK526 emerged from the hangar in March 1983 resplendent in RAF 'wrap-around' camouflage and markings for the first time. In late March it replaced the previous occupant, Buccaneer S1 XK531, and became Honington's gate guardian having never seen service in either the RAF or RN.

A flying shot of XK526 on another test sortie from RAE Bedford. *(RAE Bedford)*

GLOSTER JAVELIN FAW9 XH903

RAF INNSWORTH

XH903 was the sixty-fifth of eighty-five P280 Javelin FAW7s built by the Gloster Aeroplane Company against Contract/Acft/11329/CB7(b) issued on 19 October 1954.

It was completed in early 1959 and was ready for collection from the company works at Hucclecote on 27 February of that year, being delivered from Glosters to RAF St Athan on that date, prior to a period of service acceptance checks with the resident No.19 MU. With its acceptance complete the aircraft was assigned to No.23 Squadron at RAF Coltishall, going to the squadron's detached base at RAF Horsham St Faith on 1 May 1959.

In the continual process of updating aircraft in order to maintain their service lives, the Air Ministry contracted the aircraft manufacturers to instate a modification programme. This programme was to update all the extant FAW7 aircraft to the much-improved FAW8 standard. The aircraft was thus returned to Glosters at their Moreton Valance facility on 1 June 1960 to permit this work to commence.

Javelin FAW 9 XH903 at Innsworth. *(C. P. Russell-Smith)*

Whilst this rework involved a number of minor system and equipment changes, the major modifications were the replacement of the Armstrong Siddeley Sapphire Sa7 engines of the FAW7 with the reheated Sapphire Sa7R as fitted to the FAW8. Changes to the mainplane were also carried out to incorporate a drooped wing leading edge, another feature found on the FAW8.

The manufacturer's conversion programme was completed by 30 December 1960 and the aircraft was ready for return to RAF service once more. With many of the FAW8 features incorporated into the aircraft, the designation now changed to the final service mark of FAW9. The main difference between this final variant and the FAW8 remained with the installed radar equipment. The FAW8 aircraft were all fitted with the US-built AI22 equipment and its different nose profile, whilst the FAW9 aircraft retained the British-built AI17 set of the earlier marks. In its newly modified form, XH903 was delivered to RAF St Athan for its second visit, again to No.19 MU, on 5 January 1961.

A return to flying commenced on 14 February when the aircraft was delivered to No.33 Squadron at RAF Middleton St George. This initial residency was short-lived however, as ten days later it departed to RAF Leuchars for a short period of loan to No.29 Squadron before returning to 33 Sqn on 3 March.

In October 1962, No.5 Squadron, then flying Javelin FAW5s, began to convert to the FAW9 variant and in doing so took on charge most, if not all, of 33 Sqn's aircraft, including XH903, and no doubt most of the crews. This re-equipment was completed by 21 November and coincided with the squadron's move from RAF Laarbruch to RAF Geilenkirchen and assignment to 2 ATAF; XH903 gaining the code 'G' during this period. The aircraft flew with 5 Sqn until 20 September 1963 when it suffered a Cat 3 accident. This resulted in its withdrawal from use until repairs were completed. It was returned to 5 Sqn on 10 April 1964.

On 7 October 1965, 5 Sqn disbanded as a Javelin unit prior to re-equipping with the E.E. Lightning. This effectively left XH903 without a home and it was flown to No.27 MU, RAF Shawbury on the 15th of the month for storage. With the Javelin fleet rapidly being retired from service, the number of aircraft with the MU quickly increased as they awaited disposal. XH903 was struck off charge as a non-effective airframe on 2 December 1966.

Fortunately XH903 was reprieved from the breaker's torch when on 23 August 1967 it was allocated to RAF Innsworth for display. Now with the maintenance serial 7938M, it was positioned as a gate guard during the later part of the year. Following a repaint prior to its final move, the serial 'XM903' was mistakenly applied and it remained for nearly a year before being corrected. The aircraft remains to this day where it was first placed, by the main entrance to RAF Innsworth.

GLOSTER METEOR FMk8 WH364

RAF KEMBLE

The Meteor F8 was the common mark of the type built, with a total of 1,090 being produced for the RAF, flying with some 31 fighter squadrons and many second-line units whilst in RAF service. WH364 was built by Armstrong Whitworth at Baginton as part of the 200 F8s ordered as the fifth production batch of its type, to Contract 6/Acft/5621/CB7(b). It first flew from Baginton in January 1952 and was delivered to No.29 MU at RAF High Ercall on 4 February for service preparation and eventual storage.

It remained in storage until 11 August 1952 when it was issued to No.601 (County of London) Squadron, Royal Auxiliary Air Force, based at RAF North Weald. WH364 was one of the first Meteors received to replace the squadron's previous mount, the Vampire F3. The RAuxAF regularly took their aircraft out to Malta for gun firing practice in the summer months and it was on one of these visits in June 1954 that WH364 was nearly destroyed. On 24 June, whilst flying at some 470 knots at 5,000 feet, its cockpit canopy shattered without warning, and with no little skill the pilot, Fg Off N. D. Norman (of Britten Norman fame) managed to get the aircraft back safely to the ground at RAF Takali, the damage assessed as Cat 3.

The aircraft was taken to No.137 MU at RAF Safi for repair and by the time this had been completed 610 Sqn had returned home, taking another aircraft with them in its place. This meant a further period of storage for WH364, this time at Safi. In June 1956 it came out of storage to be briefly allocated to Takali's Station Flight as a 'hack'. However, this only lasted five weeks and once again it went back into storage at Safi. It came out again in October 1957, venturing across the Mediterranean to RAF Idris in Libya, also for use by the Station Flight.

It remained at Idris for some five months before again returning to storage at Safi. In July 1959 it was allocated to the Communications and Target Towing Squadron at Takali, towing banners for visiting squadrons to shoot at, before returning once again to storage at Safi in October 1960.

It finally returned home in 1962 when it was delivered to No.5 MU, RAF Kemble on 17 August for a complete refurbishment. After the work was completed it was issued to No.85 Squadron on 4 December who coded the aircraft 'U'. No.85 Sqn was based at RAF Binbrook and was Fighter Command's fighter interception training squadron flying Canberras and Meteors as radar targets and banner towers; WH364 was, in effect, doing the same job as

Still airworthy when this shot of it was taken in June 1968, WH364 flew on with 85 Sqn for another 18 months before finally being grounded. *(C. P. Russell-Smith)*

it did in Malta. There followed five uneventful years in this unglamorous yet essential work before, on 18 November 1969, it was sent back to No.5 MU, this time for disposal.

The aircraft was placed in storage and on 3 September 1971 was finally declared a non-effective airframe. It was allocated to RAF Kemble for display in February 1972 and issued with the maintenance serial 8169M. Kemble had not had a proper gate guard for three years since Spitfire XVI TE392 had been removed to be used in the film *Battle of Britain* in 1967. Kemble had WH364 painted once again in 601 Sqn colours and put it on display on 9 February 1972. The aircraft has been refurbished a number of times since then, the most recent over the winter of 1988-9.

HAWKER HUNTER F6 'XJ673' (XE606)

RAF LAARBRUCH

Regarded by many as the definitive model of the celebrated Hunter design, the Hawker Type P1099 Hunter F6 variant first flew on 22 January 1954 with deliveries to the first units beginning in late 1956.

XE606 was built as part of a 100-strong batch of aircraft at the Hawker factory at Kingston on Thames as part of Contract 6/Acft/7144, dated 12 July 1951. It made its maiden flight on 17 May 1956 in the hands of David Lockspeiser and on 21 June 1956 was delivered to No.33 MU, RAF Lyneham, Wiltshire for service preparation.

XE606 first entered service, after a short period of storage at Lyneham, with the Air Fighting Development School (AFDS) at RAF Binbrook in mid-1957. The AFDS, which was part of the Central Fighter Establishment, later underwent a number of changes, becoming the Fighter Combat School and then later the Day Fighter Combat School.

XE606 only remained with the AFDS for a few months and in late 1957 it joined No.92 Squadron at RAF Middleton St George who coded the aircraft 'U'. In 1961 the squadron, including XE606, moved to RAF Leconfield. The aircraft subsequently remained with this unit until it began to exchange its Hunters in favour of the more advanced Lightning F2 in 1962.

After the excitement of front-line service XE606 moved to a more sedentary haven in the care of No.229 OCU, RAF Chivenor. In 1965 it was noted with this unit wearing No.63 Squadron markings and coded '2'. It also wore the markings of the other two shadow squadrons at Chivenor, Nos. 79 and 234, coded '2' and '54' respectively over the next few years.

In 1974, XE606 moved to RAF Brawdy to join the newly formed Tactical Weapons Unit (TWU) where it arrived still wearing the markings of 234 Sqn, although by now coded '11'.

Sometime later the aircraft went to No.5 MU at RAF Kemble for conversion to F6A standard. This entailed fitment of some FGA9 items such as the facility for carrying 230-gallon underwing fuel tanks, a tail parachute and various modifications to the cockpit ventilation and oxygen system. But unlike the production FGA9, the F6A or F6A/Interim FGA9 as it was known, retained the original 10,000 lbst Avon 203 turbojet. After this work was completed the aircraft returned to Brawdy where it took up the markings of No.79 Squadron who recoded it '11' again.

In 1984, with the introduction of the Hawk T1 and therefore the gradual running down of the Hunter fleet, XE606 was passed to

RAF Laarbruch for use as a Battle Damage Repair Trainer (BDRT), where upon its arrival it was allocated the maintenance serial 8737M

One of the current squadrons based at Laarbruch is No.20 Squadron, whose current equipment is the Tornado GR1; in earlier times it had flown Hunters in the Far East. Therefore, to save XE606 from the normal fate of BDRT airframes, it requested and was granted the aircraft for use as a gate guardian/display aircraft.

The Hunter moved to 20 Sqn's premises on 7 December 1984 where it was transformed into 'XJ673:XX'. This was 20 Sqn's Commanding Officer's personal Hunter when the squadron was part of the Far East Air Force from 1 September 1961 to 13 February 1970, flying from RAF Tengah, Singapore. The aircraft carries a squadron leader's pennant on the nose wheel door and the name 'Sqn Ldr Calvert' (who was OC 20 Sqn from 1 September 1961 to 8 April 1964) below the cockpit. Because the aircraft had had a change of role it was given a new maintenance serial 8841M.

The original XJ673, having served with Nos.14 and 66 Squadrons, had been on 20 Sqn's strength at Tengah, where it became the Squadron Commander's aircraft (hence the code XX) until 2 April 1969. On that day, as part of a four-ship detachment, it experienced electrical and hydraulic problems on route from Hong Kong to Tengah. The pilot attempted to divert to Clark AB in the Philippines for an emergency landing, but unfortunately the engine flamed out about five miles from the runway, forcing the pilot to eject, luckily without injury.

An immaculate-looking 'XJ673', at RAF Laarbruch. *(RAF Laarbruch)*

ENGLISH ELECTRIC CANBERRA B(I)8 XM264

RAF LAARBRUCH

Characterised by its fixed fighter-type canopy, this, the final bomber variant of the English Electric Canberra was an attempt to emulate the DH Mosquito but in jet form. The prototype B8, VX185 (a conversion of the only B5) first flew on 23 July 1954 with production aircraft entering service with No.88 Squadron as part of 2 ATAF in RAF Germany from May 1956.

XM264 was built by the English Electric Aircraft Co. at their Preston factory as part of Contract 6/Acft/6445, and was part of an order manufactured to replace aircraft that had been sold to overseas customers such as Peru and India. These aircraft were built between August 1958 and April 1959.

XM264 first entered service with 88 Sqn at RAF Wildenrath, West Germany in late 1958 where it became part of the Light Bomber Force. It was painted in the standard camouflage scheme of green and grey upper surfaces with a gloss black underside, and carried 88 Sqn's 'writhing snake' badge on the fin.

On 1 January 1961, XM264 changed ownership when it was transferred to No.16 Squadron and marked with the squadron's black and yellow fuselage band. It remained with 'The Saints' until August 1965 when it returned to Wildenrath, this time joining No.14 Squadron. By mid-1966, XM264 had acquired the code 'B' and although still in its original camouflage scheme, had, in common with others, been painted with large white serials on the fuselage sides.

In May 1967 it went to No.23 MU at RAF Aldergrove for a major servicing, returning still coded 'B' to 14 Sqn later that year. No.14 Sqn finally bade farewell to the aircraft in September 1968 when it was returned to its manufacturer for extensive modifications.

After these modifications had been completed XM264 returned once again to Germany (via 23 MU) in April 1971, but now with its gloss black undersides repainted with a light grey scheme. It rejoined 16 Sqn at Laarbruch. Once it had been accepted by 16 Sqn the aircraft was once again painted with the squadron's black and yellow fuselage band, a 'saint badge' on the fin and a nose sharkmouth, the markings it still carries.

In 1972 the RAF Germany Canberra force began to run down and by February 1972 XM264 had been grounded, 16 Sqn itself disbanding as a Canberra unit on 6 June 1972 when it reformed as a Buccaneer squadron. With its flying days now finished the aircraft began the next phase of its life acting as a surface decoy

Close-up view of Canberra B(I)8 XM264 at Laarbruch. It carries the famous 'sharks mouth' markings of 16 Sqn. *(RAF Laarbruch)*

at Laarbruch and as such was issued with the maintenance serial 8227M.

Following the trend that seemed common among RAF Germany-based units, 16 Sqn re-acquired the aircraft with the aim of restoring it to its former glory for eventual display at the main gate. Unfortunately, after completion of the project in 1981, it was found that it would be impossible to locate the aircraft at the gate due to the large number of trees that would have to be felled to accommodate the aircraft. Therefore, in order that 16 Sqn's efforts would not go to waste, it was decided that the Canberra should stay with the squadron, displayed outside their hangar where it remains today.

GLOSTER JAVELIN FAW4 XA634

RAF LEEMING

After the Second World War the Air Ministry issued Specification F44/46 for a fighter capable of 525 knots at 25,000 feet to intercept aircraft day or night, up to at least 40,000 feet. This Specification led directly to the Meteor NF series from Armstrong Whitworth (under licence from Glosters) whilst Glosters worked on a more advanced design, Project P280 of delta configuration. An updated Specification F4/48 was issued, and the Javelin was born.

XA634 was one of only fifty FAW4s built; they were delivered between September 1955 and July 1957 and were part of Contract 6/Acft/8336 dated 14 July 1952, which was the main Javelin production order. The FAW4 was essentially an FAW1 but with the following modifications: (1) An all flying tailplane, which reduced stick loads at high speeds and improved pitch control at all speeds and altitudes; (2) Two rows of vortex generators on the wings to reduce buffet; (3) The inclusion of the British AI-17 intercept radar.

XA634 was ready for collection at the main Gloster factory at Hucclecote near Gloucester on 18 May 1956. It was not issued for RAF use, however, but was retained by the manufacturers at their Moreton Valance airfield for trials. Subsequently it was loaned to Flight Refuelling Ltd. at Tarrant Rushton where it was fitted with a flight refuelling probe on the port wing. In this configuration it flew with Canberra and Valiant tankers making many 'dry' contacts, but this particular location for the 'in-flight refuelling probe' proved to be unsuccessful and later trials showed that the best place for the probe was above the starboard engine, a fit that was used on some FAW9 aircraft.

After these trials were complete the aircraft was returned to Moreton Valance where it had a modified nose cone fitted. This meant the removal of its radar installation and the new nose cone was fitted with a long 'Pitot type probe'. At this time it was also used to conduct trials using dummy Firestreak missiles.

XA634's flying life was not particularly long; in early 1960 the aircraft was grounded and declared non-effective. On 2 June 1960 it was transported by road to No.12 SofTT at RAF Melksham, Wiltshire; it was given the maintenance serial 7641M and became a training airframe. XA634 remained at Melksham until 1965 when it was transferred to the growing museum at RAF Colerne for display. With the closure of Colerne in June 1976 and the break-up of the Museum, XA634 was on the move again, this time to 27 MU RAF Shawbury in Shropshire. Its stay

XA634:L in the markings of 137 Sqn. In 1988 the aircraft underwent a complete restoration before returning back to display *(RAF Leeming)*

at Shawbury was to be quite brief and, later in the year, it was allocated to RAF Leeming for display.

After transportation to Leeming, it was placed on display in the position it now holds, outside the Officers Mess, and painted in the colours of No.137 Squadron. These markings represented Leeming's past association with No.228 OCU which had been based there operating Javelin FAW5 and T3s from June 1957 until it disbanded on 19 September 1961, and whose shadow squadron number for reinforcement of the front-line Javelin force was 137.

MCDONNELL DOUGLAS PHANTOM FG1 XT864

RAF LEUCHARS

With over 5,000 built, the F4 Phantom has proved to be one of the most successful post-war military aircraft, although it is now beginning to reach the end of its operational life. XT864 had two distinct careers, first with the Royal Navy but latterly with the Royal Air Force.

The Phantom was originally ordered as the F4H-1 for the US Navy, with the prototype 'BuAe 142259' first taking to the air on 25 May 1958 from the McDonnell Douglas facility at St Louis, Missouri. The first F4As entered service with US Navy squadrons VF101 and VF121 in early 1961, but it wasn't until the introduction of the F4B in October 1961 that the type entered front-line service on board the USS *Saratoga*.

British interest in the Phantom began in February 1964 when the decision was taken to order the type for the Royal Navy as a replacement for the DH Sea Vixen FAW1. An initial order was placed with McDonnell Douglas for 143 F4Ks, although enventually, only forty-eight were delivered. After some early difficulties, mainly due to the British wanting to install its own equipment, a compromise was reached with the only major difference between the types being the installed engine. The British version would be fitted with two Rolls-Royce Spey 25R engines rated at 12,250 lbst or 20,515 lbst with reheat. instead of the General Electric J79 in the US versions. This gave the British type a larger rear fuselage containing bigger jet pipes. The first F4K as the Americans called it, 'XT595', first flew from St Louis on 27 June 1966; it was essentially an aircraft based on the F4J. Some other differences included an extendable nose leg to afford higher angles of attack on take-off and a folding radome so that it would fit on the 54-foot interdeck lifts on the RN aircraft carriers.

Eventually the first three F4Ks arrived at RNAS Yeovilton (HMS *Heron*) on 29 April 1968, becoming the first exported Phantoms. On arrival they were designated Phantom FG Mk1 and formed the basis of No.700P Naval Air Squadron (NAS) who would carry out the task of trials flying. Unfortunately, out of the forty-eight aircraft delivered only twenty reached the RN, the rest being diverted to the RAF.

XT864, like all the British Phantoms, was built at St Louis and received the line number 2,475. It arrived at Yeovilton on 22 July 1968 and following acceptance by the Aircraft Support Unit

(ASU) it joined No.700P NAS on 3 September and was coded 'VL:724' (VL for Yeovilton). The aircraft stayed with this trials unit until 7 January 1969 when it was transferred to No.767 NAS prior to 700P NAS disbanding later that year. On joining its new unit it received the code 'VL:151'. Its role with 767 NAS was to train new Phantom pilots in fighter/ground attack, the two main roles of the aircraft, and apart from several brief visits back to the ASU for modification and servicing it stayed with them until 24 September 1971.

Phantom FG1 XT864 here flown by 767 NAS at Yeovilton prior to joining the Navy's only front line Phantom unit 892 NAS. *(C. P. Russell-Smith)*

On that date the aircraft re-entered the ASU once again but this time for preparation prior to its issue to No.892 NAS, the Royal Navy's only front-line Phantom unit. It eventually joined them on 4 October, replacing XV567, and was to remain with them for the rest of their existence. The aircraft was issued with the code 'R:011' (R for HMS *Ark Royal*) and was used primarily for fleet air defence with a secondary role of ground attack. Following a visit to the BAe facility at Holme-on-Spalding-Moor (HOSM) in March 1973 the aircraft was recoded 'R:007'.

Apart from operating their Phantoms from HMS *Ark Royal*, No.892 NAS had its shore base at RAF Leuchars sharing its facilities with another Navy unit, the Phantom Training Flight (PTF) and of course the RAF. XT864 was noted at Leuchars on several occasions, in particular from 5 November 1975 when it underwent fuel tank repairs and a mainplane replacement. This work took until 2 February to complete when the aircraft returned to its squadron. It was also noted at RAF St Athan in March 1977 being resprayed. By this time, however, decisions at higher levels were to have a dramatic effect on the Royal Navy's air defence. The decision was taken to scrap HMS *Ark Royal* in 1978 — leading to the disbandment of 892 Squadron.

HMS *Ark Royal* began its final cruise in September 1978 to the Mediterranean; XT864 was on board still coded 'R:007' and successfully completed all that was asked of it. On 27 November 1978 it flew off the 'ARK' for the last time and was delivered to RAF St Athan where it was officially transferred to the RAF together with the rest of the Royal Navy's Phantoms. On arrival at St Athan the aircraft was put into short-term storage until its turn came to be de-Navalised. The most obvious difference following this work was a new paint scheme, a change from Extra Dark Sea Grey and White to the RAF's grey/green camouflage. The aircraft was then delivered to RAF Leuchars on 10 September 1979 to join No.111 Squadron who coded it 'J'. 'Treble One's' primary role was for the air defence of the Northern Region.

On 11 February 1982, XT864 was flown to RAF Scampton for a most unusual journey. The aircraft had to go once again to Holme-on-Spalding-Moor for a rebuilding programme following

Seen landing at Yeovilton following another training sortie with 767 NAS, XT864:VL:151 showing its clean lines for the camera. *(C. P. Russell-Smith)*

the expiry of its fatigue life. The aircraft was put through a well-proven method of delivery to the facility on the other side of the River Humber. It was dismantled and transported by road to the factory, a regular occurrence and usually carried out at quiet periods, normally early on a Sunday morning. After completion of the work it returned to Scampton by the same method where it underwent flight testing prior to its return to Leuchars. It returned to 111 Sqn on 16 March 1983, this time remaining with them until 6 June 1986 when it flew to St Athan for a major servicing. The aircraft returned to 'Treble One' on 7 October although now coded 'BJ'.

This was the aircraft's last extended visit away from Leuchars where it continued in its air defence role. In 1988 it was announced that 'Treble One' would re-equip with the Tornado F3 sometime in 1989. Following some Cat 3 damage in December 1988 when its tailplane was forcibly removed by a refuelling bowser, it was considered fitting a complete new tailplane outboard of the transport joint abeam the jet pipes from another Cat 3 airframe. Unfortunately, because all Phantoms were hand-built in batches without jigs, this idea was shelved. The aircraft was subsequently grounded and issued with the maintenance serial 8998M.

On 1 August 1989 the aircraft, painted in its 111 Sqn markings, replaced Lightning F1a XM144 as the gate guard at RAF Leuchars thus becoming the first of its type to be preserved by the RAF.

HUNTING PERCIVAL PROVOST T1 XF545

RAF LINTON-ON-OUSE

The Hunting Percival Piston Provost was produced in response to Air Ministry Specification T16/48 with the prototype (designated Type P56) first flying on 23 February 1950. The type was powered by an Alvis Leonides 126 radial engine rated at 550 hp and the first production aircraft entered service with the Central Flying School (CFS) Basic Training Squadron at RAF South Cerney. By the spring of 1960 the last of some 461 of these trainers had rolled off the production line and the type remained in service until replaced by a direct descendant, the Jet Provost.

XF545 was one of a batch produced under Contract 6/Acft/9850 by the parent company at Luton. It carried the construction number PAC/56/576 and following initial test flights was declared ready for collection on 20 May 1955. Four days later it was delivered to No.12 MU at RAF Kirkbride where, following acceptance by the RAF, it was put into long-term storage.

It re-appeared on 31 May 1957 and was immediately delivered to No.27 MU at RAF Shawbury where it again underwent service

Piston Provost T1 XF545 (7975M) seen here at the Finningley Battle of Britain display in September 1967. *(C. P. Russell-Smith)*

preparation, this time mostly involved with bringing it up to the latest modification standard. Following this work it was painted in the standard Training Command colours of silver with yellow 'T bands' and on 26 August 1957 was allocated to No.2 FTS at RAF Hullavington. Its stay with this unit proved to be a short one because on 18 November it was transferred to the newly formed No.41 Group Maintenance Command at RAF Syerston.

XF545 remained at Syerston until 4 March 1960 when, as with many of its type, it joined by far the largest user of the piston Provost, No.6 FTS at RAF Ternhill. On arrival it was coded 'P-Z' and had its yellow 'T bands' replaced with liberal amounts of 'Dayglo'. It served with 6 FTS until 20 July 1961 when, in company with many others, it was withdrawn from use to make way for the introduction of the Jet Provost. After removal from Ternhill it found its way back to No.27 MU once again and was put into store.

On 4 August 1965 after more than four years at Shawbury it was declared non-effective stock but this was just a paperwork exercise because it remained in store for another two years. On 16 June 1967 it left Shawbury to join the growing RAF Museum Regional Collection at RAF Finningley, where on arrival it was issued with the maintenance serial 7975M.

XF545 remained at Finningley until February 1977 when, together with the rest of the collection, it was removed to make way for the forthcoming Queen's Silver Jubilee celebrations. It was then taken to RAF Swinderby where once again it was put into long-term store.

It remained at Swinderby until September 1983 when it moved to its present home. Following restoration to display standard it was repainted in its No.6 FTS colours once again and given the code 'O-K' and put in the position it retains.

FOLLAND GNAT T1
XM708
RAF LOCKING

Painted in the markings of the Red Arrows, for which the Gnat will for ever be remembered, XM708 is now the only survivor of its type to have served with them to be displayed as a gate guard.

The Gnat was originally developed as a single-seat day fighter, but, when it was realised that this version would have no future with the RAF (although some did fly with overseas airforces), the parent company, Folland, managed to successfully develop a two-seat trainer version to Specification T185. This retained the type's outstanding manoeuvrability — it had a maximum roll rate of 200 degrees per second.

XM708, construction number FL513, was built by the parent company at Hamble as part of Contract 6/Acft/15434. This was a pre-production order for fourteen aircraft that were to be used for development flying prior to the aircraft's release to service. After initial flight testing at the company's Chilbolton airfield, XM708 was declared ready for collection on 19 June 1962.

Five days later it was delivered to the RAF Handling Squadron at A&AEE Boscombe Down for use, amongst other things, in the preparation of the aircraft's handling notes. It stayed with them until 10 May when it moved on to join the Central Flying School (CFS) at RAF Little Rissington; on arrival it was coded '99'. The Gnat took over the task that was previously carried out by the venerable Vampire T11, providing advanced flying training following on from initial training on the Jet Provost. It remained with the CFS for the next ten years but wasn't always used in its primary role. The Red Arrows were officially part of the CFS and it wasn't unusual for them to borrow Gnats as required. XM708 fell into this category when it was on the team in the summer of 1969.

On 9 February 1972, XM708 returned to Hawker Siddeley (who had by now absorbed Folland Aircraft) for a complete overhaul. This work took until 1 September to complete, after which it changed ownership, going to No.4 FTS at RAF Valley; on arrival it was coded '18'.

On 9 March 1973 it suffered a Cat3 flying accident that required the attentions of No.71 MU from RAF Bicester to effect repairs. They were obviously extensive because the work took until 23 November to complete and, a little over a month later, on 21 December it rejoined 4 FTS. XM708 remained at Valley for the rest of its flying career until in 1977, with the introduction of the Hawk T1, the type was gradually replaced.

XM708 photographed in 'Red Arrows' colours at RAF Lossiemouth in July 1969. *(C. P. Russell-Smith)*

XM708 retired in November 1977 when it made its last flight from Valley to RAF Abingdon. After a few days the aircraft was dismantled by No.71 MU (now based at Abingdon) and taken by road to No.1 School of Technical Training at RAF Halton, arriving on 2 December. It was to be used as a ground instructional airframe and was issued with the maintenance serial 8573M.

In 1986 RAF Locking relinquished Spitfire F21 LA198, one of its then three gate guards, to RAF Leuchars in Scotland as part of a Spitfire shuffle. This left a gap at Locking that, after negotiations, was filled by XM708. After suitable preparation for display and resplendent once again in Red Arrows markings, the aircraft went on display on 5 August 1986.

In December 1989, XM708 became the only gate guard at Locking as a result of a policy change by the MOD to allow only one gate guard per station; Locking's Canberra and Meteor were removed.

BLACKBURN BUCCANEER SMk1 XK532

RAF LOSSIEMOUTH

Although at first it might seem unusual that an aircraft in Royal Navy colours should grace the gate of an RAF Station, RAF Lossiemouth was for many years RNAS Lossiemouth or, in Navy terms, HMS Fulmar, and it was at Lossiemouth that XK532 first entered military service.

XK532 was built by Blackburns (later to become part of the Hawker Siddeley group) at Holme-on-Spalding-Moor (HOSM) near Hull, as one of twenty prototype and pre-production aircraft to Naval requirement ASR NA.39; to cover production this was later amended to Admiralty Specification M.148T. It made its first flight from HOSM on 31 May 1961 but because it was part of the first development batch it was retained by the company for trials.

It was not long before the Royal Navy began to take delivery of its new strike fighter (later nicknamed 'the brick' because of its robust construction). On 3 August 1962, XK532 joined No.700Z Naval Air Squadron (NAS) who were (and still are) the traditional Navy trials squadron with responsibility for accepting new types of aircraft into service. The aircraft was coded 'LM:681' and flew with the squadron at RNAS Lossiemouth until 30 January 1963 when 700Z NAS was renumbered 809 NAS; XK532 was recoded 'LM:228'.

The aircraft remained with this front-line Navy squadron until 11 March 1964 when it returned to HOSM for a refit and modernisation. This was followed by a period of development flying at RAE West Freugh from August 1964 to May 1965 after which it once again returned to HOSM. Its next port of call was again Lossiemouth but this time it went to the RN Aircraft Handling Unit there, who took it on charge on 23 June 1965. It remained with them for about a month when on 20 July, it moved round the airfield to join No.736 NAS in the training role; soon after arrival it was coded 'LM:632'. This was really a return to one of its former units because when No.809 NAS disbanded in March 1965 they briefly became No.709 NAS before finally becoming No.736 NAS.

On 15 July 1966 the aircraft's effective flying life was deemed to have finished so it was grounded and handed over to the Naval Aircraft Support Unit (NASU) at Lossiemouth for a brief period of storage until a decision on its future could be made. On 26 September it was declared a Class 1 Instructional Airframe and given the naval maintenance serial A2581 before moving to RNAS Arbroath (HMS *Condor*). In April 1967 after briefly returning to Lossiemouth, it went to RNEC Manadon as a training airframe for apprentices and on 22 February 1968 it was further downgraded to a Class 2 instructional airframe.

In early 1982 RAF Lossiemouth entered into negotiations with Manadon to have the aircraft transferred north for eventual display as a gate guard. However, one of the problems encountered was how the aircraft would actually be moved there. Because transportation by road was out of the question due to the narrowness of some of the roads it would have to use, it was decided to transport it by sea. The aircraft (still in its No.736 NAS colours) was taken to Plymouth and dismantled for the journey to Lossiemouth where it arrived on 1 February 1984. On 16 August, after six months refurbishing by the engineering staff on the station, the aircraft was placed on display by the main gate in No.736 NAS colours.

Buccaneer S1 XK532 represents RAF Lossiemouth's past links with the Navy. It carries No.700Z NAS markings. *(C. P. Russell-Smith)*

On 14 April 1988 the aircraft enjoyed a brief period of limelight when the station celebrated the thirtieth birthday of the first flight of the Buccaneer. As part of this it was removed from its position on the gate and put in a line-up of thirty Buccaneers on one of the runways. The aircraft was returned to the gate later in the month.

Whirlwind HAR10 XD184 was originally intended for display at RAF Larnaca but by mid-1986 was put on display at Akrotiri. *(J. A. Simpson)*

Spitfire PR.XIX PM651:X began a second spell as the gate guard to RAF Benson in 1971. Its PR Blue colour scheme represents an aircraft of No.541 Sqn. *(J. A. Simpson)*

The RAF Memorial Chapel at Biggin Hill was guarded by two aircraft. This Hurricane II LF738 and Spitfire XVI SL674. The Hurricane is currently undergoing restoration at Rochester. *(Via J. A. Simpson)*

In 1984 SL542 was refurbished, following the work it was returned to the markings '4M-N' it carried when it flew with No.695 Sqn at RAF Horsham St Faith in 1948. *(Via J. A. Simpson)*

The Dept of Air Warfare now only display this Canberra B2 since the removal of a Hunter. It represents the record-breaking ARIES II aircraft WH669 although the aircraft's correct serial is WJ637. *(J. A. Simpson)*

Close-up of the nose inscription of WH669 at RAFC Cranwell, showing the aircraft's achievements. *(J. A. Simpson)*

No.1 S of TT at RAF Halton is guarded by Hunter F6 XF527.

RAF Kemble display Meteor F8 WH364 in 601 Sqn R.Aux AF markings. It is seen here in 1989 removed from its position on the main gate, for maintenance. *(J. A. Simpson)*

The position vacated by Spitfire F21 LA198 at RAF Locking was taken up by Gnat T1 XM708 displayed in Red Arrows colours. *(John Kyte)*

Shackleton MR2c WL738 stood guard at Lossiemouth from April 1974 in No.8 Sqn markings. In March 1990 WL738 was scrapped on site. *(J. A. Simpson)*

Lancaster BVII NX611/YF-C was a long time guardian at RAF Scampton. The markings are those carried by Guy Gibson on the Dams Raid. *(J. A. Simpson)*

RAF Swinderby is guarded by Vampire T11 XD506. *(J. A. Simpson)*

On display at RAF Turnhouse as a memorial to the airmen of No.603 Sqn R.Aux AF Spitfire XVIe RW393 has now been replaced by a glass fibre replica. *(J. A. Simpson)*

Wattisham's gate guard, Lightning F1A XM192 in 'Treble One' colours. *(J. A. Simpson)*

In the markings of No.85 Sqn, a unit long associated with RAF West Raynham, the station have Javelin FAW 9 as their gate guard. *(S. Donald)*

A fine shot of 'WT720:B' on display at Sealand. The aircraft is displayed in No.74 (Tiger) Squadron markings. *(Ray Milburn)*

DE HAVILLAND COMET C2 XK699

RAF LYNEHAM

In 1964, soon after a spate of tragic accidents suffered by the Comet 1, BOAC cancelled its order for twelve Comet 2 aircraft because of their inability to cross the North Atlantic non-stop. The RAF stepped in and took over the order and added three more aircraft.

Originally ordered under Contract 11809, DH106 Comet C2 XK699 first flew on 2 February 1957 at Hatfield. With its test programme complete, it was delivered to No.216 Squadron based at RAF Lyneham on 20 February 1957. No. 216 Sqn, although not the world's first military jet transport squadron (that honour went to No.412 Squadron RCAF who flew three Comet series 1 aircraft modified to series 2 standard), had received its first Comet (T2 XK670) on 7 July 1956 and were well into operational flying by the time XK699 arrived.

With the advent of the Comet C2, RAF Transport Command passengers began to enjoy speed and luxury hitherto unheard of and the regular routes to Australia and Christmas Island (connected with Britain's H-bomb tests) were flown in much reduced times: Lyneham to Adelaide (10,500 miles) took well under 30 hours of flying and the 19,000-mile round trip to

After many hours of restoration work XK699 took its place as RAF Lyneham's gate guard in the summer of 1987. *(J. Kyte)*

Christmas Island and back was flown in only four days with 45 flying hours.

In October 1959, 216 Sqn upheld a tradition of Transport Command by naming their aircraft. They chose star formations and XK699 became 'Sagittarius'.

In February 1962, 216 Sqn began to receive the much larger Comet 4c, although this was not the end of the road for the Comet 2. Its excellent serviceability did much to restore the Comet's good name and it was not until 1967 that the last operational Comet C2 flight took place, when XK698 arrived back at Lyneham on 1 April. However, XK699 had the honour of making the last ever flight of a Comet 2. On 14 June 1967 the aircraft was flown to RAF Henlow, Bedfordshire, and landed successfully on Henlow's grass runway. It was retained for preservation by the RAF Museum and on 19 June 1967 it was allocated the maintenance serial 7971M.

The aircraft remained at Henlow, one of the RAF Museum's reserve stores, until 1986 when, under the Museum's policy of loaning aircraft for display purposes, a team from No.71 MU at RAF Abingdon dismantled XK699 and moved it back to Lyneham by road on 17 October 1986. The task of restoring the aircraft fell to Lyneham's Aircraft Engineering Section who rebuilt the aircraft and prepared it for display. It was restored to its former glory as a Transport Command aircraft and made one final journey across Lyneham's sports field to the position it holds today.

One final honour was to befall the aircraft; in September 1987, HRH The Princess Royal dedicated the aircraft to RAF Lyneham.

HAWKER HURRICANE IIc 'BN230' (LF751)

RAF MANSTON

Hurricane, a name that conjures up images of the Battle of Britain, exploits in Russia and tank busting in the Middle East. Although it was to be credited with more 'kills' during the Battle of Britain than the Spitfire, the Hurricane never received the acclaim of its Supermarine counterpart.

The type was originally designed to Air Ministry Specification F36/34 as the 'Fury Monoplane', with the prototype 'K5083' first taking to the air on 21 February 1935. No.111 Squadron was the first squadron to re-equip with Hurricane Is in January 1938 at RAF Northolt replacing their Gloster Gauntlet IIs.

LF751 was built by Hawkers at Langley in early 1944 as part of Contract 62305. It was fitted with a Rolls-Royce Merlin XX engine giving 1,280 hp and was initially delivered to No.22 MU at RAF Silloth for service preparation. By 8 April 1944 it was on the strength of No.1681 Bomber Defence Training Flight (BDTF) at RAF Long Marston where it joined a mixed batch of other aircraft including Spitfires, Martinets and Tomahawks. It was used by the flight to simulate enemy aircraft so that air gunners (under training in the Heavy Conversion Units) could practise the art of air defence against attacking fighters.

On 8 August 1944, No.1681 BDTF was disbanded in conjunction with the many Heavy Conversion Units that required its services. LF751 subsequently moved on to No.24 Operational Training Unit (OTU) where it joined 'C Flight' at RAF Honeybourne. This time it was used to provide the OTU's Wellingtons with practice fighter evasion tactics, something akin to its job with

LF751 at RAF Henlow in 1967, it was used as the master mould for replica Hurricanes used in the 'Battle of Britain' film. *(M.A.P.)*

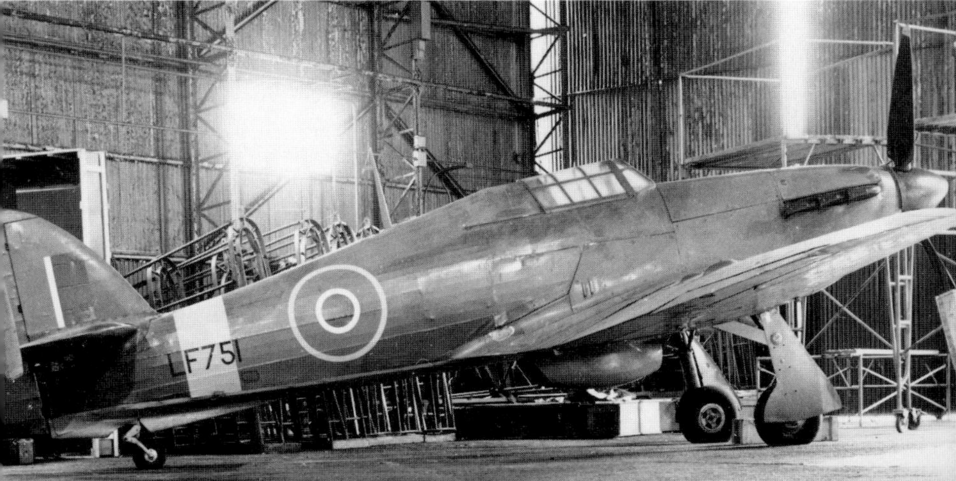

1681 BDTF. On joining 'C Flight' it was coded 'FB-B' and was one of eight aircraft, four Hurricanes and four Martinets, that made up the flight. The aircraft remained with the OTU to the end of the Second World War when, in conjunction with many thousands of other aircraft, it was declared surplus to requirements. It went to RAF Waterbeach for use as a ground instructional airframe and was allocated the maintenance serial 5466M.

It remained at Waterbeach, latterly on display until August 1957 when, following a refurbishment using components from Hurricanes Z3687 and PG593 (which also supplied parts to keep the still airworthy LF363 flying at the annual Battle of Britain flypasts), it was transferred to HQ Fighter Command at RAF Bentley Priory. Shortly after its arrival the aircraft was dedicated to the memory of those pilots of Fighter Command who had given their lives in the Second World War.

LF751 remained at Bentley Priory until 1967 when it was used as a master mould for the dummy Hurricanes that were constructed for the film *The Battle of Britain*. Following completion of the work the aircraft returned once again to Bentley Priory where it lay undisturbed until 1974. This time it was removed to No.71 MU at RAF Bicester for a much-needed complete restoration to display standard. In early 1975 it was back at Bentley Priory restored once again to its No.24 OTU markings of 'FB-B'.

In 1985, after nearly thirty years on display outside the now No.11 Group Headquarters, it was removed for the last time from its long-held position. It was taken to Rochester Airport where a team from the Medway Branch of the Royal Aeronautical Society began another complete restoration of the aircraft to display standard.

Three years' work were to follow consisting of some 12,000 man hours and expenditure of £15,000, resulting in a pristine airframe once again. It was finished as 'BN230:FT-A' of No.43 Squadron as flown by Squadron Leader Danny Le Roy Du Vivier and returned to the RAF on 22 April 1988. At the ceremony were the restoration team leader, Lewis Deal, Air Chief Marshal Sir Patrick Hine and Captain W. J. Cornelius who represented the widow of Sqn Ldr Du Vivier.

By May 1988 the aircraft had joined Manston's Spitfire in the now renamed Spitfire and Hurricane Memorial Building. This had originally been opened by Dame Vera Lynn on 7 October 1987 to house another of Medway's projects, Spitfire TB752.

In early 1989, the decision was made to purchase some plastic replica Hurricanes, and because this was the only Hurricane available that could be used as a master mould it was temporarily removed from display. (The Battle of Britain Flight at RAF Coningsby who had two airworthy Hurricanes would not allow them to be used.) Following this work and following a brief visit to RAF Abingdon to repair some minor damage it was back on display later in the year.

VICKERS SUPERMARINE SPITFIRE LF XVIe TB752

RAF MANSTON

The MkXVI version of this famous aircraft was a redesignation of the parallel built MkIX adapted to take the American-built Packard Merlin 266. TB752 was part of the seventeenth order for Spitfire MkIXs and XVIs, Contract B1981687/39 dated 19 April 1944, and was built by Vickers at their Castle Bromwich factory. It was part of a batch built between December 1944 and June 1945, and was first delivered to No.33 MU at RAF Lyneham on 21 February 1945. After acceptance it was issued to No.66 Squadron at RAF Linton-on-Ouse and was coded 'LZ-F'.

On 18 March 1945, 66 Sqn began the step-by-step march across Europe, their first port of call being Schijndel (B85) in Holland. The squadron carried out their first operational sortie the following day escorting a force of Mosquitoes from No.2 Group on a ground attack sortie to first, Coesfeld, then later in the day, to Dulmen. This was the daily routine for the next week or so until 25 March when, returning from an armed reconnaissance sortie, the pilot, Plt Off Hugo, found he couldn't lower the port undercarriage leg. The ensuing accident caused Cat A damage to the aircraft; Hugo escaped unhurt. A team from No.409 Repair and Salvage Unit (R&SU) carried out the repairs but because the pace of the war was moving so quickly 66 Sqn left TB752 behind. On 19 April it was allocated to No.403 (Wolf) Squadron, RCAF.

No.403 Sqn, commanded by the famed Wg Cdr J. E. (Johnnie) Johnson was also a ground attack unit and whilst with them TB752 scored a number of 'kills'. On 20 April, flown by Sqn Ldr H. P. M. Zary DFC, it destroyed a ME Bf109 on the ground; four days later there followed a FW189, again on the ground, but this time TB752 didn't get away unscathed. It suffered flak damage to its starboard wing which caused the pilot, Fg Off D. Leslie, a certain amount of difficulty in landing the aircraft. The damage this time was assessed as Cat B and a team from No.410 R&SU carried out the repairs. By 1 May it was back with 403 Sqn and whilst being flown that day by Fg Off R. Young it destroyed a FW190 on the ground. On 2 May, this time flown by Fg Off F. W. Town, it got its first airborne kill when it shot down a Heinkel He111K.

On 5 July the aircraft was again transferred to No.410 R&SU for further repairs, returning to the squadron two days later. It remained with them until the war in Europe ended.

At the end of the war in Europe TB752 returned to No.29 MU at RAF High Ercall for storage, arriving there on 2 August 1945. It made a brief appearance at the RAF Scampton Battle of Britain display in September 1949 before returning to storage at High Ercall on the 29th.

It remained in storage for a further two years until 19 April 1951 when it was issued to No.102 Flying Refresher School (FRS) at RAF North Luffenham. It only stayed with them for about a month and then moved to No.103 FRS at RAF Full Sutton, remaining there until 24 August 1953 when it again returned to No.29 MU, this time for refurbishment.

TB752 on display outside the Officer's Mess at RAF Manston in the mid 1950s. *(M.A.P.)*

Following this work and resplendent in a shiny new all-silver finish with black spinner, it was issued to No.5 Civilian Anti-Aircraft Co-Operation Unit (CAACU) at RAF Llanbedr on 23 November 1953, where it was flown by civilian pilots as a target for civilian anti-aircraft gunners. Coded 'F', it remained in this role for just over a year when on 25 November 1954 it again went into storage, this time with No.33 MU at RAF Lyneham. On 13 December it was declared non-effective and struck off charge.

Unusually, this wasn't quite the end of its flying days because in 1955 it joined several other Spitfires at RAF Kenley to be used in the making of the film *Reach for the Sky*, the life story of Gp

Capt Douglas Bader. At the end of filming it was finally grounded, allocated the maintenance serial 7256M, and transferred to RAF Manston for display purposes, arriving on 28 September 1955. It was originally displayed outside the Officers Mess but moved to the main gate some time in 1956, having its maintenance serial strangely changed to 7279M.

It remained on display at the main gate until 7 July 1978 when, badly in need of restoration, it was dismantled by a team from No.71 MU at RAF Abingdon and taken to Rochester Airport to undergo a fourteen-month restoration by the Medway Branch of the Royal Aeronautical Society. The team found many signs of neglect including a seized engine, vast amounts of corrosion, and total delamination of the wooden propellers, amongst other things. After some 8,000 man hours and an outlay of £4,000 the task was complete. The aircraft was returned to its 66 Sqn markings of 'LZ-F' (also showing its four kills gained whilst with 403 Sqn), given a new maintenance serial, 8080M, and delivered back to Manston in 1979. Immediately upon its return a fund-raising effort was begun to have a purpose-built building constructed to display the aircraft. The following year with the money raised, the aircraft was moved into its new home where it remains to this day.

This building was originally called the Spitfire Memorial Building but in 1988 when Manston took delivery of Hurricane IIc BN230 (LF751) it was formally re-dedicated by Dame Vera Lynn on 7 October and renamed the Spitfire and Hurricane Memorial Building. These two aircraft are now the only ones of their type now displayed as gate guards at any RAF station; all of the rest were removed during 1989 as part of a policy change by the MOD.

HANDLEY PAGE VICTOR K2 XH673

RAF MARHAM

Originally built as a Victor B2, XH673 was ordered as part of Contract 11303. This order consisted of the final batch of Victor B1s and the first batch of eight Victor B2s (XH668 to XH675). These eight aircraft were delivered in 1961 and spent the early part of their lives at A&AEE Boscombe Down where they were used in the trials required for C(A) release.

XH673 finally entered RAF service on 1 February 1962 with the newly re-formed No.139 Squadron as part of the Wittering Wing. The aircraft was painted overall white with the Wing's squadron badges on the fin. Together with Nos.100 and 543 Squadrons the Wing's role was nuclear strike, at first with free-fall bombs, then later with the Blue Steel stand-off missile. The fleet of Victors were later painted in grey, green and white when they changed from high level to low level penetration.

In 1967, when the Royal Navy took over the Nuclear Deterrent role from the RAF, the problem remained of what to do with the apparently redundant Victor bombers. The decision was taken to disband the Wittering Wing, 100 Sqn going on 1 October 1968 and 139 Sqn on 31 December. (543 Sqn remained as a strategic reconnaissance unit for a few more years.) The surplus Victors were delivered to the Handley Page airfield at Radlett to await a decision on their fate.

Awaiting its next tanking sortie, XH673 on the ramp at Marham in January 1980. *(C. P. Russell-Smith)*

The sudden withdrawal of the Valiant from service in January 1965 created a gap in the UK's airborne refuelling force. This had been partially filled by the conversion of the earlier Victor B1s to Victor B(K)1A2P and later K1 three point tankers. Unfortunately these earlier mark of Victors suffered from a lack of power in hot and high conditions. So, in order to capitalise on available resources, the decision was taken to convert the more powerful Victor B2s into three point tankers, thereby providing the RAF with a tanker force capable of operating in most areas of the world.

The initial planning work was carried out by Handley Page, with either XM715 or XL614 being nominated as the prototypes. Unfortunately, Handley Page were experiencing financial difficulties in 1969, mainly caused by the escalating cost of Jetstream development work. This caused the Official Receiver to be called in and by February 1970, Handley Page had ceased to exist.

This was a setback to the plans to solve the RAF's tanker problem but as no formal contract had been issued to the parent company, the conversion task was put out for tender. The contract was eventually awarded to Hawker Siddeley Aviation, who initially prepared all stored aircraft (XH673 included) for one flight only to either Chattendon or Woodford for conversion.

The main bulk of the conversion work entailed fitting fuel tanks in the photo-flash bay, the deletion of the bomb bay mechanisms and doors, and the installation of two large fuel tanks in the bomb bay. Other work included reduction of the wing span to 113 feet and the upward movement, by three degrees, of the aileron neutral position.

After completion of the programme, known collectively as MOD 5000, the first delivery took place on 7 May 1974 when XL233 was delivered to No.232 OCU at RAF Marham, Norfolk. XH673 was the seventeenth conversion and joined No.57 Squadron at Marham when they started re-equipping with K2s on 7 June 1976. Only one other squadron received the type and that was No.55 Squadron who were also based at Marham. The three units spent the next six years engaged in routine tanking sorties from their Norfolk base, occasionally ranging as far away as RAF Akrotiri in Cyprus in support of the RAF's air defence force. The peaceful routine was rudely interrupted in April 1982 when Argentine forces invaded the Falkland Islands.

As part of Operation Corporate many of the Victor force were deployed to Ascension Island in the South Atlantic to provide tanking and navigational support for air operations in the war zone. XH673 was with 57 Sqn on 29 March and by early April it was engaged in flight refuelling trials with Vulcan bombers, which were hastily exercising a long-since redundant system. On 5 May, in company with Vulcan B2 XM715, XH673 made its first sortie south; flying from Marham via Banjul in the Gambia to Ascension, returning to Marham the next day. There then followed another brief period of trials, this time in conjunction with hurriedly modified Nimrod and Hercules aircraft, before undergoing routine maintenance. It re-appeared on 12 May having been modified to carry Omega and Loran Navigational Aids plus a Radar Warning Receiver. After its test flight for these items was completed it again departed for Wideawake airfield on Ascension.

Its first task there was to escort two No.1(F) Squadron Harrier GR3s to HMS *Hermes* which was entering the Total Exclusion Zone at the time. On 1 June, XH673 was part of a fleet of tankers used to provide fuel for Vulcan XM597 on 'Black Buck 6', a mission to destroy radar systems in the vicinity of Port Stanley. After a few more support sorties throughout June the aircraft finally returned to Marham at the end of the month.

Victor K2 XH673 was put on display in early 1987 following the expiry of its fatigue life. It carries both 55 and 57 Sqn markings. *(C. P. Russell-Smith)*

On arrival at Marham the aircraft was prepared for major servicing and sent to RAF St Athan. When it arrived back at Marham it had been repainted in the new toned-down scheme of hemp and light grey. It rejoined 57 Sqn and remained with it until it disbanded in 1986.

Because it was a fatigued expired airframe it was grounded and allocated for display purposes. It was issued with the maintenance serial 8911M, and put on display inside the camp at Marham in the spring of 1987. It sports Nos.55 and 57 Squadron markings either side of the fin.

GLOSTER METEOR F8 WK654

RAF NEATISHEAD

The Gloster Meteor F8 was a direct descendant of the Meteor F4, the first aircraft flying on 12 October 1948. The main difference distinguishing it from the earlier type was an altered tailplane, a fully blown clear canopy and slightly longer length.

WK654 was built as part of the last production batch of 343 Meteor F8s by the parent company at Hucclecote to Contract 6/Acft/6066/CB7(b). This particular batch was built between 1951 and 1954, WK654 being ready for collection at Hucclecote on 21 March 1952. It was initially delivered to No.20 MU at RAF Aston Down from where, after service preparation, it was delivered on 7 May to No.247 Squadron at RAF Odiham. They coded it 'E'.

With the disbandment of 247 Sqn as a Meteor unit on 1 June 1955 the aircraft joined No.46 Squadron, also at Odiham, on the 27th of the month. 46 Sqn was actually a night fighter unit flying NF12 and NF14 variants of the aircraft. WK654 was therefore probably used as a squadron hack as there is photographic

WK654 replaced Spitfire LFXVI TE476 as the gate guard at RAF Neatishead in December 1969. *(M.A.P.)*

evidence of it painted in Odiham Station Flight's striking red colour scheme. Whilst in this role it was coded 'X'. On 15 November 1955 it had a Cat 3 flying accident which needed a team from No.49 MU, RAF Colerne to carry out repairs. These were completed by 29 February 1956 and it was returned to 46 Sqn that day.

The aircraft moved again on 5 August 1959, this time to the All Weather Fighter Combat School (AWFCS) at RAF West Raynham where it was used to train pilots in the art of air-combat tactics. Whilst with this unit it retained the code 'X'. The AWFCS later became the Day Fighter Leaders School (DFLS) as part of the Central Fighter Establishment (CFE).

On 7 September 1962 it suffered another Cat 3 accident. The repairs this time were carried out by No.71 MU from Bicester and were completed on 24 November; four days later it returned to the DFLS. It suffered a third Cat 3 on 29 May 1963 and this time it was repaired by No.60 MU, RAF Leconfield. The repairs were completed on 1 August and once again it returned to the DFLS.

On 5 August 1964 it was transferred across the airfield to join No.85 Squadron, still retaining its code 'X', but now acting as a target tug; as such it was now an F(TT)8. It suffered yet another accident on 16 September 1966; the repairs were again carried out by 60 MU and were completed on 3 November, the aircraft returning to 85 Sqn five days later.

WK654 continued its service uneventfully until 1 December 1969 when it was retired to No.5 MU, RAF Kemble, where three weeks later it was struck off charge and declared non-effective stock. It remained at Kemble until April 1976 when RAF Neatishead, who were looking for a new gate guard (their previous guard, Spitfire LF XVI TE476 had been removed for the Battle of Britain film in 1967 and not returned), acquired the aircraft.

After transportation by road from Kemble on the 9th of the month, and now with a maintenance serial 8092M, it was painted in 247 Sqn colours and put on display in its current position.

HAWKER HUNTER FMk1
WT694

RAF NEWTON

The last pure classic fighter to come from the design genius of Sir Sydney Camm, the Hawker Hunter first took to the air in May 1953, and entered service with the RAF and No.43 Squadron in July 1954.

WT694 was manufactured at the Hawker Siddeley Aircraft plant at Kingston as part of Contract SP/6/5910/CB7(a) dated for 14 March 1951. It first flew from the company's airfield on 29 October 1954 in the capable hands of Hugh Merrywether. After initial testing and a brief period of storage, WT694 was issued to No.54 Squadron at RAF Odiham on 2 March 1955. Its stay at Odiham was short and in September 1955, 54 Sqn complete with WT694 moved to RAF Stradishall, Suffolk.

The Hunter Mk1's service in front-line squadrons was relatively short-lived and replacement by later variants of this excellent aircraft began. In common with others, WT694 embarked on a new career with the Day Fighter Leaders School (DFLS) at RAF West Raynham, Norfolk, where on arrival it was coded 'Y'. WT694 remained with them until early 1956 when it was on the move again, this time to No.229 OCU at RAF Chivenor.

WT694 ceased its flying career on 22 November 1957 when it was passed to No.1 S of TT, RAF Halton, for ground instructional purposes and was given the maintenance serial 7510M.

When its useful life as an instructional airframe was over, it became a display aircraft, first appearing on the gate at RAF Debden, where it was painted in the markings of 43 Sqn coded 'Y' and, when Debden closed in 1975, moving by road to RAF Newton, Nottinghamshire. The aircraft was placed on display at the main gate in the position it holds today and remains in the (incorrect) markings that were applied at Debden.

In the markings of the first squadron to receive the Hunter F1, No.43 Sqn, WT694. *(J. A. Simpson)*

GLOSTER METEOR NF Mk14 WS776

RAF NORTH LUFFENHAM

The Meteor NF14 was the latest of the line to be produced and was itself a development of the NF12. The prototype NF14 (WM621 — a converted NF11) was first flown on 23 October 1953 by Flt Lt W. H. Else and only four months later, in February 1954 deliveries of the type began to reach the RAF.

In comparison to earlier variants, the main external difference of the type was its two-piece fully transparent cockpit canopy replacing the heavy framed hood used hitherto. Other less obvious changes were a revised windscreen, and a lengthened nosecone containing the latest American-built AI Mk21 (APS-21) Air Intercept Radar.

WS776 was built by Armstrong Whitworth's at Baginton, Coventry as part of Contract No.6/Acft/6412/CB5(b), eventually 100 of the type were produced serialled WS722–WS760, WS774–WS812 and WS827–WS848, WS776 was completed and declared ready for collection on 9 February 1954. In comparison to today's high technology aircraft it is interesting to note that the 100th and final production NF14, WS848, was delivered to the RAF Central Fighter Establishment on 26 May 1955, just seventeen months after the first flight of the prototype.

On 22 February 1954 within two weeks of being completed, WS776 was issued to No.8 Maintenance Unit (MU) RAF Little Rissington for a short period of storage prior to delivery to an operational squadron, and on 16 June 1954 the aircraft joined No.25 Squadron at RAF West Malling, Kent who coded it 'K'.

No.25 Squadron had been retained as a permanent night fighter unit at the end of the Second World War, flying Mosquitos until converting to Vampires in 1951. The squadron continued to be based at West Malling, where a further conversion to Meteor night fighters took place in April 1954, just two months before WS776 was taken on charge. Although little is known about WS776 during this period, as it was a new type to the squadron, it must be assumed that a considerable amount of training, including practice interceptions (PIs) were carried out.

No.25 Squadron were forced to leave West Malling on 30 September 1957 for nearby RAF Tangmere to allow runway modifications to be carried out and although they soon returned, less than a year later the squadron was disbanded on 2 July 1958. WS776 was transferred to No.85 Sqn, another famous night fighter unit, at RAF Church Fenton, North Yorkshire where it was coded 'J'.

Similar to No.25 Sqn, No.85 Sqn remained as part of the post-war establishment of Fighter Command eventually converting to Meteors in September 1951, whilst also based at West Malling. Three years later the unit took delivery of NF14s in addition to the NF11 and 12s it already flew. WS776 spent only a short time with them because they too were disbanded on 31 October 1958, to re-form a month later as a Javelin unit.

It would appear from WS776's next role that there was some uncertainty as to the future of the Meteor, especially as many squadrons who previously flew this version were re-equipping with the Javelin, but on 25 November 1958, less than a month after No.85 Sqn disbanding, WS776 was allotted to No.92 Sqn at RAF Middleton St George.

No.92 Sqn was primarily equipped with Hunter F6 aircraft, so the actual role of WS776 is uncertain, but it has been suggested that the aircraft was employed on target towing duties which would seem a waste of a valuable radar-equipped aircraft. Furthermore there is no indication that any NF14s were converted to target towing aircraft as were some of their earlier variants. It is perhaps more reasonable to assume that WS776 was used for practice interceptions (PIs) with the Hunters. In addition there is no information available as to whether WS776 was ever painted in No.92 Sqn markings. In the end WS776 remained with No.92 Sqn for nearly seven months until being transferred to RAF Leeming on 15 June 1959 where it was issued to No.60 Sqn (Detachment), who were starting to work up on the type. The main element of No.60 squadron was based at RAF Tengah, Singapore, flying Venoms in the fighter/ground attack role, but were in the process of running down prior to a change of aircraft and aircrew. According to the squadron historian at the time, numerous strings were pulled and the 'old-boy' network frequently used to gather together at Leeming the required crews. The criteria considered necessary for aircrew to join this new squadron were:

1. At least one tour in the Night/All Weather role.
2. Meteor qualified.
3. Not Javelin trained.

The final point was of particular importance because by mid-1959 all UK-based Night/All Weather squadrons were flying Javelins of various marks (apart from No.72 Sqn which was still in the process of converting). On 11 and 12 June 1959, pilots from No.72 Sqn RAF Church Fenton, ferried a mixture of five NF12s and five NF14s to Leeming. A further two NF14s arrived from RAF Middleton St George, one of which was WS776. In addition to the Mk12s and 14s the unit also acquired four Meteor T7s from various units for refresher flying and training in instrument flying. Soon after arrival the Mk12s and 14s were all painted with No.60 Sqn markings consisting of a silver lightning flash on a black rectangle either side of the fuselage roundel. Forward of the pilot's cockpit on the port side, the white head of the 'Kabuli Markhor' outlined in black was also added. With the exception of WS775, which had a natural metal finish, and was the Squadron Commander's (Sqn Ldr R. Knight) aircraft, all the night fighters had the standard Fighter Command dark green/dark grey camouflage with light grey undersurfaces. Tail fins continued to display the aircraft letter in black as used by No.72 Sqn, repeated on the nose wheel door. During its time with the squadron WS776 was coded 'J', but whether this was a continuation from its time with 85 and 92 Sqns is difficult to determine.

WS776: K displayed in No.25 Sqn markings. *(S. Donald)*

By 19 August 1959 No.60 Sqn (Detachment) had completed its work up, therefore from 21 August pilots of the Ferry Squadron began to fly away the now redundant Meteor NFs. Generally the Mk12s went to No.49 MU RAF Colerne for scrapping, whereas the NF14s went to No.5 MU RAF Kemble to be modified for other duties. Consequently, WS776 left the squadron on 24 August and was flown to Kemble.

The aircraft remained stored at Kemble for nearly a year until 26 July 1960 when it was returned to flying duties at RAF Leeming joining No.228 Operational Conversion Unit (OCU). This OCU was primarily equipped with Javelins whilst WS776 served with them, but there was still a requirement to train

Meteor crews for night fighter squadrons operating in Germany. Although information is scarce, it is probable that WS776 operated in a role similar to that during its time with No.60 Sqn (Detachment).

Eventually, some six months later, on 25 January 1961, WS776 was ferried to No.33 MU RAF Lyneham and retired from service. After a brief stay the aircraft was issued to RAF North Luffenham on 3 May 1961 for display purposes and issued with the maintenance serial 7716M. Some thirty years later the aircraft still stands outside the main camp entrance, a reminder of North Luffenham's one-time role as the Night and All-Weather Fighter Operational Conversion Unit which trained Meteor and Vampire crews. This particular unit remained operational from 1955 until January 1957 when it amalgamated with No.238 OCU. When first displayed, WS776 was painted in No.238 OCU markings and coded 'Z' but since the aircraft was never based at North Luffenham it is likely that this was done to represent a type flown from the station. At some point prior to May 1973 the aircraft was recoded 'K' and painted in No.25 Sqn markings consisting of a broad silver bar edged top and bottom with black either side of the fuselage roundel. (The white code letter on the fin should ideally be smaller and on a black disc.) Today the aircraft is still depicted in these same markings.

WESTLAND WHIRLWIND HAR 10 XR453

RAF ODIHAM

RAF Odiham has for many years been the home of the RAF's tactical helicopter force, and as part of the force No.230 Squadron was based there, most recently from 1 January 1972 until 14 October 1980, when it returned to one of its former homes, RAF Gutersloh in Germany. This squadron's markings are carried by XR453.

Built as part of the second production order for fifteen Whirlwind HAR 10 and HCC12s, XR453 was constructed as a HAR 10 under Contract KF/2N/042 by Westlands at their Yeovil factory. It received the construction number WA403 and was completed in November 1962, being declared ready for collection on the 23rd of the month.

Six days later, on the 29th, it was delivered to RAF Ternhill, Shropshire and joined the Central Flying School (CFS) the following day, although it was immediately put into storage. After a short period in store it was soon in service being used to train future helicopter pilots for the RAF. On 7 February 1963 it suffered a Cat 4 accident which required the aircraft to be returned to Yeovil for repair; following a lengthy road journey the subsequent repairs took from 26 February until 31 December to complete.

Whirlwind HAR 10 XR453 shortly after going on display at Odiham in June 1987. *(C. P. Russell-Smith)*

On completion of the work, XR453 was put into store once again, this time at Yeovil, prior to it being taken by sea to Cyprus. Once in Cyprus the aircraft joined the combined 1563 Flight and 230 Sqn detachment supporting the UN peace-keeping force on the island. It stayed on the island until March 1965 when the 230 Sqn aircraft were sent to RAF Labuan in Borneo; XR453 was one of these aircraft. On arrival the squadron quickly took up duties supporting British forces during the Indonesia/Malaysia confrontation. It remained in Borneo until November 1966 when, with its duties completed, it sent its aircraft (XR453 included) back to the UK by sea to RAF Odiham where it was back on strength by 30 November. On 10 March 1969 the squadron moved to RAF Wittering, retaining XR453 coded 'W' for a further two years until it was disbanded on 3 December 1971 (re-forming at Odiham on 1 January 1972). The Whirlwind was replaced in the support helicopter role by the Anglo-French Puma HC1, and on 17 December 1971 XR453 flew to No.15 MU at RAF Wroughton for storage, although on 26 February 1972 it was transferred by road to RNAY Fleetlands for further storage where it remained until 29 May 1974.

It then began the next part of its career when it returned to the training role with the CFS, first at Ternhill and later at RAF Shawbury when Ternhill closed in 1976. XR453 remained on their strength until 12 December 1979 when the CFS began to re-equip with the Wessex HC2; on the following day XR453 was grounded and placed into storage across the airfield with No.27 MU having completed 5,466 flying hours.

The aircraft remained in storage until 1986 when it was allocated to RAF Odiham for display. It was issued with the maintenance serial 8873M and taken by road to Odiham where, after being resprayed in the more appropriate camouflage colour scheme that it wore when with 230 Sqn, and given the code 'A', it was placed on display in September 1986.

XR453 in 230 Sqn colours at Coningsby in January 1969.
(C. P. Russell-Smith)

GLOSTER METEOR T7 WF784

RAF QUEDGELEY

This particular aircraft, recently repainted, has had a most interesting life. It was originally ordered as one of eighty-nine aircraft as part of Contract 6/Acft/5044/CB7(b), that were built by Glosters at Hucclecote. It was declared ready for collection on 13 April 1951 and initially issued to No.26 Squadron at RAF Wunsdorf in West Germany as part of 2 ATAF. Whilst with this unit (who flew Vampire FB5s) it was used as the squadron hack, carrying out general communications and meteorological flights. Its life wasn't without incident; it suffered a Cat 3 accident on 11 August 1951 and after repair it returned to the squadron on 19 March 1952. It then moved with the squadron when they redeployed to RAF Oldenburg in August 1952, prior to receiving the Sabre Mk4.

On 5 February 1954 it joined No.130 Squadron (also a Sabre unit) at RAF Bruggen, remaining with it until 5 June when it was the victim of another flying accident. Flown by Fg Offs O'Neill and Hancock the aircraft was on a routine instrument training sortie; the flight had been uneventful but after travelling about 1,000 yards on its landing run the aircraft's port undercarriage collapsed. Fortunately the crew were unhurt but the aircraft was declared Cat 4, and because the damage was severe it had to be returned to the UK for repair. It arrived at Tarrant Rushton on 12 August for the work to be carried out by Flight Refuelling Ltd, which was completed by 31 January 1955. The next day it flew to No.20 MU at RAF Aston Down prior to its reissue to the RAF.

On 20 February it joined the Ferry Training Unit (FTU) at RAF Benson to be used to convert pilots onto jet aircraft. It continued in this role until 6 March 1958 when it was once again the victim of a flying accident.

This time flown by Master Pilot J. A. Trigg and his pupil Major E. Geiskopf, USAF, the aircraft was on a routine training sortie practising circuits and landings. On its planned final approach, with the student in control, about 100 feet high and 200 yards from the runway threshold, the aircraft started to sink rapidly. Mst Plt Trigg immediately took control but failed to prevent the aircraft from hitting the top of a tree. This inflicted damage to the port wing leading edge, flaps and undercarriage but didn't prevent the aircraft landing safely. Both crewmen were unhurt and the aircraft was assessed Cat 2. The repairs were carried out by a team from No.71 MU at RAF Bicester and were completed by 7 May; the next day it rejoined the FTU.

WF784 was next on the move on 11 March 1959 when it went

Meteor T7 WF784 is unusual in that it also displays its Support Command maintenance serial 7895M under its main serial. *(J. Kyte)*

to No.33 MU at RAF Lyneham, for storage. It moved to No.5 MU at RAF Kemble on 21 July and from there, on 31 August, it was issued to the College of Air Warfare (CAW) at RAF Manby to be used to train pilots in the art of fighter tactics. It was involved in another accident on 11 March 1960; although the details are not known it was assessed Cat 3. The repairs this time were carried out by No.60 MU from RAF Leconfield and were completed by 28 April. The following day it rejoined the CAW.

Its stay at Manby lasted until 23 February 1961 when it returned to No.33 MU for storage. It transferred to No.19 MU at RAF St Athan on 22 November where it remained until early 1963, when it received one last flying assignment. It joined No.5 Civilian Anti-Aircraft Co-operation Unit (CAACU) at RAF Woodvale for use as an airborne target by civilian anti-aircraft gun crews. It remained with them only until 17 September when it returned into storage, this time with No.5 MU.

On 23 July 1965, WF784 was declared non-effective stock, struck off charge and put up for disposal. On 30 November it was issued with the maintenance serial 7895M (which is still displayed on the airframe) and taken to No.1 Site of No.7 MU at RAF Quedgeley where it has been displayed ever since.

HAWKER SIDDELEY GNAT T1
XR571
RAF SCAMPTON

XR571, although displayed in the markings of the Red Arrows outside the headquarters of this world-famous aerobatic team, unfortunately never flew with the team. Bearing the construction number FL561 it was built at Hamble by Hawker Siddeley Aviation Ltd. as part of the second production batch of Gnats to Contract KC/2B/05.

It first took to the air on 4 October 1963 and on 31 October the RAF were informed that it was ready for collection. On 11 November it was delivered to RAF Valley to join No.4 Flying Training School (FTS). It was coded '23' and immediately went into use as an advanced trainer taking over the role previously carried out by the venerable Vampire T11.

It suffered the first of two accidents on 3 August 1966. On this occasion it was repaired by a team from No.60 MU, and following this work it rejoined 4 FTS on 17 November. It flew on with 4 FTS undergoing bouts of routine maintenance about

XR571 in No.4 FTS colours at Alconbury in August 1971.
(C. P. Russell-Smith)

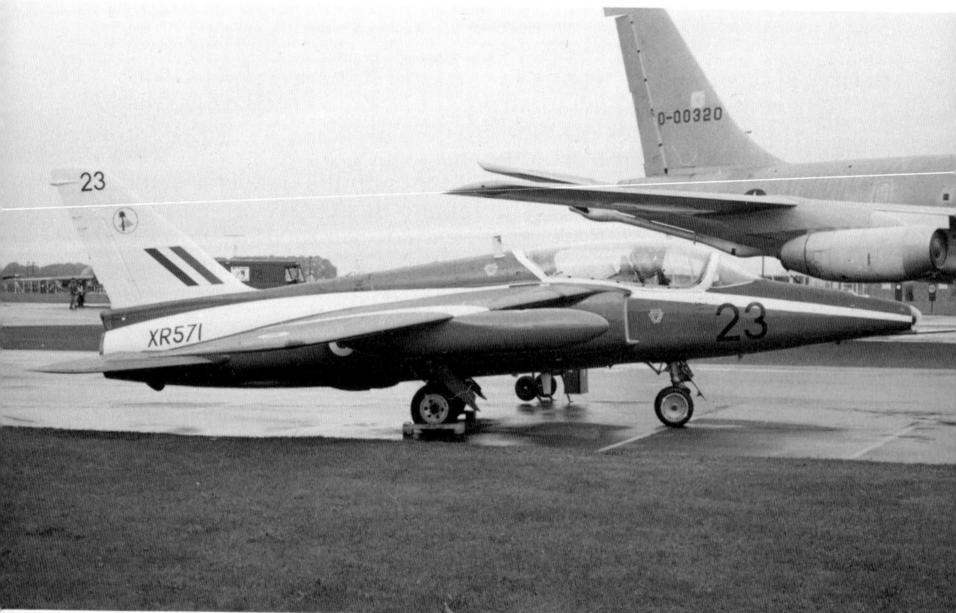

every two years until 16 May 1972 when it returned to its manufacturers for reconditioning. This work took until 19 January 1973 to complete after which it returned to Valley and 4 FTS.

On 28 October 1975 it was involved in its second accident. The aircraft was so damaged that it was assessed as uneconomical to repair, particularly as the Hawk T1 was now beginning to enter service at Valley as a replacement for the Gnat. Therefore XR571 was declared Cat 5 the following day.

On 19 November it was delivered by road to No.5 MU at RAF Kemble where it was issued with the maintenance serial 8493M and almost immediately the task of converting it to display standard was begun. By 27 July 1976 the aircraft had taken up residence on the gate at HQ RAF Support Command, RAF Brampton. Sometime later it returned to Kemble for a short period of display with the Red Arrows, before being taken by road to RAF Cosford on 2 November 1980 to join the expanding Aerospace Museum collection.

On 31 January 1984 it was on the move again when it was allocated to HQ CFS at RAF Scampton. By June it had been put in the position it is in today, outside the entrance to the Red Arrows' hangar.

HAWKER HUNTER F51
WT720 (E-408)
RAF SEALAND

Under the guise of Hunter FMk4 WT720, of No.74 Squadron, this aircraft is in fact an ex-Royal Danish Air Force (RDAF) aircraft which was ordered against Contract HAL/54/D-017 dated 3 July 1954, and was one of thirty Hunter F51 aircraft built at Kingston on Thames for the RDAF. These aircraft were built to FMk4 standard, but without the leading edge extensions, and powered by the Rolls-Royce Avon RA14 Mk115 turbojet.

Having made its first flight on 14 March 1956, in the hands of test pilot Frank Bullen, the aircraft was delivered from Kingston via Dunsfold to the RDAF maintenance base at Vaerlose on 18 August 1956. RDAF squadron Esk724 was formed in 1956 to operate the Hunter at Karup with a detachment at Vaerlose, and E-408 soon became operational. In 1958 the squadron moved to a more permanent operating base at Skrydstrup, where they remained until disbandment.

In 1966, the Danish Hunter force began to run down and the first unit to go was the detached flight at Vaerlose. Two causes for this rundown can be identified: the first was the cost, and lack of spares for the Hunters, and second, the passing of the 1966 Danish Defence Act which limited the number of aircraft in front-line service. Over the next few years, Esk724 soldiered on with a depleting force of Hunters and, by 1973, they had only ten operational aircraft with the rest being used as a source of spares. The end was not long in coming for Esk724; in 1974, as part of further Government defence cuts, the squadron was disbanded on 31 March, and the Hunters were placed in store at Aalborg to await disposal.

All the remaining Hunters, including E-408, were purchased by Hawker Siddeley in early 1976, and were returned to the UK: E-408 arrived at Dunsfold on 10 April 1976 to await possible refurbishment and resale. Whilst at Dunsfold it was allocated the 'B' class manufacturer's serial G-9-436; no buyer could be found for the ex-Danish aircraft and they remained there until they could be dispersed to collections, museums and, in the case of E-408, RAF Brawdy in Dyfed, Wales.

On 28 February 1978, E-408 was acquired by Brawdy who wanted a Hunter for display. It was repainted in the markings of 43 Squadron, coded 'B', (unusually without a serial) issued with the Support Command Serial 8565M, and placed on display at Brawdy's main gate. It remained there until 1984 when it was replaced by the more appropriate Hunter FGA 9, XE624, and was put up for disposal. Shortly afterwards it was acquired by the

Department of Air Warfare at RAF Cranwell, where it arrived in December 1984.

With the permission of the Commandant, AVM E. H. Macey, the aircraft was restored to display standard and painted in the markings XF979:A; these were representative of an aircraft flown by the College of Air Warfare when it was based at RAF Manby from 1955 to 1960. With its restoration complete, it was placed on display outside Trenchard Hall, the present home of the Department of Air Warfare. (The real Hunter FMk4, XF979, was built at Blackpool in 1956 and served with the College of Air Warfare before being repurchased by Hawkers in 1968; they resold it to Jordan in 1971 as an FGA Mk73B.)

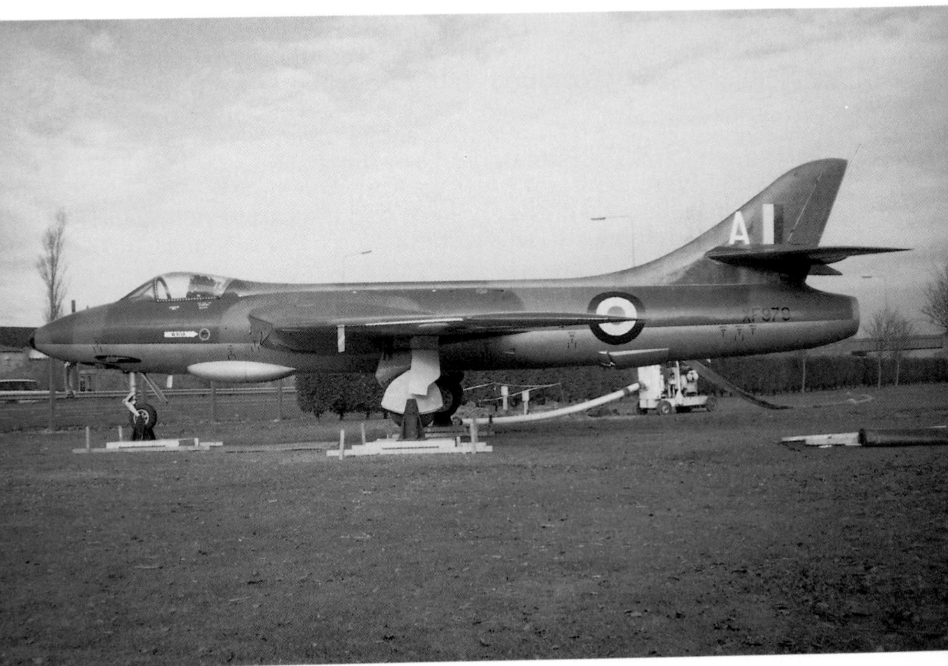

Hunter F51 'XF 979' shortly after its arrival from Cranwell in early 1989. *(R. Milburn)*

In November 1988 the aircraft was reallocated to RAF Sealand for display as a result of the change of policy by MOD. It was dismantled on 15 November 1988 and moved to Sealand on the following day. It was initially displayed as XF979 but by mid-1990 it had undergone a total restoration and repaint into the markings it now carries. WT720 first flew on 27 January 1955, and delivered to the RAF at No.33 MU on 1 March 1955. Shortly thereafter it joined 74 Sqn coded 'B'. Later it joined 111 Sqn and was finally Struck off Charge in November 1964, having amassed 613.10 flying hours.

WESTLAND WHIRLWIND HAR 10 XP351

RAF SHAWBURY

To those in difficulties in the mountains and around the coastline of Great Britain the sight of a bright yellow helicopter coming to their rescue always brings a sense of relief. The most common was the Sikorsky-designed, Westland-built Whirlwind, the first helicopter built in any great numbers for the RAF and RN. In its final form, the HAR 10, it at last gained a powerplant equal to the tasks set for it, although it was still plagued by a lack of range not overcome until the introduction of the Sea King HAR 3.

XP351 c/n WA369 was built by Westlands at Yeovil as part of Contract KF/2N/037/CB25(a); unlike earlier batches, aircraft from this order were built as HAR 10s from the outset. The most noticeable difference between these and the earlier Whirlwinds, was the elongated nose fairing containing a Rolls-Royce Gnome turboshaft engine in place of the Pratt & Whitney piston engine.

Following initial flight testing, XP351 was declared ready for collection on 2 March 1962 and five days later it was issued to No.22 Squadron. This squadron was responsible for a large percentage of SAR cover of Britain's coastline and because of this, was a widespread unit. It had its headquarters at RAF St Mawgan with detached flights at Chivenor, Felixstowe, Tangmere, Thorney Island, Valley, Manston and Coltishall and regularly rotated its aircraft between these flights. XP351 spent the next six years at many of these flights engaged in SAR duties as the situations arose.

On 3 May 1968 the aircraft flew to the RNAY Fleetlands for a much-needed major servicing. The greater part of this work took the form of corrosion control due to the majority of the aircraft being constructed from magnesium alloy. Although this material saved a large amount of weight in the aircraft's construction, unfortunately it was very susceptible to the effects of seawater. The work was completed by 10 October 1968 and the next day XP351 rejoined 22 Sqn.

The aircraft returned once again to SAR duties and it wasn't for another three years that it was grounded for any length of time. On 2 November 1971 it was the victim of a Cat 3 flying accident, which took a team from No.71 MU at RAF Bicester four months to repair; on 14 March 1972 the aircraft rejoined the squadron. Its stay this time with 22 Sqn was somewhat brief because on 30 November it was loaned to MOD(PE) for a series of trials. It was employed in the testing of an upgraded avionics system, and an improved Auto-Stab hover system which were

XP351 at West Raynham on 16 June 1971 taking part in a NATO SAR Meet. *(C. P. Russell-Smith)*

designed to improve the efficiency of the helicopter. Also tested was an improved fuel management system although this was not its primary task; the aircraft remained with MOD(PE) until 9 May 1973, rejoining 22 Sqn the following day. Another two years passed by, during which the squadron had reduced its number of outposts to just four — Brawdy, Chivenor, Coltishall and Valley, with its headquarters now at RAF Thorney Island.

XP351 served with 22 Sqn until 8 September 1976 when it was found that the aircraft was in need of further large-scale repair work. This took until 2 November to carry out, after which it became a training aircraft joining the SAR Training School at RAF Valley. This unit was (and still is) responsible for the training of aircrew in all aspects of the SAR role. For the next three years it was used in this unsung but vitally important role, when on 26 February 1979 it was allocated to No.2 FTS at RAF Shawbury.

Unfortunately its entry to the fleet at Shawbury was temporarily delayed because first it had to undergo some minor repairs; it finally joined the school on 13 March. With this change of role there also came a change in colour scheme. It received the standard Support Command training scheme of red, white and grey, together with the code 'Z', and was soon put to use training new pilots for the RAF helicopter fleet.

It remained with 2 FTS until 9 February 1981 when it was finally grounded after a long and interesting career. It was decided not to scrap the aircraft but instead use it as a familiarisation trainer. It received the maintenance serial 8672M and was soon put to its new role. Unfortunately, it was also used as a 'Christmas tree' to keep the remaining few Whirlwinds airworthy and this caused the aircraft to be soon re-classified as a Battle Damage Repair Airframe, a role it remained in until chosen to replace Sycamore HR14 XG540 as a gate guard at Shawbury.

Fortunately for the restoration team, XP351 had suffered very little damage during its use as a BDR machine, therefore repair work to bring it up to display condition was largely a cosmetic exercise. In December 1987 the aircraft took up its post by the entrance to RAF Shawbury as a reminder of the contribution the Whirlwind made to the history of the RAF.

GLOSTER JAVELIN FAW2
XA801
RAF STAFFORD

This particular mark of Javelin was unusual in that it was produced in parallel with Javelin FAW4. The only major difference between the two types was the type of Airborne Intercept (AI) Radar carried. The Mk4 was fitted with the British built AI-17 set, whilst the Mk2 was fitted with the American AI-22.

XA801 was built at Hucclecote by Glosters as part of an order for thirty aircraft, to Contract 6/Acft/8336. After completion, it was declared ready for collection on 21 June 1957, and three days later was issued to No.46 Squadron at RAF Odiham, who coded it 'F'. No.46 Sqn, together with 89 Sqn, at RAF Stradishall, were the only squadrons to equip with this mark of Javelin. In fact, 46 Sqn were the first Javelin-equipped squadron in the RAF, and so didn't waste much time converting to the new mark.

This was ably demonstrated the following August when they took their new aircraft to RAF Leconfield to participate in the first Fighter Command Gunnery Meet in company with the Hunters of 34 Sqn, representing No.1 Group. The aircraft took part in various exercises including ranging and tracking cine-camera missions followed by two air-to-air target tracking missions. But, despite their intensive training, 46 Sqn could only manage

A brand new XA801 at Benson in August 1957. *(C. P. Russell-Smith)*

Javelin FAW 2 XA801:F still retains the No.46 Sqn colours it wore whilst operational at RAF Odiham. *(J. A. Simpson)*

a total of 837 points out of 2,000 (mostly due to problems with the AI-22 radar). No.46 Sqn moved to RAF Waterbeach in July 1959 when Odiham closed as a fighter station, and XA801 flew on without incident from its new base until 26 April 1960 when it suffered a Cat 3 flying accident. The aircraft was repaired at Waterbeach by a team from Glosters and returned to 46 Sqn on 20 June.

The aircraft flew on for a further year until 20 June 1961 when it was delivered to No.19 MU at RAF St Athan (prior to 46 Sqn disbanding ten days later). On arrival it was placed into store. The aircraft was declared non-effective on 4 July 1961 and issued with the maintenance serial 7739M, although it remained in store. On 21 January 1962 it was allocated to RAF Stafford for display and five days later, still bearing its 46 Sqn 'Arrowhead' motif, it went on display at the main gate where it still stands.

HAWKER HUNTER FMk5
WP190
RAF STANBRIDGE

This particular aircraft is worth more than a passing glance, not only because it is one of only two Hunter Mk5s to have survived, but also because it is one of the few aircraft still on RAF charge to have taken part in the Suez crisis.

WP190 was built by the Armstrong Whitworth Aircraft Company at Baginton, to Contract SP/6/6315/CB7(a) (the only production order for the Sapphire-engined Mk5, 105 aircraft being built). WP190 was part of the batch WP179–WP194. It was initially delivered to No.5 MU at RAF Kemble on 22 July 1955 for service acceptance and on 13 August it was issued to No.1 Squadron at RAF Tangmere, who coded it 'K'.

No.1 Sqn had recently converted from the Meteor F8 but their new Hunters were plagued by many problems, these lasting for many months resulting in a poor serviceability record. The most serious problems were cracks in the undercarriage oleos (which caused several accidents) and tailplane control failures.

In May 1956 tensions in the Middle East increased and 1 Sqn, together with No.34 Squadron, the other Tangmere unit, were put on standby for immediate deployment to Cyprus. On 7 May when the Suez Crisis erupted Operation Quickfire was put into effect, twenty-five Hunters (including WP190) of the Tangmere Wing staging to RAF Akrotiri, as part of the massive French and British build-up. Upon arrival the aircraft were painted with yellow and black recognition stripes in similar fashion to the D-Day invasion stripes of the Second World War.

On 1 September the Hunters moved from Akrotiri, which was at bursting point, to RAF Nicosia, although conditions there weren't much better. From 21 October, the Hunter squadrons were tasked with maintaining an Operational Readiness Flight, being scrambled on many occasions to investigate straying aircraft. These were mostly civilian strays or aircraft from the US Navy Sixth Fleet. This was to remain the Hunters' primary task even throughout the fighting in October (although they also provided fighter affiliation training against Canberra bombers). On 12 November, No.1 Sqn lost its only aircraft of the campaign when EOKA terrorists badly damaged WP180 on the dispersal at Nicosia.

With the ceasefire on 6 November many of the Canberra and Valiant force returned home, but the Hunters remained a further two months still providing air defence. They finally left Nicosia on 21 December arriving back at Tangmere on the 24th.

Hunter F5 'WP180' is one of only two aircraft still on RAF charge that took part in the Suez Crisis. *(S. Donald)*

WP190 remained with 1 Sqn for a further eighteen months until 11 July 1958 when it was retired to No.5 MU. It was immediately declared non-effective and in early August was issued to RAF Bircham Newton for ground instruction at the Equipment Officers Training School (EOTS), becoming 7582M. In 1962 it moved to RAF Upwood with the school for display/ instruction purposes in their hangar. It remained there until 1974 when the EOTS closed and then moved to RAF Stanbridge for display on the gate. After this move it was allocated another maintenance serial, becoming 8473M. In 1976 the aircraft was refurbished and at some stage it was decided to paint the aircraft as WP180 (the one blown up). Unusually, this marking was only applied to the fuselage because, under its wings, it carried the correct serial WP190. The former marking was later removed and the correct one applied.

GLOSTER JAVELIN FAW1
XA553
RAF STANMORE PARK

Designed to Air Ministry Specification F4/48 for a two-seat 'all-weather fighter' and initially known as the Gloster GA5, XA553 is one of only two Mk1 Javelins left extant, the other being in the RAF Cosford Museum.

XA553 was ordered under Contract 6/Acft/8336, dated 14 July 1952. This was the main production order for the Javelin and was divided between the Gloster Aircraft Co. Ltd at Hucclecote and the Armstrong Whitworth Co. Ltd at Baginton, Coventry. It was the tenth production Javelin and one of only forty Mk1 aircraft built. It was ready at Hucclecote on 28 April 1955 but was destined never to fly with the RAF.

The Ministry of Aviation had only three Javelin prototypes and it became necessary to divert eleven aircraft from the main production batch for trials. XA553 was one of these and it was retained by Glosters to fly exclusively from their test airfield at Moreton Valance from 28 September 1955.

XA553 has been on display at RAF Stanmore Park since 20 May 1963. *(M.A.P.)*

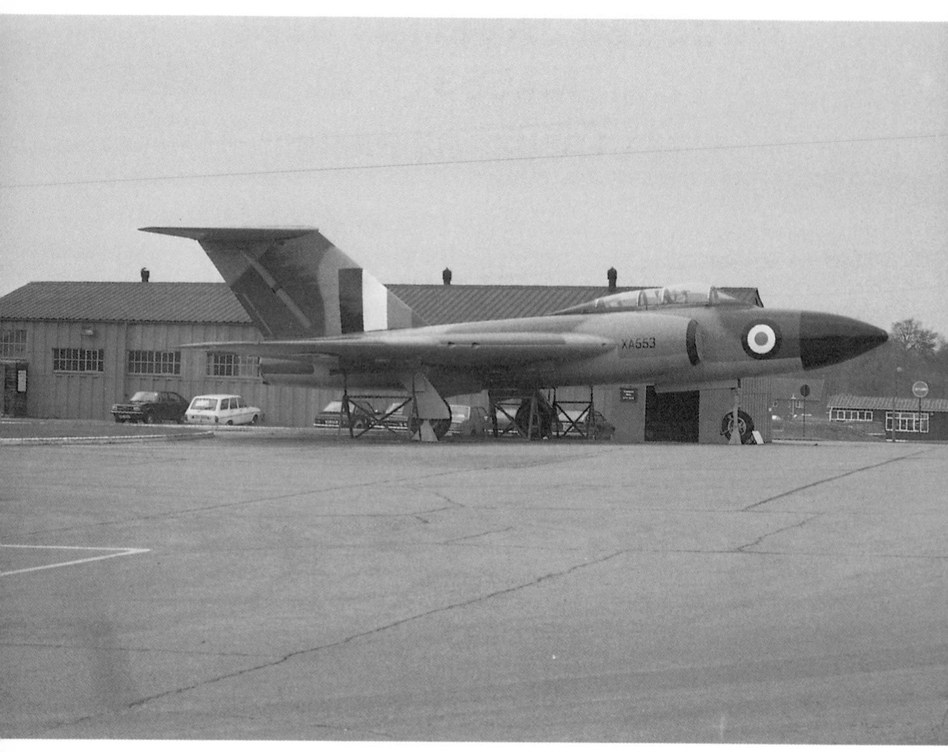

Javelin FAW 1 XA553 never served with the RAF. It has been RAF Stanmore Park's gate guard since arriving from RAF Yatesbury. *(J. A. Simpson)*

XA553 was not one of the more famous of the test airframes and records of its trials work are scarce. However it is known that it carried a modified nose radome which was more blunt and slightly smaller than the standard Mk1. This was probably a trial for the FAW2 which was to carry the American AI-22 radar; the AI-22 had a smaller radome than the British AI-17 radar. Nothing else is known about its flying life at Moreton Valance which was shortlived; in July 1957 it was declared non-effective and grounded.

On 13 August 1957 the aircraft was delivered to RAF Yatesbury as a ground instruction airframe for training RAF Instrument Fitters; it became 7470M.

XA553 remained at Yatesbury for just under six years and, with the closure of the station in 1963, it was given to Stanmore Park for display. After preparation it was positioned at the station entrance on 20 May 1963 where it has remained to this day.

AVRO SHACKLETON AEW2 WL795

RAF ST MAWGAN

On 24 November 1981 at RAF Lossiemouth, Sqn Ldr Chris Booth (later Wing Commander and last C.O. of Shackleton-equipped No.8 Sqn) throttled up the four Rolls-Royce Griffon powerplants of Shackleton WL795 for its last flight. The aircraft was flown south to RAF St Mawgan, arriving some two hours later. Upon landing the aircraft was officially handed over to the then Station Commander, Group Captain Phillips.

The story of this aircraft began with the issue of Air Ministry Contract 6/Acft/6129 to A. V. Roe Ltd at Woodford for a batch of forty Shackleton MR Mk2 anti-submarine aircraft. The aircraft was duly completed and, following its first flight on 17 August 1953 and subsequent test flights, it was declared ready for collection by the RAF on 31 August.

On 8 September it was delivered to No.23 MU at RAF Aldergrove in Northern Ireland for service preparation, and on 14 October it passed into the hands of the Command Aircraft Preparation and Modification Flight for this work to be carried out. This little-known unit completed the work by 30 October after which WL795 entered a brief period of storage before being issued to No.204 Squadron at RAF Ballykelly on 6 January 1954.

This anti-submarine/reconnaissance squadron had formed five days earlier and WL795 soon entered an uneventful period of maritime flying which included the usual round of anti-submarine warfare (ASW), navigation and rescue-training exercises many of which were to last up to fifteen hours in duration; sortie lengths of up to twenty-four hours were also not uncommon. This changed on 13 March 1954 when the aircraft suffered a ground accident which rendered it Cat 3(R) and left it grounded until 13 September. The following day, now fully serviceable, it returned to 204 Sqn.

On 28 February 1955 the aircraft was selected to be fitted with an uprated set of ASW equipment and there followed a series of trials designed to test its use in a working environment. These trials lasted until 24 March when the aircraft was returned to its original configuration and passed back to its squadron four days later.

On 11 November 1958, WL795 transferred its allegiance to a new squadron when it moved around the airfield at Ballykelly to join No.269 Squadron. The unit only remained in existence until the end of the month because on 1 December it was renumbered No.210 Squadron. The aircraft was used in a similar manner to that with its previous unit, and remained with 210 Sqn until 23 November 1959 when it returned to 204 Sqn.

This second stay with 204 Sqn only lasted for a couple of weeks because on 15 December it flew to Woodford for conversion to Phase 1 standard. This work included replacing its engines with the slightly more powerful Griffon 58s and the fitting of more modern avionics equipment. WL795 remained at Woodford until 6 December 1960 when, with the modifications completed, it was declared ready for collection once again.

By the 20th it had arrived at RAF Hal Far in Malta where it joined No.38 Squadron and was soon coded 'T'. It remained in Malta for the next six years uneventfully carrying out its ASW role far and wide over the Mediterranean before once again returning to the UK. This time it went to Hawker Siddeley Aviation Ltd, arriving on 21 July 1966 at Langar for Phase III update. This is rather interesting because it didn't undergo a Phase II update similar to the rest of the Shackleton fleet. The modifications brought the aircraft's avionic fit up to that contained in the Shackleton MR3.

The work took until 13 July 1967 when it was declared ready for collection. By 1 August it had arrived in Singapore where it was taken on strength by No.205 Squadron at RAF Changi, who

WL795:G at Luqa, on its way from RAF Changi to No.5 MU at Kemble to be put into storage. It still retains 205 Sqn markings. *(C. P. Russell-Smith)*

coded it 'G'. As before it was used in its primary role together with the secondary one of an air-sea rescue (ASR) support aircraft. One such incident involved Bristol Britannia XM519 'Capella' which had suffered an engine overspeed problem many miles from land and declared a 'MAY DAY'. Aircraft from 205 Sqn (WL795 included) shadowed the struggling Britannia until it made a safe landfall at RAF Gan, a small island in the Indian Ocean.

One of its major tasks during its time at Changi was in support of units fighting in the Borneo Confrontation. As part of Operation Hawkmoth it was often required to patrol the coastal waters of the Far East to try and prevent Indonesia-aligned communist terrorists from landing in North Borneo, Sabah, Brunei, Sarawak and the Malaysian Peninsula. On one such 'Hawkmoth' sortie it had the pleasure of chasing away Indonesian submarine No.408 from the protectorates. These often lengthy sorties continued until the cessation of hostilities in August 1966 when the squadron resumed its normal peacetime ASW and ASR duties.

WL795 returned to the UK in early 1971 and by 2 February it had arrived at No.5 MU, RAF Kemble for storage. It languished until 4 February 1972 when it was allocated to Hawker Siddeley once again, this time going to Bitteswell for conversion to AEW2 standard.

The requirement for an RAF AEW force had initially arisen because of the impending retirement of the Royal Navy's Gannet AEW3 carrier-based aircraft. This had resulted in a gap in Britain's air defence coverage. Therefore the decision was taken to convert twelve low fatigue-life Shackletons to fulfil this role. After the conversions had been completed the most obvious difference was the addition of an external radome that contained the APS 20 radar scanner (taken from the Gannet). As well as the AEW associated changes the opportunity was taken to update the aircraft's normal avionics systems.

WL795 was flown to Bitteswell for conversion on 4 February and became the eighth aircraft to be modified. It re-appeared some six months later and, following a brief return to Kemble for painting, it joined No.8 Squadron at RAF Kinloss on 12 October. Before becoming operational, the aircraft went to Lossiemouth, then still the shore base for the Navy's remaining Gannet force, for the installation of its radar equipment. This work took seven days and on 19 October it rejoined 8 Sqn at Kinloss. On 14 August 1973, 8 Sqn as a whole moved the eleven miles down the Moray coast to RAF Lossiemouth, this location becoming the unit's permanent home.

In the early days 8 Sqn gave their aircraft names taken from the *Magic Roundabout* TV programme; WL795 was not left out and soon carried the name 'Rosalie' under the cockpit. It uneventfully carried out its air defence role until it became a victim of John Knot's defence cuts in 1980. The aircraft had a high fatigue rear wing spar (a common Shackleton problem) so on 8 July it was finally grounded and withdrawn from front-line service.

Following its last flight and achieving a grand total of 11,883 flying hours, St Mawgan planned to use the aircraft for crash rescue training. However, because of the station's long association with the Shackleton, the Station Commander decided it would be better put to use as a gate guard. The aircraft was issued with the maintenance serial 8753M and placed in external store until time could be found to prepare it for display.

Shackleton 'MR2' WL795:T at St Mawgan in April 1989. *(J. A. Simpson)*

On 21 March 1988, as the base Nimrods were away at RAF Marham whilst the runway was being relaid, the opportunity was taken to move the aircraft into the station's maintenance hangar. It was decided to reconvert it back to MR2 standard by removing the APS 20 radome and fitting a set of lengthened bomb doors. Fortunately a set of these doors were still on charge at Lossiemouth. Following a year's hard restoration work, which included a complete rub down of the airframe, the aircraft was once again repainted as a Maritime Reconnaissance variant, given the code 'T', and put on display in late April 1989.

By December 1989 it became the only remaining Shackleton gate guard when RAF Lossiemouth were forced to dispose of their version (interestingly a MR2 made to look like an AEW2) as part of the one gate guard only policy.

DE HAVILLAND VAMPIRE T11 XD506

RAF SWINDERBY

Always innovators in the aviation world, the De Havilland Aircraft Company surprised many people when they produced the twin-boom Vampire fighter and trainer series of aircraft. They originally produced the Vampire T11 as a private venture realising that a two-seat training version of their popular jet fighter might have a future. Initial design work was carried out by Airspeeds at Christchurch (a subsidiary of De Havillands) and by 1950 the company soon realised they had a winner. The Ministry of Supply soon showed similar interest and issued Specification T111P to cover production .

XD506, construction number 15271, was built as part of Contract 6/Acft/8981 by the parent company at Broughton near Chester. It was declared ready for collection on 31 March 1954 and a week later on 6 April was delivered to No.48 MU at RAF Hawarden for service acceptance. It was then issued to No.206 Advanced Flying School (AFS) at RAF Oakington who coded it 'AL'.

This unit was converting from Meteor T7s at the time and on 1 June 1954, after this was completed, became No.5 Flying Training School (FTS). XD506 retained its 'AL' code and spent the next three years training new pilots at Oakington and Gravely, its relief landing ground. In May 1957 it went to No.10 MU at RAF Hullavington for servicing and a period of storage before returning to 5 FTS in January 1959, where it was coded '36' as part of the unit's newly created numerical coding system.

No.5 FTS disbanded as a Vampire unit in 1963 but, prior to this, XD506 had transferred to the Central Navigation and Control School (CNCS) at RAF Shawbury in February 1962 where its role became that of a 'clockwork mouse' training air traffic controllers for the RAF. With this unit it was coded 'Z', which it retained when, on 11 February 1963, the CNCS was renamed the Central Air Traffic Control School (CATCS). XD506 remained with it, still coded 'Z', until August 1967 when it was withdrawn from use. Having flown 3,267 flying hours and making some 6,470 landings the aircraft was placed into store across the airfield with No.27 MU, and was given the maintenance serial 7983M. It didn't remain in store for very long because on 7 September it was allocated to RAF Finningley for display as part of the RAF Museum's regional collection held there.

Soon after arrival at Finningley it was repainted in the markings of No.616 (South Yorkshire) Squadron Royal Auxiliary Air Force, an unfortunate choice because that squadron never

Photographed at Finningley in September 1967, XD506 still wears the markings of CATCS. *(C. P. Russell-Smith)*

flew Vampires, although they had long been associated with Finningley. In July 1968 as part of the Royal Review of the RAF it was taken to RAF Abingdon and put on display; following this brief excursion it returned to Finningley.

It was moved to RAF Swinderby in 1977 when the regional collection was dispersed to accommodate the Queen's Silver Jubilee Display. After arrival at Swinderby the aircraft was refurbished, retaining the markings of No.616 Squadron, and placed on display on a plinth by the main gate. In 1985 a team from nearby RAF Waddington refurbished the aircraft, once again repainting the aircraft in the 616 Sqn markings that it still retains.

FOLLAND GNAT T1
XR534
RAF VALLEY

The unique Gnat T1 trainer originates from a private venture by the Folland Aircraft Co. who produced the Folland type 139 'Midge' aerodynamic test vehicle. This project soon expanded and the Type 140, single-seat lightweight fighter (the Gnat F1) was soon flying. Designed by W. E. W. (Teddy) Petter (who had previously designed the Westland Whirlwind fighter and English Electric Canberra bomber), the Type Fo141 single-seat fighter first flew on 18 July 1955 but failed to gain any orders from the RAF although it did serve with distinction in the air forces of India (the licence-built HAL Gnat), Finland, and Yugoslavia.

Using the knowledge gained in the earlier project the design was modified to later appear as a revitalised two-seat supersonic trainer that satisfied Air Ministry Spec.T.185D. The initial order was for fourteen pre-production aircraft, the first of which, XM691, first flew from Chilbolton on 31 August 1959. The first production aircraft (the fifteenth) was delivered in 1962 and was followed by a total production order of 105 aircraft.

Folland (Type Fo144) Gnat T1, XR534, was built at Hamble as part of a twenty-strong batch to Contract KC/2B/05, and was issued with the construction number FL545. It was declared ready for collection from Folland's Chilbolton test airfield on 28 June 1963, and after acceptance by the RAF it was delivered to its first flying unit, the Central Flying School (CFS) at RAF Little Rissington on 5 July.

The Gnat T1 replaced the venerable Vampire T11 as the RAF's advanced high-speed trainer and XR534 flew without incident until 5 March 1964 when it was declared Cat 3(R) following a flying accident at Little Rissington. The repair work, undertaken by a team from No.71 MU, RAF Bicester, was completed on 14 April and shortly afterwards the aircraft took up its duties once again with the CFS.

Its flying career continued uneventfully until 7 April 1969 when it returned to the Hawker Siddeley factory at Dunsfold for partial reconditioning; this work was completed by 20 October 1969 and it again returned to the CFS at Little Rissington who issued it with the code 'A'. It returned to Dunsfold once again the following year, this time for repair, because on 14 May 1970 it was the victim of a Cat 4 flying accident. It was eventually transferred by road to the factory and after extensive repairs it joined No.4 FTS on 16 November and was subsequently coded '65'.

A further three years passed without incident until 26

XR534 in its early CFS markings in 1968. *(M.A.P.)*

November 1973, when it again suffered another Cat 3 accident. The repairs this time were again undertaken by No.71 MU who also combined the repairs with a much-needed major servicing. In January 1974 the aircraft flew to No.5 MU at RAF Kemble for completion of its major service (a total repaint into the new Support Command red and white and grey colour scheme) prior to it rejoining No.4 FTS on 14 March 1974.

It retained the code '65' and apart from a brief loan period with the CFS from 23 September 1975 to 3 December 1975 it remained with this No.4 FTS for the rest of its operational life. With the introduction of the Hawk T1 in 1974 the Gnat fleet were gradually retired and on 12 April 1977 this fate befell XR534 when it was declared Cat 5c (spares recovery).

The disposal instructions were later changed to Cat 5 G.I/Display and on 12 December 1977 it was issued with the Support Command serial 8578M and placed on display at RAF Valley as a gate guard from that day.

AVRO VULCAN B2
XM607
RAF WADDINGTON

The Avro Vulcan was designed shortly after the end of the Second World War to meet Air Ministry Specification B35/46 which was issued on 1 January 1947. To provide data on the aerodynamics of the delta plan-form, several small delta-winged aircraft were built as research vehicles (the Avro Type 707 series); two of these can be seen in the museum at RAF Cosford. The prototype Avro 698 flew on 30 August 1952 and this led to forty-five production Vulcan B1s which entered service from July 1957. Later Vulcans were built to the B2 standard with a larger wing and more powerful engines.

XM607, a B2, was the twenty-second aircraft of the fourth production batch and was one of the last Vulcans to be built. It was ready for collection from Woodford, Manchester on 30 December 1963 and, two days later, was allocated to No.35 Squadron which operated from RAF Coningsby in Lincolnshire alongside Nos.9 and 12 Squadrons. The Coningsby Wing was originally intended to carry the Douglas GAM-87A Skybolt nuclear missile but when Skybolt was cancelled in December

XM607 at St Mawgan in March 1976. *(via J. A. Todd)*

1962 the Wing converted to the conventional non-nuclear free-fall role. Initially, the aircraft were painted in a white, anti-flash colour scheme; when the V-force concept changed from high-level to low-level penetration in 1964, the colour scheme was changed to standard grey-green camouflaged upper surfaces and white undersides.

In 1964, the Coningsby Wing moved to RAF Cottesmore in Rutland and with the advent of centralised servicing early the following year, the aircraft ceased to belong to a particular squadron. In January 1969, the Cottesmore Wing moved to RAF Akrotiri in Cyprus but XM607 remained in the UK and was transferred to the Waddington Wing which comprised Nos.44, 50 and 101 Squadrons: No.9 Squadron joined them in June 1975 when the Akrotiri Wing disbanded.

Throughout the 1970s, XM607 remained on the Waddington Wing paying occasional vists to RAF St Athan for major servicing and to Bitteswell for modifications. In 1975, with the return to squadron servicing aircraft were again allotted to squadrons and XM607 joined 44 Sqn.

In the early 1980s, the Tornado GR1 force began to build and the Vulcan force gradually ran down. By March 1982, the Scampton Wing had disbanded and, one month later, 9 Sqn ceased to exist at Waddington; the other Waddington squadrons were given a temporary reprieve by the Argentine invasion of the Falkland Islands.

XM607, still with 44 Sqn, was one of the five remaining Vulcans which had the Skybolt wing hardpoints and these were used to carry ECM pods and Martel and Shrike missiles although, in the event, Martel was never carried operationally. XM607 and XM598 left Waddington for Wideawake airfield, Ascension Island on 29 April 1982 and arrived the following day.

The first mission to be flown during Operation Corporate, codenamed 'Black Buck 1', was planned for 30 April–1 May with XM607 as the reserve aircraft but the primary aircraft had pressurisation problems — later traced to an air leak around the pilot's direct vision window — and XM607 took over. The aircraft was commanded by Flt Lt Martin Withers and, after six air-to-air refuellings, the last of which was from Victor K2 XL189 some 3,000 miles south of Ascension Island, the crew dropped twenty-one 1,000 lb bombs across the runway of Port Stanley airfield at 0446 hours local time (0746Z); one of the bombs hit the centre of the runway. At the time, this standard of accuracy was criticized in some quarters but the Vulcan's NBS and H2S radar were designed with nuclear weapons in mind and not for precision bombing from 10,000 feet. At the end of the 16-hour mission, the aircraft returned safely to Wideawake after further air-to-air refuelling. XM607 was also used for the second attack on Port Stanley airfield, codenamed 'Black Buck 2', on 4 May; on this occasion, the captain was Sqn Ldr R. J. Reeve. On 13 May, it was due to fly 'Black Buck 3' but strong headwinds caused it to be cancelled. XM607 carried out the final mission on 12 June, 'Black Buck 7'; again the captain was Flt Lt Withers and several Pucara aircraft were destroyed on Port Stanley airfield.

On 14 June 1982, XM607 returned to Waddington and flew with 44 Sqn for a further six months. It appeared at several post-Falklands air displays, including RAF Binbrook on 28 August, RAF Leuchars on 4 September and RAF Abingdon on 18 September. No.44 Sqn was the last Vulcan bomber squadron (although 50 Sqn flew converted Vulcan K2 tankers for another two years) and XM607 led a four-aircraft 'scramble' to mark the end of the operational V-force on 17 December 1982.

On 4 June 1983, XM607 was allocated for display at RAF Waddington and was given the Support Command Serial 8779M. It was placed on display near the Electronics Squadron building on 2 July and was dedicated for display by Air Vice-Marshal D. Parry-Evans during his AOC's Inspection on 14 July 1983.

On the port (left) side of the aircraft, near the cockpit, are three 'kill' markings applied shortly after Operation Corporate. As a postscript, Flt Lt Withers was awarded the Distinguished Flying Cross for his part in the 'Black Buck' raids.

ENGLISH ELECTRIC LIGHTNING FMk1A XM192

RAF WATTISHAM

This particular Lightning is probably one of the most famous of its type built, because in 1962 it was the subject of an Airfix construction kit.

XM192 was built as part of the first production batch by the English Electric Co at their Salmesbury factory and was given the construction number 95090, it being the twenty-fourth production airframe. It made its first flight on 25 May 1961 when, flown by J. K. Isherwood, it was delivered to the company test airfield at nearby Warton. After completing its test programme it was issued on 28 June to No.111 Squadron at RAF Wattisham, who coded it 'K'.

As was common with the Lightning force at the time, the aircraft retained its natural metal finish but with squadron markings applied either side of the nose roundel. In the case of 'Treble One' this was a black lightning flash edged in yellow together with a 'Maltese cross' on the fin. These were the markings being carried when it was chosen by Airfix in 1962 to be the subject of a 72nd scale model kit.

No.111 Sqn's early years of service with the F1A were spent in extensive in-flight refuelling exercises with Valiant tankers. This was because the Lightning F1A was fitted with a removable in-flight refuelling probe in an effort to increase the poor range of the Lightning.

In December 1964, 111 Sqn began to re-equip with the more advanced Lightning F3 and because of this XM192 was transferred to RAF Coltishall to join No.226 OCU to train new pilots for the Lightning force. As was the norm on the OCU, XM192 was coded '192' this being displayed on the tail or nose of the aircraft in large black figures. It remained in this second-line role on the strength of No.145 Squadron (one of the shadow units designated to the OCU the other being No.65 Squadron) until 26 August 1965 when it went to No.60 MU at RAF Leconfield for a major servicing. This took until 7 June 1966 to complete after which it returned to Coltishall to rejoin No.226 OCU.

XM192 was a common sight at many airshows throughout the next three years in its 145 Sqn markings until 1 October 1969 when it was transferred to RAF Binbrook, joining the locally based Target Facilities Flight (TFF). In this role it acted as a high-speed target for No.5 Squadron, the locally based Lightning unit. It was painted with a blue bar either side of the nose roundel together with a large blue Lion on the tail (taken from Binbrook's station badge). It only remained at Binbrook for a few months after which, in early 1970, it moved back to Wattisham to join their TFF. Its markings changed to black and yellow bars either side of the nose roundel and Wattisham's station badge on the tail.

A winter shot of XM192 at Wattisham in 1984. *(J. M. Webber)*

This was to be XM192's last productive assignment, albeit lasting for three years, and on the last day of 1973 the flight disbanded. With a grand total of 2,186 flying hours the aircraft was sent to Leconfield for storage and disposal. It was saved from destruction when it was allocated to Wattisham for display, and on 27 September 1974, resplendent once again in the markings of 111 Sqn, it was delivered to Wattisham and presented by 'Treble One' to the station for display at the main gate.

ARMSTRONG WHITWORTH METEOR NF(T)14 WS807

RAF WATTON

Possibly the most elegant of the Meteor family, 100 of this type were built in response to Air Ministry Specification F44/46 (later rationalised to F4/48) and was the culmination of a series of aircraft that began with the NF11. This particular mark, which can trace its origins directly back to the NF12, was built as the Gloster Type G47, but because Glosters (the parent company for the Meteor) were heavily involved with its replacement (the Javelin) the complete order was built under licence at Baginton by the Armstrong Whitworth Aircraft Co. The first NF14 entered service in May 1954 and it fell to one such NF14, WS787:G of No.60 Squadron at RAF Tengah to carry out the last front-line sortie of a RAF Meteor on 17 August 1961.

As previously stated the NF14 was a direct descendant of the earlier NF12 version with the most obvious difference being the latter type's fully blown clear canopy. Armament took the form of four wing-mounted cannons guided by the American-built APS-21 radar system contained in the slightly longer nose radome.

WS807 was built as part of Contract 6/Acft/16412/CB5(b) at Baginton and following initial test flights was declared ready for collection on 25 March 1954. Five days later it flew to No.8 MU at RAF Little Rissington for service acceptance. Following acceptance the aircraft was put into short-term store at Kemble prior to joining No.46 Squadron in August 1954.

No.46 Sqn was based at RAF Odiham and operated a mixed batch of NF12s and NF14s. WS807, coded 'N', was painted with the squadron's distinctive 'Arrowhead' motif which it carried on its fin. The Meteor force remained operational at Odiham until the introduction of another Gloster product, the Javelin FAW1, and 46 Sqn became the first operational unit to receive this aircraft. By mid-1956 the unit had replaced most of their Meteors, although a few, WS807 included, soldiered on to the end of the year.

On 10 January 1957, WS807 finally left No.46 Sqn and flew to RAF Lyneham (a well-known Meteor graveyard) to be put into storage with No.33 MU. On 10 April 1958 it moved to another Meteor graveyard, No.12 MU at RAF Kirkbride, remaining there until September before moving south again, this time to No.49 MU at RAF Colerne. At Colerne it was selected to be the recipient of a special trials fit resulting in it being converted to NF(T)14 status. The fit was designed to help train navigators, with most of the conversion work aimed at removing the radar and replacing it with ballast. Its paint scheme was also modified and although it retained its basic camouflage pattern it had large dayglo strips placed in strategic positions indicating to other aircraft that it was now a trainer. By 12 March 1959 the aircraft was declared ready for issue once again and following another visit to Kirkbride was put into temporary store with No.12 MU.

This Meteor NF(T)14 in the arrowhead markings of No.46 Sqn is used to guard the gate of Eastern Radar at RAF Watton. *(J. A. Simpson)*

On 30 June, WS807 returned to flying duties once again when it was issued to No.2 Air Navigation School (ANS) at RAF Thorney Island. Soon after arrival it was coded 'J', the letter appearing on the aircraft's fin and nose wheel door. No.2 ANS was in the process of replacing its ageing Vampire NF(T)10s with Meteors although it only retained the latter type for about three years. On 15 January 1962, No.2 ANS moved to RAF Hullavington where shortly after arrival it re-equipped with the Vickers Varsity T1.

WS807 managed to survive this re-equipment programme and was transferred instead to No.1 ANS at RAF Stradishall where it retained its 'J' coding. Its uneventful flying career lasted for another two years but on 3 March 1964 this changed when it suffered a Cat 3 flying accident. It was subsequently repaired at Stradishall and resumed flying duties on 1 May. On 23 June it was the victim of yet another accident. This time, although again declared Cat 3, it was deemed beyond local skills so a team from No.71 MU at RAF Bicester were tasked to carry out the repairs. One month later it rejoined No.1 ANS to give further uneventful service until it was retired to No.5 MU, RAF Kemble on 26 January 1966.

On 8 March it was declared a non-effective airframe and although it remained at Kemble it had effectively been struck off charge. This state of affairs lasted for the next eighteen months until 11 October 1967 when it was issued with the Support Command maintenance serial 7973M and allocated for display duties.

Following a complete refurbishment it was allocated to Signals Command at RAF Watton (now Eastern Radar) and took up its duties later in 1967. It was initially displayed in a natural metal scheme but following another refurbishment in 1976 it was returned to the colours it first flew in, as 'N' of 46 Sqn.

ENGLISH ELECTRIC LIGHTNING F2 XN769

LATCC RAF WEST DRAYTON

Unique as the only remaining example of its type remaining on RAF charge, this particular aircraft spent most of its operational flying career overseas with 2 ATAF in West Germany.

The Lightning F2 variant of the mighty Lightning was essentially very similar to the earlier F1A version but with a number of minor modifications. It had an improved navigation system, a liquid oxygen system, a steerable nosewheel and a standby DC generator. An intake duct fitted for the DC generator was the only external means of distinguishing it from the F1A.

XN769, construction number 95122, was built at Salmesbury by the English Electric Co. as part of an order for fifty-five Lightning F2s as part of Contract KC/2D/03/CB7(b). The order was eventually reduced by eleven aircraft and was completed by late 1963. The aircraft first flew, in the hands of Dougy de Villiers, to the nearby company airfield at Warton and following testing was declared ready for collection on 30 August 1963.

On 30 September instead of joining an operational squadron XN769 was flown to No.33 MU at RAF Lyneham and was put into store. This remained its fate for the next two years and it was not until 5 August 1965 that it joined No.92 Squadron who coded it 'Z', at RAF Leconfield. Together with No.19 Squadron these were the only two operational units to fly this mark of Lightning (a few were used by the Air Fighting Development School). Shortly after arriving at Leconfield 92 Sqn was allocated to 2 ATAF in West Germany to provide local air defence; on 30 December 1965 the squadron moved to RAF Geilenkirchen, following 19 Sqn who had moved to RAF Gutersloh three months earlier.

XN769 joined 19 Sqn briefly on 28 September 1966 and although it only stayed with the squadron until 11 January 1967, it was coded 'X'. When the aircraft rejoined 92 Sqn it was reissued with the code 'Z'. On 22 January 1968, 92 Sqn joined 19 Sqn at Gutersloh following the decision to centralise the RAF Germany air defence force at one station.

On 26 February 1971, XN769 suffered a Cat 3 flying accident which required the skills of No.431 MU from RAF Bruggen to effect repairs; these were completed by 19 March and the aircraft rejoined 92 Sqn. In July 1971 it was returned to Salmesbury for some minor modifications, returning to Germany the following month. In September the aircraft left Germany for the last time when it flew to No.60 MU at Leconfield and was put into storage.

XN769 had been grounded at Leconfield by the time this photograph of it was taken in July 1974. *(C. P. Russell-Smith)*

Many Lightning F2s were modified to F2A standard (which made them equivalent to the F6) but a few were declared surplus to requirements. XN769 fell into the latter category and on 30 November 1963 was declared a non-effective airframe and put up for disposal. Fortunately it didn't suffer the attentions of the scrap merchants because in early 1974 it was allocated to RAF Leconfield for display. On 1 May 1965, after a period of preparation which included painting it in both 19 and 92 Sqn markings it went on display inside the camp.

In April 1976 with the impending closure of Leconfield, the aircraft was once again declared surplus; again it was saved when RAF West Drayton declared an interest in displaying it. It was dismantled by a team from No.71 MU at RAF Abingdon and taken by road to West Drayton for display outside the London Air Traffic Control Centre, and in October it became the station's first and so far only gate guard. In the mid-1980s it was refurbished and repainted in a very distinctive silver and blue colour scheme once worn by 19 Sqn.

GLOSTER JAVELIN FAW8 XH980

RAF WEST RAYNHAM

Destined to be the last totally new variant of the Javelin, the FAW8 first entered service with the RAF on 26 October 1959. This mark was radically different from its predecessors in that it was the first British production aircraft to feature a limited reheat facility for its Sapphire 7R engines. These engines gave the aircraft a very much enhanced performance at altitude although fuel consumption increased, requiring the installation of two extra under-fuselage fuel tanks.

Other changes included an improved windscreen rain dispersal system and the replacement of the cartridge engine start system for one which used the volatile but more efficient 'Avpin'. Aerodynamic improvements included wing drooped leading edges and pitch and yaw dampers fitted to the flying control system. It was originally fitted with the American AI-22 Radar which proved to be so unreliable that earlier British sets were

A fully armed XH980:A on the gate at RAF West Raynham. *(M.A.P.)*

removed from redundant FAW2 and FAW4 aircraft when they became available and installed in their place.

XH980 was one of 60 FAW8s built by the parent company as part of Contract 6/Acft/11329/CB7(6) and was declared ready for collection at the firm's Hucclecote airfield on 16 October 1959. Three days later it was delivered to No.23 MU at RAF Aldergrove where it underwent service preparation and on 23 November it was issued to No.41 Squadron at RAF Wattisham. This unit had flown Javelins since 1956, originally operating FAW4s at Coltishall prior to moving to Wattisham in July 1958. They had received their first FAW8 just three days earlier and were rapidly converting to the new mark.

The aircraft suffered a Cat 3 flying accident on 22 September 1960 which required the skills of No.71 MU from RAF Bicester to carry out repairs. These were completed by 27 October and that same day it was reissued to 41 Sqn. On 10 June 1961 the aircraft was one of eight aircraft selected to take part in the Queen's Birthday flypast. During the following month, on 26 July, it returned to its manufacturer for refurbishment and modification. On completion of this work it was declared ready for collection at Moreton Valance before returning once again to 41 Sqn on 21 November. In 1962 it went with the squadron to Norway to take part in air defence exercises in conjunction with Royal Norwegian Air Force F-86Ks as part of 'Exercise Fawn Echo'.

The defence-cutting environment of the early 1960s mean that on 6 December 1963, 41 Sqn was disbanded and its Javelins prepared for disposal. However, before they finally disbanded the squadron managed a farewell flypast over St Omer in France. XH980 was delivered to No.27 MU at RAF Shawbury together with the rest of the squadron on 16 December 1963, and was immediately placed in store. It was given the maintenance serial 7867M and struck off charge on 24 February 1964, but unlike many of its contemporaries it was not reduced to scrap. Instead it was allocated to RAF Stafford for display, taking up residence on 26 November 1964 outside Youth Selection Centre (YSC), together with a Bloodhound Missile.

When the YSC closed in 1970 the aircraft was transferred by road to its current home at RAF West Raynham, where soon after arrival it was repainted in No.85 Squadron colours and coded 'A'. No.85 Sqn had been the only other operator of the FAW8, receiving its first aircraft in March 1960 at RAF West Malling. It moved to West Raynham with these aircraft in September 1960 and has a long association with this airfield.

In 1975 the aircraft was repainted in a low-visibility colour scheme but fortunately this mistake was soon remedied and it was soon returned to the correct colours. At some stage since then the aircraft was fitted with its full complement of four Firestreak missiles, the configuration it retains now.

HAWKER HUNTER FMk6
XF418
RAF WILDENRATH

Although most of the Hunters produced for the RAF were constructed at Hawker's Kingston on Thames factory, to ease production difficulties a few were built at the company's Blackpool plant and, following the successful completion of an order for Hunter F5s, the Armstrong Whitworth Aircraft Co. at Baginton was licensed to build a further production batch of 100 FMk6 aircraft.

XF418 was part of this order from Baginton, which was Contract 6/Acft/9818/CB7(a). The aircraft were originally built without the wing leading edge extensions (the famous dogtooth) and gun blast deflectors, both of which were fitted at a later date. Following initial test flights the aircraft was declared ready for collection from Baginton on 31 October 1955. It remained with Armstrong Whitworth in store for nearly a year and it was not until 29 October 1956 that it was delivered to No.33 MU at RAF Lyneham for service acceptance.

The acceptance took until 6 February 1957 to complete and the following day it joined the Day Fighter Leaders School (DFLS) at RAF West Raynham. Upon arrival, it was coded 'F' and painted with a red spine and fin to distinguish it in combat. This unit was part of the Central Fighter Establishment (CFE) and trained Fighter Command's pilots in air combat tactics. The DFLS went through a number of name changes throughout the late fifties and early sixties. It became the Day Fighter Combat Squadron in March 1958, changing to Day Fighter Combat School on 1 July 1962; this title was retained until disbandment on 31 October 1965. XF418 did not quite manage to stay with the DFCS to the end because on 28 September 1965 it was the victim of a Cat 3 flying accident.

The repairs were categorised as beyond local skills so a team from Hawkers was despatched to West Raynham to carry them out. They must have been quite extensive because it took the working party until 27 June 1966 to complete the task and, on 4 August following a brief period of storage, XF418 moved to RAF Chivenor to join No.229 OCU. No.229 OCU was responsible for training all Hunter aircrew in the RAF. On 29 September 1971 it suffered a second, but fairly minor accident; the damage was deemed Cat 2 and it was back with the OCU on flying duties by 8 October.

On 2 September 1974, No.229 OCU was disbanded at Chivenor, reforming immediately at RAF Brawdy as the Tactical Weapons Unit. XF418, now coded '16', transferred with the rest of the OCU's Hunters to continue as a training aircraft. The TWU at Brawdy was renamed No.1 TWU on 31 July 1978 when a similar unit (No.2 TWU) was formed at RAF Lossiemouth to ease the training difficulties caused by the poor weather factor at Brawdy. The TWU's role (by now the largest operator of the Hunter in the RAF, with over 70 on strength) was to teach tactical flying to pilots destined for the 'fast jet' OCUs.

On 6 April 1982, XF418 flew to No.5 MU at RAF Kemble for long-term storage but on 14 July it was removed from store and returned to No.1 TWU on 23 August. It remained at Brawdy with the TWU until, with the introduction of the Hawk T1, it was put into store at Brawdy on 20 November 1984.

This was not quite the end of XF418's flying career because on 6 December it undertook one last flight to RAF Laarbruch in Germany. It was destined to be a battle damage repair training airframe and was subsequently declared Cat 5 (GI) and issued with the Support Command maintenance serial 8842M. It did not stay long at Laarbruch when in early 1985 it moved to RAF Wildenrath where it was acquired by No.92 Squadron as a display aircraft. It was painted in the colours of the Blue Diamonds, the squadron's aerobatic team of 1961–2 and placed on display outside the squadron's headquarters later that year.

The Blue Diamonds were formed in early 1961 to replace the Black Arrows of No.111 Squadron as the RAF's premier aerobatic team. The aircraft were painted in an overall blue colour scheme with white serials and a white lightning flash. The team originally flew twelve aircraft but by the end of 1962 when they disbanded they had eighteen aircraft on strength.

XF418 as a 229 OCU aircraft at its home base of Chivenor in August 1970. *(C. P. Russell-Smith)*

HAWKER SIDDELEY HARRIER GR3 XV779

RAF WITTERING

Of all the fixed wing aircraft to have served with the RAF the Harrier is totally unique. It was and still is the only Vertical Take-off and Landing (VTOL) combat aircraft in front-line service anywhere in the world (although the Soviet Navy do have the Yakolev Yak-38 'Forger' in service).

The original concept began in the 1950s when Hawker Siddeley entered into competition for a vertical take-off aircraft. Under a design team led by Ralph Hooper the project really came to life when Dr Stanley Hooker at Rolls-Royce offered a vectored thrust engine (later named Pegasus) to Hawkers. This led directly to two privately funded P1127 development aircraft, and one of them, XP831, flown by Bill Bedford, after tethered trials made the first tentative vertical take off on 21 October 1960.

Originally the whole project was directed at producing a supersonic VTOL aircraft (the P1154) but this was eventually cancelled by a doubting Ministry of Defence. Hawkers succeeded in overcoming these initial doubts and using the lessons gained from the P1127 they produced the Kestrel FGA1 as a follow on to the P1127 and then in 1966 received the first production order for sixty Harrier GR1 aircraft against Air Staff Requirement 384.

XV779 was part of this original order and was built at Kingston on Thames as a GR1. It was completed in March 1970 and made its first flight on the 26th in the hands of company test pilot Don Riches. It initially remained with the company who carried out modifications to bring the aircraft up to GR1A standard; this entailed replacing the Pegasus 101 with the slightly more powerful Pegasus 102.

The aircraft was finally delivered to RAF Wittering on 29 May where two days later, after service acceptance, it joined the world's first Steep Take-off and Vertical Landing (STOVL) unit, No.1 Squadron. It remained with them for only a few months because later in the year the first Harrier squadrons were being formed to go to RAF Germany (RAFG). No.4 Squadron was the first nominated and in August 1970, XV779 became the first aircraft to be issued to it, being joined by thirteen others over the next few weeks. After re-equipping as a detachment at Wittering the squadron flew to RAF Wildenrath where it replaced the squadron's previous mounts, the Hunter FGA9, in the ground attack and tactical reconnaissance role.

XV779 stayed with the squadron until 12 July 1972 when, having flown just over 355 hours, it returned to Wittering for its first major servicing. After completion of this work it returned to Wildenrath, but this time joining No.20 Squadron, and upon arrival it was coded 'Q'. It was obviously a good aircraft because in early 1973 it passed 500 hours and was well on its way to 1,000 when in December 1974 it required a Cat 4 minor rebuild. This work was carried out at RAF Gutersloh and after completion it returned to 20 Sqn. It flew on for a further two years after which, in December 1976, it returned to Wittering, this time for conversion to GR3 standard.

XV779 'AB' whilst on 3 Sqn strength.

The conversion involved replacing the Pegasus 102 with the much more powerful Pegasus 103, but more obviously it had an extension built onto its nose that contained the Laser Ranging and Marked Target Seeker equipment to be used in conjunction with the Ferranti FE542 Avionics system, giving the type a far superior bomb delivery system. The work was completed in February 1977 and on completion it returned to Wildenrath once again, this time joining No.3 Squadron who coded it 'P'. Shortly after its arrival at Wildenrath the Harrier force moved to RAF Gutersloh and XV779, together with the rest of the squadron, arrived there in March.

It returned to Wittering for another major servicing from 14 March 1979, flying back to 3 Sqn some two months later. Its flying career continued to be uneventful for the next six years until 25 April 1985 when it again required Cat 4 repairs. With this work completed it returned to 3 Sqn on 13 June and in November 1986, having flown 3,397 hours of operational service, it returned to Wittering for the last time to join No.233 OCU. Its fatigue life ran out on 12 January 1987 and having

Harrier GR3 XV779 was also coded AP as a No.3 Sqn aircraft. *(M.A.P.)*

flown 3,525.20 hours the aircraft was grounded and declared Cat 5 (spares recovery).

In early 1988 it was decided to put a Harrier on display at Wittering and because XV779 was time expired it was allocated to the task. It was issued with the Support Command maintenance serial 8931M and painted in the dual markings of No.233 OCU coded 'A' on its port side and No.1 Squadron coded '01' on the other and in March 1988 was positioned by Wittering main gate.

VICKERS SUPERMARINE SPITFIRE F21 LA255

RAF WITTERING

Although graceful to fly and elegant to look at the Spitfire F20 series bore very little resemblance to the more famous earlier marks of the same aircraft. They differed in so many respects that at one time it was planned to rename the aircraft 'Victor'. For this series of Spitfires the wing platform was radically revised and large deep bath radiators were installed to provide better cooling for the Rolls-Royce Griffon G61 engine. This powerful engine drove a five-bladed propeller which in turn meant the aircraft required a larger fin to counteract the increased torque.

The evolution of LA255 is rather convoluted as its original building contract was issued in March 1942 as an order for 300 Spitfire MkVcs. This was cancelled in early 1943 but reissued later that year, this time for the F21. The aircraft was subsequently built at South Marston by the parent company as part of Contract B981687/39 and given the construction number 4388. The whole of this batch of aircraft were built between July 1944 and December 1945.

LA255 was completed in March 1945 and following its initial thirty-minute test flight by Flt Lt Loweth it was delivered to No.39 MU at RAF Colerne on 26 March by Fg Off Farley of the Air Transport Auxiliary. On 10 April it joined No.1 Squadron at Ludham where shortly after arrival it was coded 'JX-U'.

No.1 Sqn was engaged in air defence duties at the time, mostly trying to shoot down the unmanned VI 'doodlebugs'. This first association with 1 Sqn was very short because soon after LA255's arrival the squadron moved to Hutton Cranswick, leaving the aircraft behind. It joined another Ludham unit, No.91 Squadron, and although its exact code isn't known it would have had the unit's 'DL-' coding. Joining its new squadron on 29 June 1945, it was soon on air defence duties again. Its stay with 91 Sqn was also rather short-lived because by 17 July it had returned to South Marston for a refit.

The refit was completed by March 1946 and shortly afterwards it renewed its ties with 1 Sqn, this time at RAF Tangmere. Resuming the code 'JX-U' it returned to air defence duties, although by now in a peacetime role. In October 1946 No.1 Sqn began to receive the Gloster Meteor F3 and although they disposed of most of their Spitfires they retained a few as hacks and general runabouts, LA255 included. When the squadron had fully re-equipped with the Meteor it began a series of postings to many different RAF stations, although still retaining its links with Tangmere and keeping the Spitfires based there. On one sortie from Tangmere on 13 November 1946, LA255 suffered a Cat E (Cat 5) flying accident. The aircraft was deemed uneconomic to repair so following some cosmetic surgery it was allocated the maintenance serial 6490M and downgraded to an instructional airframe.

LA255 was retained by 1 Sqn throughout the next few years as a variety of aircraft such as the Harvard, Oxford (as squadron runabouts) Meteor F4s and F8s and finally the Hunter F5 came and went. It eventually became surplus in July 1958 when the squadron disbanded at Tangmere. (No.263 Squadron was renumbered No.1 Squadron at RAF Stradishall the following day.)

Because LA255 was now without an owner it was despatched to No.216 MU at RAF Cardington to begin its first period of duty as a gate guard. Its stay lasted until April 1964 when it was discovered by former squadron member Leslie Hunt. He informed the then Hunter F6-equipped No.1 Squadron of its plight and following some quick negotiations the aircraft was transported to RAF West Raynham to rejoin its former owners.

It remained at West Raynham until 18 July 1969 when 1 Sqn Harrier (designate) was formed at RAF Wittering as the world's first VSTOL squadron. Once conversion was completed the squadron took charge of LA255 and had the aircraft transported to Wittering to resume its display duties.

This might have been the end of the story, but it was decided

No.1 Sqn have used LA255 as the squadron gate guard for many years. *(M.A.P.)*

in early 1974 to use the aircraft in a series of trials in conjunction with the RAF Battle of Britain Flight. This involved installing a Rolls-Royce Griffon G57A engine from an Avro Shackleton to see if this type of engine would be suitable for use in the flight's airworthy Spitfires. The trial began on 25 September 1974 and involved bringing LA255 up to taxiing standard, but the results of the test are unknown.

Following these trials, which finished in mid-1975, LA255 returned to Wittering where it has remained jealously guarded ever since. It is only displayed outside the squadron hangar on fine days and is normally visible to the many motorists travelling south on the A1 trunk road. In 1988 the aircraft was fully refurbished and continues to carry its 1 Sqn code of 'JX-U'.

GLOSTER METEOR TMk7 WA591

RAF WOODVALE

Designed as Britain's first jet fighter the Meteor eventually spawned a number of varieties, many of them two-seaters. The first two-seater was the T7, in fact this was the only trainer version built as all the rest were night fighters.

Designed against Air Ministry Specification T1/47 the first TMk7 flew on 26 October 1948 and over 600 of this mark were later built. WA591 was part of the fourth batch of 137 aircraft built to Contract 6/Acft/2982, these being built by Glosters at their Hucclecote factory, and were delivered between August 1949 and February 1952. WA591 was one of the earlier aircraft built and was ready for collection in late 1949, initially going to No.6 MU, RAF Brize Norton for service acceptance.

Its first job was with the Central Fighter Establishment (CFE) at RAF West Raynham where it was used to convert pilots to the single-seat fighter Meteors prior to training in the use of fighter tactics. The aircraft was soon on the move, this time to RAF Driffield where it joined No.226 OCU which was in process of being renumbered No.203 Advanced Flying School (AFS). This occurred on 31 August 1949 and in its new role WA591 was coded 'FMK-O'.

As this was a period of expansion for the RAF the formation of new training schools continued apace, with WA591's next move

Meteor T7 WA591 as gate guard at RAF Woodvale on Merseyside. *(C. P. Russell-Smith)*

occurring in November 1951. It joined the newly formed No.208 AFS at RAF Merryfield, and in common with the rest of the aircraft of this unit WA591 remained uncoded.

It was on the move again in February 1952 when on the 11th of the month it joined No.215 AFS at RAF Finningley, another new unit. This was to remain its home for the next two years after which in mid-1954 it was noted on the strengths of No.12 FTS at Weston Zoyland and No.5 FTS at Oakington in quick succession.

WA591 next joined No.203 AFS in June 1954 when it renumbered to No.8 FTS and when this unit moved to RAF Swinderby on 17 August 1955 it took the aircraft with it, although it was soon replaced by the newer Vampire trainer. After Swinderby, there followed a short spell with the RAF Flying College at Cranwell and following a period of storage WA591 joined the College of Air Warfare at RAF Manby in 1962 where it was coded 'U'. WA591 continued flying until May 1965 when it was withdrawn from use and placed in storage at No.5 MU, RAF Kemble.

RAF Kemble in common with other maintenance units had a resident Technical Training School and with a maintenance serial 7917M, WA591 was placed in the hands of the training staff on 16 August 1966. This state of affairs remained until 1972 when WA591 was transported by road to a similar facility at RAF St Athan.

With more up-to-date aircraft such as the Hunter now becoming surplus, WA591 was no longer of any use as a training aid. So, on 8 December 1978 it was again moved by road, this time to RAF Woodvale where after a period of storage, restoration to display standard began in mid-1983. This restoration was completed by December 1983 and WA591 took its place on the gate as a representative of the Meteor units that had once flown from Woodvale, namely No.610 (West Lancashire) Squadron, based there in 1951, and No.5 Civilian Anti Aircraft Co-operation Unit (CAACU) which arrived from Llanbedr on 1 January 1958, remaining until disbandment on 30 May 1971.

ENGLISH ELECTRIC CANBERRA B2 WJ676

RAFH WROUGHTON

Following the successful first flight of the prototype Canberra (VN799) on 13 May 1949 the amount of orders for the aircraft received by English Electric far outweighed the company's capacity to build them. The decision was therefore taken to sub-contract the building of the RAF's first jet bomber. The companies licensed were Avros, Short Brothers, and the builders of this aircraft, Handley Page.

WJ676 was ordered as part of Contract 6/Acft/5943 which called for seventy-five aircraft to be built by the Handley Page Co. Ltd. These aircraft were built at Radlett and WJ676 was declared ready for collection from there on 30 November 1954. On 13 December it was collected by the RAF and flown to No.15 MU at RAF Wroughton for service preparation and eventual storage.

At this time more aircraft were being delivered to the RAF than they had squadrons to fly them so WJ676 was put into short-term store at Wroughton. This lasted until 28 March 1955 when it flew to RAF Gutersloh in West Germany, joining No.149 Squadron as part of 2 ATAF three days later. It remained with this unit only until 1 August 1956 when it was briefly transferred to the general strength of RAF Germany prior to it returning to the UK.

On 8 August it was allocated to No.40 Squadron at RAF Upwood as part of the Upwood Bomber Wing. Its stay with this unit was also rather brief because on 23 January 1957 it moved around Upwoods airfield to join No.50 Squadron. On 5 May 1958 whilst with 50 Sqn, it was the victim of a Cat 3(R) flying accident; the repairs were carried out by a team from English Electric and following completion, it returned to the squadron on 30 September. No.50 Sqn's role was in support of NATO, although many of its aircraft, WJ676 included, undertook 'lone ranger' sorties to Malta, Libya and bases in the Middle East. In its sorties around Britain it would engage in fighter affiliation, bombing and navigation exercises codenamed 'Marshmallow'.

On 1 October 1959, WJ676 joined No.35 Squadron who were another Upwood unit, engaged in a similar role. Some four months later, in early February, it was the victim of another Cat 3 flying accident. This time it was repaired by a team from No.71 MU, RAF Bicester and by 15 March it was back on squadron strength.

On 12 October 1961 it joined No.245 Squadron at RAF Tangmere which as part of No.90 Signal Group used the aircraft in a completely different role. This squadron carried out a variety of roles including calibration of Radio and Navigation aids that were installed at various RAF stations. On 3 August 1962 it was again declared Cat 3 and again a team from No.71 MU carried out the repairs. It returned to 245 Sqn on 14 September remaining with it until 7 December when it joined No.24 Group Comms Flight at RAF Colerne prior to joining No.12 S of TT at RAF Melksham as a ground instructional airframe. At the end of its flying career it had amassed 3105.40 flying hours.

In pristine condition, WJ676 was part of the RAF Colerne Museum in September 1965. *(C. P. Russell-Smith)*

For its new role it was issued with the maintenance serial 7796M and remained with the school until it closed on 19 October 1964. The aircraft subsequently returned to Colerne ostensibly for use as an instructional airframe but somehow managed to find its way into the station's growing aircraft museum, where it remained until its closure in 1976.

It was then transferred by road to No.15 MU at RAF Wroughton and following a brief period of storage, was restored to display standard and painted in a high speed silver finish and unofficial 35 Sqn badge (although this was later removed) and placed on display by the entrance to the PMRAFH Wroughton. In 1987 it was restored once again and repainted in the 50 Sqn colours that it still retains.

SHORT BROTHERS CANBERRA PR9 XH170

RAF WYTON

Although the Canberra should be considered an English Electric Company design, this, the final totally new variant of this versatile aircraft was a pure Short Brothers product. Using the experience gained during the building under licence of earlier Canberra B2s, PR3s and PR7s Shorts were able to successfully bid for the contract to build the high performance PR9.

The PR9 differed in many ways from its predecessors although it was evolved from the earlier B(I)8, utilising that type's fighter-style canopy. It was also fitted with a hinged nose into which the navigator would install himself. The aircraft also had a pair of Rolls-Royce Avon turbojets rated at 11,250 lb st giving the aircraft a much enhanced performance over its predecessors. The prototype subsequently first flew on 8 July 1955 with the first production model following on 21 July 1958.

XH170 was ordered as part of Contract 6/Acft/14027 and was given the construction number SH1733. It was originally to be one of fifty-three aircraft ordered but this was later reduced in number and only twenty-three were finally built. It was declared ready for collection from the company's Sydenham airfield on 29 July 1960 from where, on 4 August, it flew to No.15 MU at RAF Wroughton for service preparation. By the end of the month it had had its acceptance carried out and on 5 September it flew to RAF Wyton and was allocated to No.58 Squadron. It was initially used as a conversion trainer by the unit, familiarising the squadron's pilots to the type's uprated engines and the powered flying controls.

On 2 May 1962 the aircraft flew back to its builders for modification and refurbishing; this work took until 30 August to carry out and on completion XH170 joined the MOD (PE) fleet for trials work, keeping the aircraft busy until 31 October. It was then returned to No.15 MU for a major servicing. On 22 March 1963 it moved on to No.5 MU at RAF Kemble for repainting, changing it from its previous natural metal scheme to the new grey/green and PRU blue scheme. With the work completed it returned to No.15 MU where it was again prepared for RAF use.

On 26 April 1963, it joined the strength of the Near East Air Force in Malta where it was issued to No.39 Squadron. This had been the first RAF unit to receive the Canberra PR9 in 1962. Life at RAF Luqa was routine and apart from a visit to Shorts for further Mods in January 1964, it remained with the squadron in the sun until 2 July 1970. On that day it suffered a Cat 3 accident which required a team from No.103 MU at RAF Akrotiri to carry

XH170 of 39 Sqn, landing at Luqa in 1969. *(C. P. Russell-Smith)*

out the repairs. They took some four months to complete and on 11 November the aircraft was declared serviceable once again. Shortly afterwards it returned to the UK and rejoined 39 Sqn who had by now moved to RAF Wyton.

On 8 May 1973 it returned to Shorts once again for a much-needed major servicing; this work was completed by 31 October when it again rejoined 39 Sqn. The next few years passed uneventfully although it went for a further servicing to Shorts in October 1976 and Mods in April 1980, each time returning to 39 Sqn.

XH170 began its last stint with the squadron on 15 December 1980 and remained on active strength for just over a year, after which, on 27 January 1982, it was grounded and declared non-effective stock. No.39 Sqn subsequently disbanded on 1 June 1982, although most of the Canberra PR9s joined the newly re-formed No.1 Photo Reconnaissance Unit shortly afterwards. Once all useful spares had been removed from the aircraft, it was declared Cat 5 ground instruction/display, for which purpose it was issued with the Support Command Maintenance serial 8739M.

It then went on display at Wyton's main gate, initially with two other variants of the Canberra, but now just with a Bloodhound missile.

FORMER RAF GATE GUARDS

Aircraft type	Serial	Station
Auster AOP9	WZ729	Seletar
Beaufighter TF10	SR910	Stafford
Beverly C1	XH124	Hendon
Buccaneer S1	XK531	Honington
Canberra PR3	WE163	Manston
Canberra T4	WH840	Locking
Canberra B2	WJ642	Upwood
Canberra B6RC	WT305	Wyton
Canberra PR7	WH773	Wyton
Canberra PR7	WT520	Manby, Swinderby
English Electric P1a	WG760	Henlow
English Electric P1a	WG763	Henlow
Gannet T5 (Hybrid)	XG882	Lossiemouth
Gnat T1	XM698	Leeming
Gnat T1	XR571	Brampton
Hastings C2	WD477	Lindholme
Hawker P1052	VX272	Cardington
Hunter Prototype	WB188	Melksham
Hunter F1	WT612	Credenhill
Hunter F1	WT651	Credenhill
Hunter F1	WT694	Debden
Hunter F1	7501M (WT694)	Debden
Hunter F4	WV398	Spitalgate
Hunter F5	WP147	Weeton
Hunter F51	E-408 (as XF979)	Brawdy, Cranwell
Hurricane IIc	LF686	Bridgnorth
Hurricane IIc	LF751	Bentley Priory, Waterbeach
Hurricane IIcb	LF738	Biggin Hill
Jet Provost T3	XN602	Brampton
Jet Provost T4	XP634	Linton-on-Ouse
Javelin FAW1	XA549	Swanton Morley
Javelin FAW1	XA553	Yatesbury
Javelin FAW4	XA629	Ternhill
Javelin FAW4	XA639 (really XH764)	Manston
Javelin FAW4	XA706	Leeming
Javelin FAW6	XA820	Acklington
Javelin FAW6	XA821	Hartlebury
Javelin FAW8	XH980	Stafford
Javelin FAW9R	XH764	Manston
Javelin FAW9	XH900	Swinderby
Lancaster B1	R5868	Scampton
Lancaster B VII	NX611	Scampton
Lightning F1a	XM144	Leuchars
Lightning F2	XN769	Leconfield
Lightning F3	XP748	Binbrook
Meteor Prototype (Gloster type F9/40)	DG202	Yatesbury
Meteor F3	EE405	Bridgnorth, Hednesford
Meteor F3	EE419	Coltishall
Meteor F3	EE424	Coltishall
Meteor F4	?	Sylt

Aircraft type	Serial	Station
Meteor F4	EE549	Innsworth
Meteor F4	RA449	Weeton
Meteor F4	VW790	Hornchurch
Meteor T7	WG981	Stafford
Meteor T7	WL360	Locking
Meteor F8	WK968	Odiham, Acklington
Meteor F8	WL168	Heywood
Meteor FR9	WH546	Khormaksar (Aden)
Meteor NF12	?	Leeming
Meteor NF14	WS739	Church Fenton
Meteor NF14	WS760	Brampton
Meteor NF14	WS774	Upwood
Meteor NF14	WS777	Buchan
Meteor NF14	WS787	Tengah
Meteor NF14	WS788	Leeming, Patrington
Meteor NF14	WS792	Carlisle
Meteor NF14	WS840	Bishops Court
Meteor NF14	WS844 (really WS788)	Leeming
Mosquito TT35	TA722	Hartlebury
Proctor MkIII	BV631	Bishops Court
Sabre F4	?	Oldenburg
Sea Vixen FAW2	XP921	Credenhill (ntu)
Skeeter	XM555	Ternhill, Shawbury
Shackleton MR2	WL738	Lossiemouth
Spitfire Vb	AB871	Credenhill
Spitfire	AR614	Hednesford
Spitfire Vb	BL614	Credenhill
Spitfire Vc	BM597	Bridgnorth, Church Fenton, Hednesford, Linton-on-Ouse, Padgate, West Kirby
Spitfire Vb	EP120	Bircham Newton, Boulmer, St Athan, Wattisham, Wilmslow
Spitfire IXc	MK356	Hawkinge, Locking
Spitfire IX	MK732	Gutersloh
Spitfire IX	ML427	Castle Bromwich
Spitfire XIV	MT847	Cosford, Freckleton, Middleton St George, Weeton
Spitfire XIV	RM694	Binbrook
Spitfire XIV	RR263	Kenley
Spitfire XVI	RW382	Church Fenton, Leconfield, Uxbridge
Spitfire XVI	RW386	Halton
Spitfire XVI	RW388	Andover, Benson, Colerne
Spitfire XVI	RW729 (really RW382)	Leconfield
Spitfire XVI	SL542	Coltishall, Duxford, Horsham St Faith
Spitfire XVI	SL574	Bentley Priory
Spitfire XVI	SL674	Biggin Hill
Spitfire XVI	SM997	Seletar
Spitfire XVI	TB252	Acklington, Bentley Priory, Boulmer, Leuchars, Odiham
Spitfire XVI	TB308	Bishopbriggs
Spitfire XVI	TB382	Ely, Middleton St George
Spitfire XVI	TB544	Padgate

Aircraft type	Serial	Station
Spitfire XVI	TB752	Hawarden, Middle Wallop, Scampton
Spitfire XVI	TD248	Sealand
Spitfire XVI	TE184	Cranwell
Spitfire XVI	TE288	Church Fenton, Dishforth, Rufforth
Spitfire XVI	TE311	Tangmere. Wattisham
Spitfire XVI	TE353	Ternhill
Spitfire XVI	TE356	Bicester, Cranwell, Kemble, Leeming, Little Rissington
Spitfire XVI	TE384	Syerston
Spitfire XVI	TE392	Church Lawford, Credenhill, Kemble, Waterbeach, Wellesbourne, Mountford
Spitfire XVI	TE400	Honiley
Spitfire XVI	TE407	Thorney Island
Spitfire XVI	TE462	Ouston
Spitfire XVI	TE476	Coltishall, Horsham St Faith, Neatishead
Spitfire	TP205	Changi
Spitfire XIX	PM651	Andover, Benson, Hucknall, Leconfield, Uxbridge
Spitfire XIX	PS853	Binbrook, Wattisham, West Raynham
Spitfire XIX	PS915	Brawdy, Leuchars, West Malling
Spitfire F21	LA198	Leuchars, Locking
Spitfire F21	LA226	Biggin Hill, Little Rissington
Spitfire F21	LA255	Cardington, West Raynham, Tangmere
Spitfire F22	PK624	Abingdon, Northolt, North Weald, Uxbridge
Spitfire F22	PK664	Binbrook, Waterbeach, West Raynham
Spitfire F24	PK683	Changi
Spitfire F24	PK724	Gaydon, Norton
Supermarine 510	VV106	Cardington
Swift	?	Jever
Sycamore HR14	XG540	Shawbury, Ternhill
Sycamore HR14	XJ385 (really XG540)	Shawbury, Ternhill
Tempest F2	SN219	Leeming, Middleton St George
Tempest/Typhoon ???	?	Tengah
Valiant B(K)1	XD818	Marham
Vampire F1	TG349	Credenhill
Vampire F1	VF301	Debden
Vampire F3	VF272	Bircham Newton
Vampire FB5	VT801	Bridgnorth
Vampire FB5	VT812	Cardington
Vampire FB5	VZ304	Carlisle
Vampire FB5	WA275	Cranwell
Vampire FB5	WA295	Carlisle
Vampire T11	WZ544	Spitalgate
Vampire T11	XD382	Shawbury
Vampire T11	XD386	Swinderby
Vampire T11	XD393	Sealand

Aircraft type	Serial	Station
Vampire T11	XD515	Linton-on-Ouse
Vampire T11	XD613	Cosford
Vampire T11	XE874	Valley
Venom FB1	?	Butzweilerhof
Venom NF2	WX853	Debden
Venom NF3	WX905	Yatesbury
Venom FB4	WR539	Kai Tak
Victor K2	XL189	Waddington
Vulcan B2	XH563	Scampton
Vulcan B2MRR	XJ782	Finningley

ABINGDON

Spitfire F22 PK624 was displayed by the main gate of this Oxfordshire maintenance unit from July 1970 to March 1989. It carried the code 'RAU-T', recalling its link with No.614 (County of Glamorgan) Squadron, Royal Auxiliary Air Force. It was a victim of the policy change in 1989 and eventually went into storage at RAF St Athan following a brief period of storage at Abingdon.

ACKLINGTON

Spitfire LF MkXVIe TB252 was displayed outside the main gate here between at least September 1959 and July 1969. For most of the time it was camouflaged and marked with the letters 'RR-M'. It stood on its wheels throughout this period but, from about 1964, its tail was raised into a flying attitude. During the early part of TB252's presence there, Acklington was the home of Fighter Command's Northern Armament Practice Camp, but more latterly was the home of 6 FTS flying Jet Provost T3 and T4 aircraft. TB252 moved on to Boulmer when Acklington closed in 1969.

Javelin FAW Mk6 XA820 wearing the standard fighter camouflage was displayed at the entrance to No.71 MU site during 1964 at least when the crash and recovery element of this Bicester-based unit had outstation detachments to deal with commitments

Spitfire LF XVIe TB252/RR-M on display in No.407 Sqn colours at RAF Acklington in October 1964. *(C. P. Russell-Smith)*

in various parts of the country. When the MU site closed XA820 moved to RAF Disforth to be used as an Instructional Airframe.

ANDOVER

Spitfire LF MkXVIe RW388 was displayed at the entrance to Headquarters Maintenance Command at this station from at least July 1963 to sometime in 1967. Throughout that period, the aircraft was painted silver and stood on its wheels. When the Headquarters closed upon reorganisation, RW388 moved to Stoke and is now displayed as a memorial to R. J. Mitchell.

Spitfire PR MkXIX PM651 is also reported as having been on display at RAF Andover but no details are known. This aircraft was subsequently displayed at RAF Benson for many years.

BENSON

Spitfire LF MkXVIe RW388 is reported to have been displayed here but details are not known.

Spitfire PR MkXIX PM651 was displayed here on two occasions, the first between June and July 1954 when it moved to RAF Hucknall; then again from 1971 to late 1989. Latterly it was displayed in PRU blue and coded 'X'. It can now be seen displayed in the RAF Museum. In late 1989 it was replaced by a plastic replica, Spitfire VIII displayed as PR MkXI 'EN343'.

BENTLEY PRIORY

Hurricane IIc LF751 was displayed for many years within the grounds of HQ Fighter Command (later HQ 11 Group). It

Spitfire XVI SL574 at RAF Halton in late 1989. *(J. A. Simpson)*

arrived from RAF Waterbeach sometime in late 1961 following refurbishment using the parts of several other Hurricanes and was only removed in 1986 when it was found that it was suffering badly from the effects of the British weather. Following restoration at Rochester Airport it went to RAF Manston displayed as 'BN230'.

Spitfire LF MkXVIe SL574 was also displayed here between November 1961 and 1986. Following a decision to exchange this aircraft with the Eagle Association of America for a P51 Mustang, it moved to RAF Halton for refurbishment and duly went to America in October 1989. Whilst on display at this station it carried the code 'AZ-B'.

When SL574 moved to Halton it was replaced by TB252 from RAF Leuchars as part of a three-way Spitfire shuffle also involving Locking. It remained on display until August 1988 when it became one of the first aircraft removed as part of the MOD's change of policy. It is currently undergoing restoration to flying condition by HFL at Audley End. It was replaced by a Mk1 glassfibre replica Spitfire VIII which is displayed as 'K9926'.

BICESTER

Spitfire LF MkXVIe TE356 was displayed on the parade ground of this maintenance unit from at least April 1958 until sometime during 1967. For the early part of this period it was painted silver and carried the code '8Q-Z' belonging to 34 Sqn whose emblem of a yellow new moon and black fox (?) was painted on the nose. After various periods of gate guard duty elsewhere it now flies again as G-SXVI and is currently owned by Warbirds of GB at Biggin Hill.

BIGGIN HILL

Hurricane IIcb LF738 was displayed outside the RAF Memorial Chapel here from September 1954 until February 1984. It was

LA226 replaced Hurricane II LF738, as one of two gate guards outside the RAF Memorial Chapel at Biggin Hill in 1984. *(K. Watson)*

displayed on its wheels and was uncoded. In 1984 it moved to Rochester Airport for refurbishment.

Spitfire F Mk21 LA226 arrived to replace LF738 in 1984 and stayed here until late 1988 when it was taken to No.27 MU at RAF Shawbury for storage as part of the MOD's policy towards its Spitfires. It was subsequently replaced by a plastic replica Hurricane IIc in 1989; this is displayed as Mk1 'L1710'.

Spitfire LF MkXVIe SL674 was also displayed outside the RAF Memorial Chapel from September 1954. In 1987 it went to Abingdon for restoration and returned carrying the code 'RAS-H' of No.612 (County of Aberdeen) Squadron, R AuxAF. In 1989 it was replaced by a plastic replica Spitfire VIII displayed as Mk1 'N3194'. SL674 subsequently moved to RAF St Athan and was put into storage.

BINBROOK

Spitfire XIX PS853 arrived from West Raynham in August 1961 for display with the CFE. In 1964 this aircraft was made airworthy once again and rejoined the Battle of Britain flight.

Spitfire F MkXIV RM694 is reported to have been displayed here during 1969 prior to the return of PK664 but no further details are known.

Spitfire F Mk22 PK664 arrived here in 1962 and originally wore the incorrect code 'VG-B'. It went for use in the Battle of Britain film in 1968 and following its return was coded 'V6-B' of No.615 (County of Surrey) Squadron, R AuxAF and displayed in a flying attitude beside the main guard room. In 1989 it moved to St Athan following the closure of Binbrook.

Lightning F Mk3 XP748 went on display in front of Station Headquarters here in September 1976. It was painted in gloss camouflage and carried Nos.5 and 11 Squadron colours either side of the fin. In 1988 when Binbrook closed the aircraft was removed to Pendine ranges to act as a ground target.

BIRCHAM NEWTON

Spitfire F MkVb EP120 was displayed at this recruit intake station in Norfolk from at least 1955 until December 1962 when the unit closed.

Vampire F Mk3 VF272 was also displayed here for a period until the base closed in December 1962. It is assumed the aircraft was scrapped on site.

BISHOPBRIGGS

Spitfire LF MkXVIe TB308 was on display here in September 1955 until at least the following year when the unit was closed. The aircraft still survives and is currently in New Zealand.

BISHOPS COURT

Proctor MkIII BV631 is reported to have been on display at this signals unit in Northern Ireland for a long period until at least

1968. Its subsequent fate is not known but in late 1969 it was noted on a scrap dump within the station so is presumed to have been scrapped on site.

Meteor NF Mk14 WS840 was displayed here from at least June 1967 until the unit closed in 1975. In 1980 it was noted derelict at Aldergrove, but then in late 1989 it was reported as undergoing refurbishment for display at Aldergrove.

BOULMER

Spitfire MkVb EP120 was displayed at the gate of this radar station in Northumberland until 1967 when it was removed for use in the film the *Battle of Britain*. It was then reissued to Wattisham for similar duties.

The replacement gate guard for EP120 was Spitfire F MkXVI TB252 which was here for a short period in 1969. In December of that year it moved on to RAF Leuchars in Scotland for a more prolonged stay.

BRAMPTON

Meteor NF(T) Mk14 WS760 (7964M) was displayed at the entrance to HQ Training Command, later HQ Support Command, from at least some time in 1970 to sometime in 1972 during which period it was painted silver with no unit markings. It later went to Duxford for display with the Imperial War Museum but is now displayed at the Newark Air Museum at Winthorpe.

Jet Provost T3 XN602 was displayed at RAF Brampton from 1973 to 1986. *(M.A.P.)*

Also displayed here between 1973 and 1986 was Jet Provost T Mk3 XN602, painted in standard training colours of red, white and grey. It was subsequently moved to Manston and is now owned by the local ATC Squadron who display it on the station parade ground.

Gnat T Mk1 XR571 was displayed here between July 1976 and at least 1980, first painted in standard training colours then in Red Arrows colours. It is now displayed outside the Red Arrows hangar at RAF Scampton.

BRAWDY

The first RAF gate guard following the transfer of this ex-Royal Naval Air Station to the RAF was Hunter F51 E-408, formerly of the Royal Danish Air Force. It was obtained from Hawker Siddeley at Dunsfold and painted in No.43 Squadron markings but without a serial. She was installed in February 1978 and remained until December 1984 when she was replaced by a more suitable mark. The aircraft then moved on to the RAF College Cranwell.

Accompanying E-408 for a while from 1980 to 1984 was Spitfire PR MkXIX PS915 which was painted in an unlikely two-tone brown camouflage. She ended up being taken to Salmesbury for a complete restoration and is now one of the Battle of Britain Memorial Flight's airworthy Spitfires.

BRIDGNORTH

At this former recruit intake centre, there are reports of three gate guards during the 1950s; these have since been identified as Hurricane IIc LF686 (which is now preserved in Washington DC), Spitfire MkVc BM597 which arrived from Hednesford when that station closed (now under restoration to fly as G-MKVC), and Vampire FB Mk5 VT801. The fate of which is unknown.

Also arriving from Hednesford following its closure was Meteor F Mk3 EE405, displayed as 5897M. Exact details of its fate are not known but it was probably scrapped on site when the station closed.

BUCHAN

At this radar station in Scotland, Meteor NF(T) Mk14 WS777 guarded the main entrance in 1963–4 but the aircraft moved on to Leuchars where it was noted at several Battle of Britain displays in the 1970s. Its fate is unknown but it was almost certainly scrapped at Leuchars.

BUTZWEILERHOF

A Venom FB Mk1 or 4 is reported to have been guarding this former vehicle maintenance unit near Cologne in 1960; no further details are known.

CARDINGTON

At least four aircraft from the collection assembled at nearby RAF Henlow prior to the siting of the RAF Museum were displayed along the front of this historic former airship station in the mid-1960s. In April 1964, Spitfire F Mk21 LA255 and Vampire FB Mk5 VT812, both painted silver, were accompanied by two prototype aircraft, Hawker P1052 VX272 (7174M) painted in two-tone naval green and Supermarine 510 VV106 (7175M) painted silver; both of these latter aircraft were displayed in their maintenance serials. All these aircraft have survived; LA255 at Wittering is owned by No.1 Squadron, VT812 is in the RAF Museum and the other two are displayed as part of the historic prototype collection in the RAF Cosford Aerospace Museum.

The unique Hawker P1052 was displayed at Cardington from May 1955 to mid-1964 when this photograph was taken. *(C. P. Russell-Smith)*

CARLISLE

During the early 1960s, two Vampire FB5s stood guard at the entrance to this maintenance unit. Both were painted silver but carried no unit markings. They were VZ304 and WA295, both of which were probably scrapped on site in 1965.

Meteor NF(T)Mk14 WS792 arrived here from Cosford in 1977 to join long-time guardian Hunter F1 WT660. It was painted in standard camouflage and carried No.85 Squadron colours. In 1989, as part of the one gate guard policy it was sold at auction to an unnamed buyer, moving to Borgue in the Highlands.

CASTLE BROMWICH

Spitfire F MkIX 6457M (ML427), reported as the last Spitfire built at the Castle Bromwich factory, was seen guarding the entrance to this former training camp in August 1958 but was probably removed shortly thereafter. It still survives and is now displayed in the Birmingham Industrial Museum.

CELLE

An unknown aircraft is reported to have been on guard here in 1957.

CHANGI

Two Spitfires are reported to have been guarding at the former Singapore transport aircraft base at unknown dates, F Mk18 (?) TP205 and F Mk24 PK683.

CHURCH FENTON

At least three Spitfires are reported to have stood guard here as well as the long-standing BM597. Spitfire LF MkXVIe RW382 (7245M) was here between at least October 1953 and August 1958 when the station operated Meteor and Hunter fighters. F MkXVI TE288 was also believed to have been here but the dates are not known. PR MkXIX PM651 was also reported here in August 1969, but this was probably a temporary stay whilst

WS739 at RAF Church Fenton in August 1970, following restoration. *(C. P. Russell-Smith)*

BM597 was being refurbished. F MkVb BM597 has had two spells as the gate guard, the first from some time in 1957 up to 1975 when it moved to nearby Linton-on-Ouse when the station went into care and maintenance, and again from 1979 until late 1988 when it was allocated to civilian ownership for restoration to flying condition. A plastic replica has since been installed as its replacement, a Spitfire VIII displayed as Mk1 'L1096'.

Apart from the several Spitfires, Meteor NF(T)Mk14 WS739 was co-located here with BM597 during the period October 1967 to at least August 1970 when the station became No.2 FTS flying Chipmunk T10s; the aircraft was painted silver and bore the markings of No.85 Sqn coded 'F', a unit which flew the type from here in the 1950s.

CHURCH LAWFORD

Spitfire F MkXVI TE392 is reported to have been guarding this former training camp from at least September 1952. Further information is not known.

COLERNE

Spitfire LF MkXVIe RW388 stood guard at this West Country maintenance unit between at least February 1952 and sometime in 1963.

COLTISHALL

Meteor F Mk3 EE424 (7248M) was on display here in October 1955, whilst sister aircraft EE419, in the overall red scheme of the RAE High Speed Flight, was here between at least July 1960 and sometime in 1969 when she was withdrawn to the charge of Abingdon for travelling display purposes.

Spitfire F MkXVI TE476 is reported to have been used as the gate guard in the 1960s but exact dates are not known.

Spitfire LF MkXVIe SL542 arrived from Horsham St Faith (Norwich Airport) sometime in the late 1960s and guarded the entrance, latterly coded '4M-N' of No.695 Sqn, until December 1988 when it was taken to St Athan for storage as part of the MOD's change of policy. In late 1989 it was replaced by a glassfibre replica Hurricane IIc displayed as Mk1 'V7467'.

COSFORD

Spitfire F MkXIV MT847 arrived here in August 1964 and was displayed in a flying attitude on the station parade square. It remained until October 1970 when it moved to the fledgling aerospace museum at Cosford where it is still on display.

Vampire T Mk11 XD613 replaced MT847 as the parade backdrop in December 1970 atop the same plinth as the Spitfire. The aircraft carried the code 'M' (from its days with CATCS) and remained in position until July 1988 when it was moved to

Cosford's airfield. The aircraft was subsequently sold to a French collector.

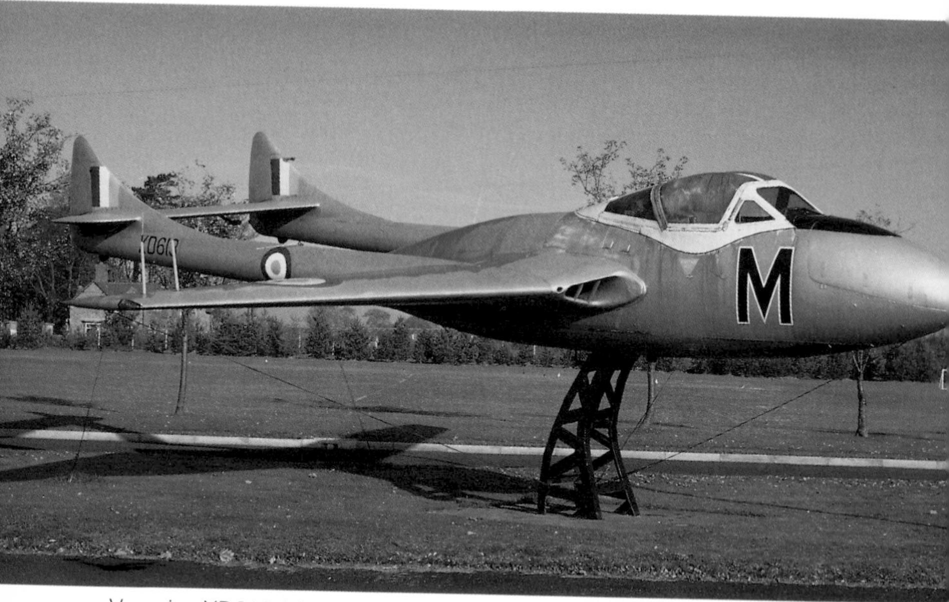

Vampire XD613:M was displayed at RAF Cosford for many years before being replaced by a Hunter in 1988. *(J. A. Simpson)*

CRANWELL

Vampire FB Mk5 WA275 was in the grounds on the main airfield site of the college area in July 1962; the aircraft was camouflaged but was in a poor condition. Its fate is not known.

Spitfire F MkXVI TE184, camouflaged and in the code 'ME-M', was displayed briefly outside Trenchard Hall Officers Mess during the summer of 1968. The aircraft subsequently returned to her home in the Finningley Regional Collection. Spitfire F MkXVI TE356 is also reported to have been temporarily displayed here in 1976 but no further details are known.

Ex-Danish Air Force Hunter 'E-408' arrived here from Brawdy in January 1985 and took up display duties outside the Department of Air Warfare. It stayed until November 1988 when it moved to Sealand. Whilst on display it carried the serial 'XF979:A' representing an aircraft of the College of Air Warfare when they were based at Manby in the 1960s.

CREDENHILL (Hereford)

Spitfire F MkXVI TE392 was displayed here between February 1970 after use in the film *The Battle of Britain*, and sometime in 1984. It is reported that this aircraft was then part of an exchange deal with the RAF Museum involving a B25 Mitchell

Bomber, TE392 moving into civilian ownership with Warbirds of GB at Biggin Hill. The aircraft is now airworthy. The B25 Mitchell was eventually installed in the Bomber Command Museum.

A number of other aircraft have also guarded this long established training station. Spitfire F MkVb AB871 and F MkVb BL614 were here from at least March 1955 until sometime in 1967 but what happened to them after that is a mystery. Also during this period, from at least 1961 until 1964, Vampire F Mk1 TG349 was displayed wearing its maintenance serial, 7203M; it is also not known what became of this aircraft. The two earlier-mentioned Spitfires were eventually joined and then replaced by a pair of Hunter F Mk1s, WT612 and WT651, both of which arrived in September 1965. They were used as parade backdrops although in the early 1970s WT612 was marked 'WT216'; both aircraft were removed in early 1983, WT612 moving initially to RAF Halton for proposed instructional duties, although this aircraft is now the gate guard at RAF Henlow. WT651 is now on display with the Royal Observer Corps at Church Lawford in Warwickshire.

DEBDEN

Vampire F Mk3 VF301 stood guard here between at least August 1963 and October 1973 when it was acquired by the Lincolnshire Aircraft Preservation Society. This aircraft is now on display with the Midland Air Museum at Baginton, Coventry in the markings 'RAL-B' of No.605 (County of Warwick) Squadron, R AuxAF.

Venom NF Mk2 WX853 (7443M) was also on display here between 1963 and at least July 1967 when she was painted overall black and wearing No.23 Sqn markings. This aircraft is now on display as part of the De Havilland Heritage Collection at Hatfield.

Hunter F Mk1 WT694 (7510M) was on display here in August 1969, painted as 'Y' of No.43 Sqn. It probably moved to its present home on the gate at RAF Newton when the RAF Police School moved with the closure of Debden in 1973.

DISHFORTH

Spitfire LF MkXVI TE288 is reported to have been displayed here but the dates are unknown.

DUXFORD

Spitfire LF MkXVIe SL542 was the gate guard at this former Fighter Command station in at least 1958. It stood on its wheels and wore an all-silver colour scheme. It eventually moved to Horsham St Faith and then to Coltishall.

ELY

Spitfire LF MkXVIe TB382 stood near the entrance to this RAF Hospital from May 1965 until sometime in 1968 when it was used in the film *The Battle of Britain*. On its return to RAF charge it joined the RAF Exhibition Flight and is currently based at RAF Abingdon.

EMBAKASI

A Venom FB Mk1 or 4 is reported to have been standing guard at the RAF Detachment site at Nairobi's main airport as late as 1971.

FINNINGLEY

The station briefly displayed Vulcan B2MRR XJ782 from mid-1986 to at least August 1987. It carried a white rose motif on its tail and it was originally hoped to move it to a more permanent position near to the main gate. Unfortunately, probably because of the expense involved in moving and restoring the aircraft, it was taken to the fire burning area where its undercarriage was blown off prior to it being scrapped.

RAF Finningley displayed this Vulcan B2 XJ780, because of the expense in preparing it for a more permanent life it was removed in 1988 and scrapped. *(J. A. Simpson)*

FRECKLETON

Spitfire F MkXIV MT847 was located at the gate of the Medical Training Establishment (hence the code MT-E) from May 1952 until August 1964. The aircraft was then displayed at RAF

Cosford as a parade backdrop and is now part of the Cosford Aerospace Museum.

GAYDON

Spitfire F Mk24 PK724 was displayed at this Warwickshire airfield from December 1961 until February 1970. It joined many other Spitfires for use in the film *The Battle of Britain* and was one of the few that made it back to its previous home. When Gaydon closed in 1970 the aircraft joined the RAF Finningley Regional Collection, and is now on display at the RAF Museum at Hendon.

GEILENKIRCHEN

A Sabre, probably a RAF Mk4 is reported to have been guarding here in 1957, but had been replaced by a Swift FR Mk5 WK295 in 1961. The subsequent fate of both of these aircraft is not known.

GIBRALTAR

Vulcan K2 XM571 was displayed here from 9 May 1984 until mid-1990 when it was cut up for scrap. It carried the markings of its last user, No.50 Sqn.

XM571 taxiing at St Mawgan, note the in-flight refuelling probe fitted. *(J. A. Todd Collection)*

GUTERSLOH

Spitfire F MkIX MK732 was on display at this RAF Germany airfield during the 1970s. In 1978 it was at Coningsby as a source of spares for the Battle of Britain Memorial Flight. The aircraft is known to be still in existence but its state of repair is not known.

HALTON

Spitfire LF MkXVIe RW386 stood guard at the entrance to the airfield here between at least May 1964 and August 1970, apart from a period removed for the film *The Battle of Britain*. Until at least June 1968 it was coded 'EH' whilst by August 1970 it had become 'RAK-A' which are the markings of No.604 (County of Warwick) Sqn, R AuxAF. The aircraft is now owned by Warbirds of GB and has been registered G-BXVI; it is not known when the aircraft will become airworthy, if at all.

HARTLEBURY

Mosquito TT Mk35 TA722 was reported to have spent some time on the gate of the Maintenance Unit here until 1963, by which time it had been joined by Javelin FAW Mk6 XA821:J. The fate of the Mosquito is unknown but the Javelin remained in place until at least September 1977.

HAWARDEN

Spitfire LF MkXVIe TB752 is reported to have stood guard at this North Wales airfield but the dates are not known.

HAWKINGE

Spitfire F MkIXc MK356 is reported to have been the gate guard at this famous Battle of Britain airfield from 1951 until the airfield closed. It then joined the museum collection at RAF St Athan, coded '21-V' of No.443 Sqn, but has recently moved to RAF Abingdon for survey to see if it can be restored to airworthiness for use by the Battle of Britain Memorial Flight.

HEDNESFORD

Spitfire F MkVb BM597 which was displayed as 5713M and subsequently spent many years as the gate guard at RAF Church Fenton, was reported here as the gate guard as early as 1945. This is the earliest instance of an aircraft being reported used as a gate guard. When the station closed it moved to Bridgnorth. Also reported here was Meteor F Mk3 5897M EE405 and possibly Spitfire AR614 (which is now under restoration in Canada) but exact details are not known. The Meteor also spent time at Bridgnorth when this station closed.

HENDON

Spitfire LF MkXVIe TE476 is reported to have been the gate guard here but the dates are not known. It was later a more permanent gate guard at Northolt. The RAF Museum has recently retired Beverley C Mk1 XH124 as its gate guard. On 19 June 1968 it was the last fixed wing aircraft to land at RAF Hendon prior to it joining the RAF Museum. Because the cost of refurbishing it was excessive it was put up for disposal in December 1989, and by February 1990 it was well on its way to being scrapped although several large pieces, notably its engines, have been saved.

HENLOW

The two English Electric P1A prototypes were displayed here for many years; WG760 from November 1966 and WG763 from mid-1963. They were displayed as parade ground backdrops when the station became the Officer Cadet Training Unit (OCTU). Both aircraft were displayed in natural metal with Air Fighting Development School markings on the nose, and were removed in July 1982 prior to the closure of the OCTU. WG760 initially moved to RAF Binbrook for restoration before going to the Cosford Aerospace Museum and WG763 to the Greater Manchester Museum of Science and Technology where it is still displayed.

EE P1A WG760 displayed at RAF Henlow, it was removed in 1982 and is now in the Cosford Aerospace Museum. *(M.A.P.)*

HEYWOOD

Meteor F Mk8 WL168 was at the gate of this Maintenance Unit north of Manchester from April 1962 until September 1963. It then spent time at Finningley and St Athan in various guises with station museums before becoming the gate guard at RAF Finningley, displayed as WH456.

HONILEY

Spitfire F MkXVI TE400 displayed as M7240 was reported as the gate guard to this former fighter station in the late 1950s. This aircraft was probably scrapped when the station closed following the disbandment of the R AuxAF in 1957.

HONINGTON

Buccaneer S Mk1 XK531 became the first gate guard here in May 1973, remaining until replaced by XK526 in 1981. XK531 had been used as a ground instructional airframe since 1969 before being placed on the gate in Royal Navy white/blue colours; she was refurbished in October 1978 in the same colours but with the emblem of No.736 Naval Air Squadron on the fin together with the Lossiemouth code 'LM'. Following removal from its position on display it spent time on the dump at Honington before being taken by road to Boscombe Down. It is now held in a compound by the Nuclear, Bacteriological and Chemical Defence Centre at Winterbourne Gunner.

HORNCHURCH

Spitfire F MkXIV RM694 stood guard at the famous Battle of Britain airfield in Essex from sometime in 1951 until 1964 when the Officer Selection Centre moved to RAF Biggin Hill and the station closed. Most of this time she was painted silver and carried the maintenance serial 6640M. In February 1953 a Meteor F Mk4 was also present painted silver without a serial number; it has been variously reported as VZ786 and VW790, but was in fact VW790 and ended up being scrapped at Little Rissington in 1968.

HORSHAM ST FAITH

Spitfire F MkXVI SL542 was here as a gate guard in 1961 and stayed until the station closed (about 1962) when it moved to nearby RAF Coltishall. Spitfire LF MkXVIe TE476 is also reported to have been here at one time.

SL542:SH-N, in 64 Sqn markings on display at RAF Horsham St Faith in 1961. *(M.A.P.)*

HUCKNALL

Spitfire PR MkXIX PM651 arrived here in July 1954 and probably remained until mid-1969 when it moved to Benson following use in the film *The Battle of Britain*. It has recently been put on display in the RAF Museum at Hendon.

INNSWORTH

Meteor F Mk4 EE549, once of the RAF High Speed Flight, was reported here in August 1965. It still survives and is currently held by the RAF Exhibition Flight at RAF Abingdon.

JEVER

A Swift F Mk2 is reported to have been standing guard here in 1957; no other details are known.

KAI TAK

Venom FB Mk4 WR539 stood guard here as a reminder of when No.28 Sqn flew the type; the actual dates are not known. This aircraft can now be seen at the Wales Air Museum at Rhoose.

KEMBLE

Two Spitfires have guarded this Gloucestershire Maintenance Unit; LF MkXVIe TE392 was here from March 1966 until September 1967 when she went for use in the film *The Battle of Britain*. In May 1969 another LF MkXVIe, TE356 replaced it, this aircraft remaining until May 1974 when it was replaced by a Meteor. Both Spitfires have survived and are now owned by Warbirds of GB.

KENLEY

Spitfire F MkXVI RR263 was on guard at this former fighter station between at least sometime in 1963 until the station closed in 1967. The fate of the aircraft is not known.

KHORMAKSAR

Meteor FR Mk9 WH546 was put on display inside the camp at the Aden airfield from June 1961. It eventually became an instructional airframe in 1963 before being scrapped.

LECONFIELD

Several Spitfires are known to have stood guard here. LF MkXVIe RW382, marked as 7245M and coded '3L-Q', was certainly here from around 1957 until 1967 when she went to Duxford for the Battle of Britain film; she returned and was present from 1969 to 1973. There are also reports that an LF MkXVIe marked 'RW729 coded DW-X', believed to be RW382, was also on display here between September 1963 and 1967; also PR MkXIX PM651 is reported to have been here at some time, probably around the time of the end of the Battle of Britain film work. Finally Lightning F Mk2 XN769 was displayed within the station from May 1975 until sometime in April 1976, when with the impending closure of the station it moved to RAF West Drayton.

LEEMING

This large North Yorkshire fighter station has had many gate guards; Tempest F Mk2 SN219 is known to have been here in the early sixties and was sighted in April 1965 coded '5R-F'. Soon afterwards she was moved to the safety of the RAF Museum and now resides in Hendon carrying the serial NV778; the airframe is in fact a composite of both aircraft.

Javelin FAW Mk4 XA706 is reported to have been on guard here in 1961 but no other details are known. Likewise, there are reports of an unidentified Meteor NF Mk12 in the same period.

Spitfire LF MkXVI TE356 accompanied by Gnat T1 XM698 stood guard by the entrance of the Headquarters of the Central Flying School from about 1978 until the mid-eighties, when the CFS moved to RAF Scampton. TE356 is now airworthy and owned by Warbirds of GB.

Meteor NF(T)Mk14 WS788 arrived from Patrington in 1974 and was originally displayed in No.68 Sqn markings. In the early 1980s, following some refurbishment work, it was marked 'WS844:JCF' of No.264 Sqn. These were the personal markings of Wg Cdr J. C. Forbes, one time CO of the squadron. It is now on display in the Yorkshire Air Museum at Elvington.

Meteor NF14 'WS844:JCF' carries 264 Sqn colours, finally ended its association with the unit in 1989 when it was put up for disposal.
(J. A. Simpson)

LEUCHARS

At least three Spitfires have stood guard here but dates are confused. Spitfire PR MkXIX PS915 was certainly here in November 1957 and also again in 1979. Meanwhile, Spitfire F MkXVI TB252 took up residence in December 1969 after being removed from the gate at RAF Boulmer and was present until mid-1986; during much of this time, she was coded 'GW-H' of No.340 Sqn. Spitfire F Mk21 LA198 arrived from Locking in March 1986 (see also Bentley Priory) and was repainted and coded 'RAI-G', of No.602 (City of Glasgow) Sqn R AuxAF. It remained in position only until 1989 when it was taken to St Athan for storage as part of the MOD's change of policy towards its Spitfires.

Lightning F Mk1a XM144 displayed in No.74 Sqn markings was a gate guard here from 1978. It was replaced by a Phantom in August 1989 and enjoyed a brief moment of glory as part of the station's annual air display that year. It has now been sold to a private collector.

TB252:GW-H, 'Lucky Nine', of No.340 Sqn at RAF Leuchars in 1978. *(M.A.P.)*

LINDHOLME

Hastings C Mk2 WD477 stood guard at this South Yorkshire airfield for a while when the station was home to the Bomber Command Bombing School who flew the last Hastings aircraft, the T Mk5 special conversions. WD477 has not survived as it was scrapped at Lindholme in the early seventies.

LINTON-ON-OUSE

Vampire T Mk11 XD515 wearing the maintenance serial 7998M stood in front of the station HQ here in the early 1970s. Later, whilst nearby Church Fenton was on a 'care and maintenance' basis only between 1975 and 1979 Spitfire F MkVb BM597 was also resident.

Jet Provost T Mk4 XP634 is also reported to have been used as a gate guard here following the removal of XD515 but dates are uncertain. XD515 has survived and is currently displayed as 'XM515' at the Newark Air Museum at Winthorpe.

LITTLE RISSINGTON

Spitfire F Mk21 LA226 wearing the code DL-E stood guard here between at least October 1958 and August 1964. During the latter part of this time, she was mounted on a pole facing the station HQ building near to the main gate.

Harvard T Mk2b FS890 stood guard here between at least August 1964 and September 1973 when she was removed to Boscombe Down as a source of spares to keep the A&AEE Harvards flying.

Finally, Spitfire LF MkXVIe TE356 arrived from Kemble sometime in 1970, probably December. She remained, displayed on a pole until the station closed in 1976 when she moved to RAFC Cranwell. This aircraft is now registered G-SXVI and is airworthy, flown by Warbirds of GB at Biggin Hill.

LOCKING

Spitfire F MkIXc MK356 stood guard here from at least sometime in 1963 until 1968. It subsequently moved to the St Athan museum and was replaced in September 1969 by F Mk21 LA198. The latter moved to RAF Leuchars in 1986 as part of a three-way shuffle of Spitfires (see also Bentley Priory).

Meteor T7 WL360 also stood guard here from September 1966 until, as part of the one gate guard policy, it was put up for disposal in December 1989 and removed. This was also the fate of Canberra T Mk4 WH840, which arrived for gate guard duties in 1974 and was put up for disposal at the same time as WL360. It eventually found its way to Seighford for a new museum.

LOSSIEMOUTH

Shackleton MR2c WL738 (masquerading as an AEW2) stood guard here from April 1974 displayed in No.8 Sqn markings. In April 1982 it was joined by Gannet T5 XG882; this 'aircraft' was constructed from the remains of three derelict aircraft, the other two being XA463 and XG889. In December 1989, as part of the one gate guard policy, both aircraft were put up for disposal, because there are no aircraft museums close by. In March 1990, WL738 was scrapped on site. XG882 was eventually removed from display in March 1991 and scrapped.

MARHAM

Valiant B(K) Mk1 XD818, veteran of the British nuclear test programme in the 1950s, stood guard near the Operations Wing HQ building between at least March 1965 and 1980. Sometime later she was dismantled and removed to the care of the RAF Museum where she now sits in Bomber Command Hall.

Now on display in the RAF Museum, Valiant B(K)1 XD818 was displayed at RAF Marham. This aircraft dropped Britain's first Nuclear Bomb on Christmas Island as part of Operation Grapple. *(S. Donald)*

MANBY

Canberra PR Mk7 WT520 was displayed here whilst it was the home of the College of Air Warfare. It arrived in October 1971 and stayed until February 1974 presumably when the station closed. It then moved to RAF Swinderby and was used as a parade backdrop for the many recruit passing-out parades held there.

MANSTON

Canberra PR Mk3 WE168 was one of four aircraft on display at this Kent airfield. It arrived in July 1969, originally intended to meet a fiery end, but was saved to be displayed within the camp carrying the markings of its last user No.231 OCU. In January 1990 it was the victim of the one gate guard policy and was scrapped.

Also displayed next to the Canberra was Javelin FAW Mk9R XH764. This aircraft arrived in May 1967 to clear customs whilst on delivery to No.27 MU at Shawbury from Cyprus. Unfortunately it aquaplaned off the runway in a fierce downpour causing damage to its undercarriage. It was subsequently acquired by the station and put on display. Originally displayed as 'XA639' (a Javelin FAW4) of No.87 Sqn, this was later rectified and the aircraft was returned to its correct No.29 Sqn identity. In January 1990 it suffered the same fate as its accompanying Canberra.

MELKSHAM

The red-painted Hunter Prototype WB188 stood guard at this West Country technical training school for some years in the 1960s until it closed. WB188 has survived and is in the Cosford Aerospace Museum as part of the collection of famous experimental and prototype aircraft.

MIDDLETON ST GEORGE

Spitfire LF MkXVIe TB382 was here as the gate guard in July 1957 until replaced in August 1959 by composite Tempest F Mk2 NV778/SN219. The Tempest moved on to Leeming when RAF Goosepool (as Middleton St George was known) closed in September 1963.

There are also reports that Spitfire F MkXIV MT847 was also displayed here sometime but dates are not known.

MIDDLE WALLOP

Spitfire LF MkXVIe TB752 is reported to have stood as the gate guard here prior to the formation of the Army Air Corps in 1957. The aircraft has survived and is now on display at RAF Manston.

NEATISHEAD

Spitfire LF MkXVIe TE476 was the gate guard at this Norfolk radar station from at least January 1960 until removal for the Battle of Britain film in 1967. Following use in the film it went to RAF Northolt for further gate guard duties.

NORTHOLT

Spitfire F Mk22 PK624 stood guard from at least September 1963 until removal for use in the Battle of Britain film. Following use in the film it moved to Abingdon in 1970 with TE476 taking its place.

Spitfire LF MkXVIe TE476 arrived from Henlow in June 1970 and was displayed by the south side gate (A40 entrance). In 1989 it was allocated for refurbishment to HFL at Audley End and it is hoped that this will result in it flying again. It has since been registered GXVIB. It was replaced by a glassfibre replica Spitfire VIII marked as MkIX 'MH777'.

NORTH WEALD

Spitfire F Mk22 PK624 is also reported to have spent time as the gate guard here between unknown dates.

NORTON

Spitfire F Mk24 PK724 is reported to have been on guard at this maintenance unit near Sheffield in 1955 but details are not known.

ODIHAM

Spitfire LF MkXVIe TB252 stood guard here in an overall silver scheme in the late 1950s until moving on to Acklington and then Boulmer.

Meteor F Mk8 WK968 became the gate guard here in January 1970 when she was painted grey and wore the white arrowhead markings of No.46 Sqn who were based at Odiham with the first Javelins from 1956. By the early 1980s, she had been camouflaged and wore the red outlined blue bars of No.247 Sqn who flew Hunters from here, also in the late 1950s. In October 1987, in an era in which preservation of aircraft had become the norm, WL968 was removed from her guarding position and scrapped on the airfield. Did the station not know that less than 10 miles away at Lasham, an aircraft preservation group were trying to rebuild a Meteor for static display and were desperate for parts, let alone a complete albeit corroded airframe?

Meteor F8 WK968 in No.46 Squadron colours at RAF Odiham in September 1970. *(C. P. Russell-Smith)*

OLDENBURG

A Sabre, probably an RAF F Mk4, is known to have been guarding this station in 1957; further details are not known.

OUSTON

Spitfire LF MkXVIe TE462 stood guard at this Northumberland station from at least September 1955, when the R AuxAF flew Vampire FB Mk5s and 9s from here, until 1968 when she was removed for the Battle of Britain film. The aircraft is now displayed in the Royal Scottish Museum of Flight at East Fortune.

PADGATE

Two Spitfires are reported to have stood guard at this maintenance unit near Warrington. Spitfire F MkVb BM597 marked as '371M', unusual because 5713M was her correct maintenance serial, was here probably before going to Bridgnorth and then for many years to Church Fenton. Much less well-known Spitfire LF MkXVIe TB544 was also here between unknown dates marked '606M' (correct number was 6062M); nothing subsequently is known of this aircraft, and she was probably scrapped on site.

PATRINGTON

Meteor NF(T) Mk14 WS788 stood guard at this storage MU near Hull from about September 1967 until the unit closed in 1974. For some period at least she wore the maintenance serial 7967M. The aircraft eventually moved to Leeming and was the gate guard there for many years.

ROYTON

Spitfire LF XVIe TE184, painted silver and wearing the code 'FJT-A' of the Central Gunnery School with whom she once served was seen guarding this training camp north of Manchester in August 1963 shortly before the site closure. It subsequently was displayed at Cranwell for a short time whilst in the hands of the Finningley Regional Collection.

RUFFORTH

Spitfire LF XVIe TE288 is reported to have stood guard at this Yorkshire MU site but no dates are known. She was later donated to the New Zealand War Museum at Christchurch where she still resides.

SCAMPTON

Lancaster B Mk1 R5868 wearing the code 'PO-S' of No.467 Sqn stood guard here from sometime in 1959 until March 1972 when she was transferred to the RAF Museum. She saw service with Nos.83, 207 and 467 Sqns and ended the war having completed 137 Ops.

Lancaster B MkIII NX611 took over from R5868 and stood guard from April 1974 until August 1988 coded 'YF-C', which was Guy Gibson's No.617 Sqn markings, after which she was dismantled and moved to East Kirby. (The code YF- was actually the Scampton Station Flight code. This was almost certainly an attempt to hide 617's existence.)

Spitfire LF MkXVIe TB752 is also reported to have stood guard here but no details are known.

Vulcan B2MRR XH563 was put on display within the camp following retirement of the type in 1982. She wore the four resident Scampton Vulcan units markings on her fin and remained on display until 1986. She was scrapped when funds could not be found to properly prepare her for more permanent display.

SEALAND

Spitfire LF MkXVIe TD248 wearing the code 'DW-A' of No.610 (County of Cheshire) Sqn RAuxAF stood guard outside the Officers Mess beside the main road that divides this Cheshire MU for a period in the 1960s. It was eventually moved to the 30 MU site across the road and remained as the gate guard until October 1988 when it was removed by HFL to Audley End for restoration to flying condition and registered G-OXVI.

Vampire T Mk11 XD393, unusually painted camouflaged, stood guard at the main entrance from at least 1962. This aircraft was probably scrapped on site when the Spitfire arrived.

In January 1967 Spitfire XVI TD248 joined No.30 MU at Sealand where it remained until 1989 when it went into private ownership to be restored. *(C. P. Russell-Smith)*

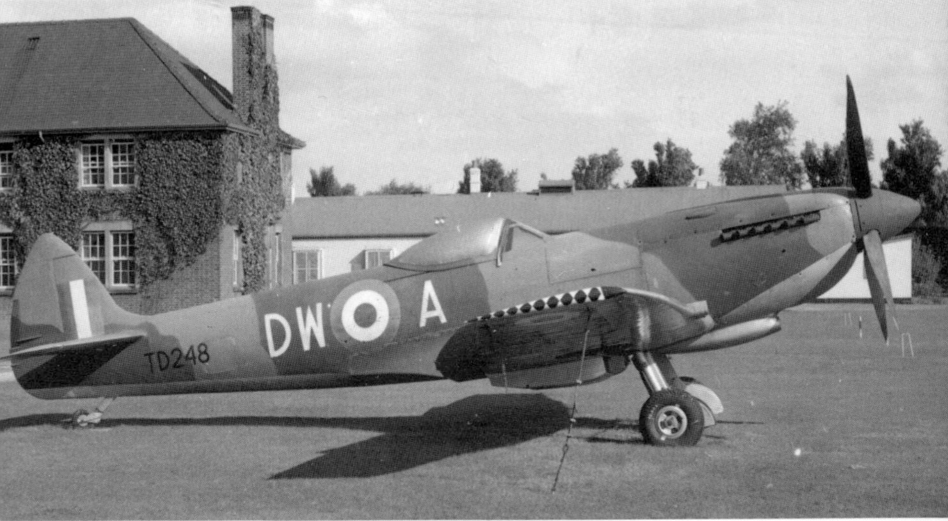

SELETAR

A Spitfire, SM997 and Auster AOP Mk9 WZ729 are reported to have stood guard here at this former Singapore airfield, but exactly when is not known.

SHAWBURY

Vampire T Mk11 was the gate guard at this Shropshire training station from May 1969. She was originally painted in a striking all-red scheme until refurbished to a more normal silver with 'T' bands in the 70s. In September 1989 the aircraft fell victim to the one gate guard policy, was sold at auction and moved to Ripley.

Skeeter AOP Mk12 XM555 arrived from Ternhill in 1977 and was displayed until September 1983 when it moved to the Cosford Aerospace Museum.

Sycamore HR Mk14 XG540 also moved in from Ternhill in 1977 carrying the serial 'XJ385 coded S-J'. The aircraft was later repainted with its correct serial retaining the code 'S-J', but then even later still this code was changed to 'S-Y'. The aircraft remained on display until 1988 when she was replaced by a Whirlwind and is now privately owned at Drighlington in Yorkshire.

When Ternhill closed in 1977 XM555 moved to nearby RAF Shawbury, where this shot of it was taken in 1978. *(M.A.P.)*

SPITALGATE

Vampire T Mk11 WZ544 stood guard at the entrance to this former WRAF recruit training centre some 10 miles south of

Cranwell from about 1963 until sometime in 1966 when she was put onto the airfield for fire-fighting practice.

Hunter F Mk4 WV398 replaced the Vampire and was here throughout 1968. Before the station closed in 1973, she was bought back by Hawker Siddeley Aviation in their attempt to satisfy demand from overseas customers for reconditioned Hunters and temporarily became G-9-411. WV398 must be one of the very few gate guardians worldwide to have returned to operational flying after standing guard: in March 1973, she went to the Swiss AF as a T Mk68 serialed J-4203 and is still flying.

STAFFORD

Beaufighter TF10 SR910 was the gate guard at this maintenance unit from about November 1951 until about 1959 when the aircraft is presumed to have been scrapped.

Meteor T Mk7 WG981, with the code 'O-T' it carried while serving with the CFS at Little Rissington, replaced the Beaufighter from about February 1957 until it too was scrapped in May 1962.

Javelin FAW Mk8 XH980 went on guard here outside the Youth Selection Centre together with a Bloodhound Missile in November 1964; she remained until moving to her present location at West Raynham in 1970.

ST ATHAN

Spitfire MkVb EP120 is reported to have been a gate guard at this South Wales MU between unknown dates.

SWANTON MORLEY

Javelin FAW Mk1 XA549 wearing the code 'M' and the markings of No.87 Sqn stood guard here from February 1962 to an unknown date.

SWINDERBY

Vampire T Mk11 XD386, wearing her maintenance serial 7629M and the crest of 8 FTS, stood guard at the entrance to the domestic site of this station from the time when 8 FTS still operated Vampires here in 1963 until some years later when the recruit training centre was established.

Javelin FAW Mk9 XH900 wearing maintenance serial 7811M and the code 'A' she wore during her service with the Guided Weapons Trials Squadron stood guard beside the parade ground on the airfield side of the hangars between at least September 1968 and the end of 1969.

Canberra PR Mk7 WT520, originally in No.81 Sqn markings then later No.31 Sqn markings, was also used as the parade ground guard from February 1974 following its arrival from Manby. The aircraft was offered for sale in 1989 although by early 1990 it had not moved on.

Vampire T11 XD386/7629M arrived at RAF Swinderby in February 1960. Little is known of its subsequent fate but this shot was taken in September 1963. *(C. P. Russell-Smith)*

SYERSTON

Spitfire LF MkXVIe TE384 is reported to have stood guard here in the period 1963 to 1967 when the station closed as the home of 2 FTS. This aircraft has survived and is displayed in Australia, latterly at Narellan.

SYLT

A former Belgian Air Force Meteor F Mk4 or 8, which force landed and was written off at this former RAF armament practice camp station in northern Germany, is reported to have been standing guard here in 1957.

TANGMERE

Spitfire LF MkXVIe TE311 stood guard at this famous fighter station from at least 1963 to 1967. During this period, the station was on care and maintenance only and subsequently closed. The aircraft is now in the hands of the RAF Exhibition Flight at Abingdon and is used as a travelling exhibit.

Spitfire F Mk21 LA255 is also reported to have stood guard here between unknown dates, probably during the station's post-war active period up to about early 1961.

TENGAH

Either a Tempest or a Typhoon is reported to have been standing guard at the former operational base in Singapore during 1956.

Meteor NF Mk14 WS787, resplendent in the markings of No.60 Sqn and coded 'G', stood guard here between September 1961 when she was retired from operational duty to sometime in 1967 when the base was closed. This aircraft flew the last operational RAF Meteor sortie but wasn't saved because it was eventually scrapped on site.

TURNHOUSE

Spitfire LF MkXVIe RW393 was displayed at this Scottish airfield for many years as a memorial to the fallen airmen of No.603 Sqn R AuxAF. It was removed and put into storage in 1989; a plastic replica Spitfire VIII replaced it in early 1990, and is displayed as Mk1 'L1070'.

TERNHILL

Spitfire LF MkXVIe TE353 stood guard at this former airfield in Shropshire until 1960. The aircraft's fate is not known.

Javelin FAW Mk4 XA629 took over guard duties between March 1961 and until at least June 1963. This aircraft's fate is also not known.

Skeeter AOP Mk12 XM555 was present as the gate guard between sometime in 1974 until 1977 when the airfield closed. When the resident 2 FTS/CFS helicopter training unit moved to nearby Shawbury they took the Skeeter with them.

Sycamore HR Mk14 XG540 was also used as a gate guard and followed the Skeeter to Shawbury. This aircraft wore the serial XJ385 during its use as a gate guard and was coded 'S-J'.

THORNEY ISLAND

Spitfire LF MkXVIe TE407 is reported to have been guarding here but no details are known. The fate of this Spitfire is not known.

UPWOOD

Canberra B Mk2 WH723, allocated the maintenance serial 7628M but wearing the ficticious serial WJ642 and the markings of No.35 Sqn who once flew Canberras from here, stood guard between April 1960 and at least November 1977 during which time the station was principally the Supply and Administrative Officers training school. The aircraft eventually went to the Proof and Experimental Establishment on Foulness Island and has almost certainly succumbed by now.

Meteor NF(T) Mk14 WS774, maintenance serial 7959M but not worn, had also taken up guard duties by July 1974 and remained until at least 1979. This aircraft moved to the gate at RAF Hospital Ely where she still remains.

UXBRIDGE

Spitfire PR MkXIX PM651 is reported to have been guarding here in July 1954 but this directly conflicts with a reported sighting of her as the gate guard to Hucknall; her subsequent history is unclear until she arrived at Benson but see reports of time spent at Andover, Church Fenton, and Leconfield as well as Hucknall.

Spitfire F Mk22 PK624, wearing the fictitious serial WP916 (a Chipmunk) was reported guarding here in 1961. This aircraft subsequently spent time at Northolt and North Weald before becoming a long-term gate guard at Abingdon.

Spitfire LF XVI RW382 in April 1984 shortly before it was repainted as NG-C of No.604 Sqn. *(J. A. Simpson)*

Spitfire LF MkXVIe RW382 arrived from Leconfield in April 1973 and became a more permanent gate guard. It was originally coded 'Q-31' but this was later removed. By April 1988 the aircraft had been re-coded 'NG-C', markings it carried whilst flown by No.604 (County of Middlesex) Sqn R AuxAF. On 26 August 1988 the aircraft was removed and became the property of HFL at Audley End who are currently restoring it to flying condition on behalf of a U.S. owner.

VALLEY

Vampire T Mk11 XE874 arrived from No.27 MU at Shawbury in the mid-1970s and became the gate guard at this Anglesey airfield. Apart from the odd time when it formed part of the station's static display at air displays it remained on show until late 1989. It suffered the fate of many other gate guards when as part of the one gate guard policy it was put up for disposal; it was subsequently purchased by a Scottish collector.

Whirlwind HAR 10 XP361 was put on display in mid-1984. It was removed in early 1990 and its fate is not known. It is possibly in use at Valley as a ground instructional airframe.

WADDINGTON

Victor K Mk2 XL189 joined Vulcan XM607 in 1987 as a combined display in recognition of their exploits in the Falklands conflict in 1982, outside the Avionics buildings at the former bomber station near Lincoln. This aircraft was the final southbound airborne tanker when XM607 undertook Black Buck 1, the first bombing mission to the Falkland Islands. In 1989 as part of the one gate guard policy, the aircraft was removed onto the airfield at Waddington and scrapped.

Victor K2 XL189 at a snowy Marham in 1979. This aircraft took part in the 'Black Buck 1' mission to Port Stanley on the night of 30 April/1 May 1982. It carries 55 Sqn markings. *(M.A.P.)*

WATERBEACH

A Spitfire and Hurricane stood guard together here from at least August 1957 until September 1961 when the station closed to be subsequently occupied by the Army. Both aircraft were painted silver overall without markings except for the Spitfire which carried its serial underwing only. Hurricane F MkIIc, rebuilt from components including LF751, was moved on to Bentley Priory where she spent a long period on guard, and Spitfire F Mk22 PK664 was moved to Binbrook where again she spent a long period mounted on a pole near the main gate.

Spitfire LF MkXVIe TE392 is reported to have replaced the two aircraft in September 1961 but no further reports are to hand. This aircraft subsequently guarded Kemble and Credenhill.

WATTISHAM

Three Spitfires have guarded this Suffolk fighter station over the years; LF MkXVIe TE311 and PR MkXIX PS853 have both been reported at some stage but actual dates are not known. TE311 is in the hands of the RAF Exhibition Flight at Abingdon, while PS853 is currently airworthy with the Battle of Britain Memorial Flight.

Spitfire F MkVb EP120, veteran of many combat missions which saw it shoot down at least six enemy aircraft, arrived following use in the Battle of Britain film. It was displayed outside the Officers Mess in a dubious two-tone brown colour scheme and carrying the code 'QV-H' of No.19 Sqn. The station had a policy of only displaying the aircraft outside during the summer months but nevertheless they had to give it up in 1989 as part of the MOD's new policy towards its veteran aircraft. It currently resides in storage at St Athan.

WEETON

Meteor F Mk4 RA449, wearing her maintenance serial 7221M and the markings of No.611 Sqn R AuxAF, stood guard at this Lancashire technical training station between at least March 1963 and 1966 when the site closed.

Also reported as being present during 1964 was Spitfire F MkXIV MT847 but further details are not known.

Hunter F Mk5 WP147 is another aircraft reported to have been used as a gate guard here in 1963, but again details are not known.

WELLESBOURNE MOUNTFORD

Spitfire LF MkXVIe TE392, wearing the fictitious serial VZ477 and the code 'JF-O', is reported as the gate guard at this Warwickshire training school in 1952. She subsequently guarded a variety of other stations — Waterbeach, Kemble and Credenhill.

WEST KIRBY

Spitfire F MkVb BM597, wearing the unusual marking '3140D', is reported to have stood guard at this former RAF station in the Wirral but the dates are not known.

WEST MALLING

Spitfire PR MkXIX PS915 is reported to have been used as the gate guard from August 1957 at this Kent fighter station. Further details of its service at this station are not known but it eventually became the gate guard at Brawdy and is now airworthy with the Battle of Britain Memorial Flight.

WEST RAYNHAM

Three Spitfires are reported to have been used as gate guards at this Norfolk airfield. PR MkXIX PS853 arrived following use by the fledgling Battle of Britain Flight at North Weald in May 1958 and departed in August 1961 with the CFE to Binbrook; it is now airworthy with the Battle of Britain Memorial Flight. This aircraft was replaced by F Mk22 PK664 the following month which remained until sometime the following year; it eventually became the gate guard at Binbrook remaining there for many years. Finally, No.1 Sqn had their own gate guard/ squadron mascot whilst based there flying Hunters in the late 1960s; this aircraft, Spitfire F Mk21 LA255, is still owned by them, but is now at Wittering.

WILMSLOW

Spitfire F MkVb EP120 was the gate guard at this Cheshire MU but the actual dates are not known.

WYTON

Canberra B Mk6 RC WT305 was one of three versions of this aircraft to have been used as gate guards. The aircraft served for many years with No.51 Sqn in whose markings it was displayed. It took up gate guard duties in November 1976 and as part of the one gate guard policy was scrapped in November 1989, although its nose was saved by a Derby owner.

Another Canberra which suffered the same fate was PR Mk7 WH773. This aircraft, which was the prototype PR7, ended its days with No.13 Sqn at Wyton in whose markings it was displayed from June 1981 to November 1989. It was also removed in late 1989, and is now near Gatwick.

YATESBURY

Gloster F9/40 DG202, the progenitor of the Meteor, stood guard at this Wiltshire technical training school beside the main A4 Bath road between at least March 1958, when she wore her maintenance serial 5758M, and February 1960 when she was wearing DG202 and her prototype marking. Such an historic aircraft was preserved from the scrapman and is now in the famous prototypes collection within the Cosford Aerospace Museum.

Venom NF Mk3 WX905, wearing her maintenance serial 7458M and the markings of No.23 Sqn, had taken over guard

Gloster F9/40 DG202 in February 1960 showing the aircraft after a repaint into its true serial. *(C. P. Russell-Smith)*

duties from DG202 by November 1961 and is assumed to have remained there until the camp closed in 1962. This aircraft has survived; for many years it was held at the RAF Museum reserve store at Henlow. It is now reported to be with the Newark Air Museum at Winthorpe.

Javelin FAW Mk1 XA553 was also reported to have stood guard here in 1961 but further details are not known.

SELECTED INDIVIDUAL HISTORIES

BEVERLEY C Mk1 XH124 RAF MUSEUM HENDON

Built at Brough by Blackburn as part of second production batch.

1–4–57 made first flight
30–4–57 ready for collection
1–5–57 to 27 MU, RAF Shawbury
5–57 to 30 Sqn, RAF Dishforth, coded 'G'
21–5–59 to 84 Sqn, Aden on loan
1–8–59 to 30 Sqn
21–10–59 30 Sqn to Nairobi, Belgian Congo relief work
7–61 30 Sqn to Bahrain, Kuwait Crisis
12–3–62 to Dishforth for wing reskinning
30–8–62 to 30 Sqn
1–9–64 30 Sqn to RAF Muharraq
16–12–64 to 32 MU, RAF St Athan for refurbishment
? to 242 OCU, RAF Thorney Island
2–3–67 to 47 Sqn, RAF Abingdon
4–4–67 to 27 MU, RAF Shawbury for storage
14–6–68 to RAF Abingdon for 50th Anniversary of RAF air display
19–6–68 last flight to RAF Hendon (last fixed wing aircraft to land there). 4,478 flying hours
20–6–68 SOC, became 8025M displayed outside RAFM
12–89 put up for disposal.

CANBERRA B6 MOD WT305

Built at Preston by English Electric to Contract 6/Acft/5786.

11–5–55 ready for collection at Salmesbury
16–5–55 to 33 MU, RAF Lyneham, storage
6–5–57 to 192 Sqn, RAF Watton
25–6–58 to Boulton Paul
26–6–58 to English Electric for mods
16–3–59 work complete
25–3–59 to 51 Sqn, RAF Watton
31–3–61 51 Sqn to RAF Wyton
11–4–73 loan to MOD (PE)
2–4–75 to 51 Sqn, RAF Wyton
15–11–76 non effective stock Cat 5(GI), 8511M
12–76 RAF Wyton gate guard
26–4–87 adopted by Cambridge Girl Venture Scouts
6–11–89 scrapped at Wyton.

HURRICANE IIcb LF738

Built at Langley by Hawkers to Contract L62305/39/c parts 13/19.

29–9–43 ready for collection

29–9–43 to 22 MU, RAF Silloth; store
19–3–44 to 1682 BDT Flt, RAF Enstone, coded 'HU– '
10–4–44 to 22 OTU, RAF Wellesbourne Mountford, coded 'LT– '
23–9–44 22 OTU disbanded, probably joined Station Flight
7–45 ground instructional, RAF Biggin Hill, 5405M
19–9–54 on display as gate guard to Biggin Hill
74 to No.71 MU, RAF Bicester for rebuild
2–84 to RAE Society Medway Branch for restoration.

LIGHTNING F1a XM144

Built as part of first production batch at Preston by English Electric Co.; construction number 95040.

14–3–60 first flight at Warton
30–9–60 to 74 Sqn, RAF Coltishall, coded 'J'
6–61 re-coded 'G'
9–63 to 226 OCU, RAF Coltishall, coded 144
29–9–64 Cat 3 wheels up landing at Coltishall
17–6–65 to 33 MU, RAF Lyneham for storage
4–7–66 to 60 MU, RAF Leconfield, became 'Golden Arrow' and used as station hack between 12–67 and 5–68
5–68 to RAF Wattisham TFF, coded 'B' named 'Jinx'
8–69 renamed 'Felix'
8–71 to RAF Leuchars TFF, coded 'X'
4–72 to 23 Sqn, Leuchars
4–73 to Leuchars TFF
7–74 non-effective airframe, became a surface decoy at Leuchars
5–78 became gate guard at Leuchars, as 74 Sqn 'J'
9–89 replaced by Phantom FGI, appeared at Leuchars Battle of Britain air display, immediate future unknown.

LIGHTNING F3 XP748

Built at Salmesbury; 30th F3 built; construction number 95176.

4–5–64 first flight, retained by English Electric
4–8–65 to 56 Sqn, RAF Wattisham, coded 'M'
31–5–67 56 Sqn to RAF Akrotiri
16–7–69 to 60 MU, RAF Leconfield for major servicing
29–2–70 to 111 Sqn, RAF Wattisham, coded 'G'
3–11–72 to 11 Sqn, RAF Binbrook, coded 'P'
31–3–75 last flight (2,252.20 hours)
5–75 Binbrook store
9–76 allocated to Binbrook for display, 8446M painted in 5 and 11 Sqn colours
6–88 Binbrook closed, aircraft to Pendine Ranges, Wales.

LANCASTER B VII NX611

Built at Longbridge by Austin Motors, first production B VII.

4–45	ready for collection
16–4–45	to 38 MU, RAF Llandow for storage
19–12–45	to Longbridge for tropical mods
2–46	to 38 MU
31–5–51	to Woodford for maritime mods; ASV & Lifeboat
5–52	to 38 MU with new serial WU-15 for French Navy
6–52	to 24 Flotille, Esc de Servitude 55S, Lann Bihoue
62	to Le Bourget for refurbishment by UTA
11–62	to Esc 9S, Noumea in New Caledonia
8–64	acquired by HAPS, Biggin Hill and flown to Bankstown Airport, Sydney, for storage
25–4–65	aircraft left Sydney for UK
13–5–65	arrived at Biggin Hill
6–5–67	air test following refurbishment, flown by Neil Williams, re-serialled NX611 civilian registration G-ASXX
19–5–67	to RAF Scampton for 24th anniversary of Dams Raid
11–68	HAPS wound up, NX611 sold to Reflectaire
30–3–69	to Lavenham, Suffolk
7–2–70	to Hullavington
26–6–70	to Squires Gate, Blackpool (last flight) for display
4–72	sold by auction to Lord Liford of Nateby. Offered to RAF Scampton as a replacement for R5868
8–73	over nine-day period Scampton engineers moved aircraft from Blackpool to Scampton for restoration
10–4–74	gate guard at Scampton as 'YF-C', Guy Gibson's aircraft
5–88	moved by road to East Kirby.

LANCASTER I R5868

Built at Trafford Park by Metropolitan Vickers, assembled at Woodford.

20–6–42	ready for collection
29–6–42	to 83 Sqn, RAF Scampton, coded 'OL-Q'
8/9–7–42	first Operation, to Wilhelmshaven
15–8–42	83 Sqn to RAF Wyton
14/15–8–43	last Operation with 83 Sqn (77th)
8–43	to 467 Sqn RAAF, Bottesford, coded 'PO-S'
27/28–9–43	first Operation with 467 Sqn
10–43	loaned to 207 Sqn, RAF Langar, coded 'EM- '
11–10–43	207 Sqn to RAF Waddington
3–44	after about 88 OPS marked up 'No enemy plane will fly over the Reich territory' — words of Goering
3–8–44	to Avro, Woodford for refurbishment
17–11–44	work complete

3–12–44 to 467 Sqn, coded 'PO-S'
23–4–45 137th and last OP., to Flensburg, 795 hrs 25 min on OPS, 466 tons dropped
23–8–45 to 15 MU, RAF Wroughton for storage
16–3–56 struck off charge
59 to RAF Scampton as gate guard, 7325M, into 83 Sqn colours
24–11–70 to 71 MU, RAF Bicester for refurbishment
12–3–72 to RAF Museum, Hendon, into 467 Sqn colours 'PO-S'.

METEOR NF(T)14 WS792

Built at Baginton by Armstrong Whitworth to Contract 6/Acft/6412.

8–3–54 ready for collection
11–3–54 to 8 MU, RAF Little Rissington
10–1–57 to 33 MU, RAF Lyneham
2–1–58 to 27 MU, RAF Shawbury
4–2–58 to 33 MU, RAF Lyneham
4–3–60 to 12 MU, RAF Kirkbride; converted to NF(T)14
8–4–60 to 2 ANS, RAF Thorney Island, coded 'K'
14–1–62 to 1 ANS, RAF Stradishall, coded 'K'
12–12–62 Cat 3 accident
31–12–62 repaired by 71 MU
1–1–63 to 1 ANS
19–1–66 to 5 MU, RAF Kemble
8–3–66 non-effective stock
19–6–67 2 S of TT, RAF Cosford for GI, 7965M
? Cosford Aerospace Museum
13–4–77 RAF Carlisle as gate guard
21–9–89 sold by auction to a Scottish buyer.

METEOR T7 WL360

Built at Hucclecote as part of Contract 6/Acft/6066.

21–4–52 ready for collection
22–4–52 to 215 AFS, RAF Finningley
31–10–52 to 210 AFS, RAF Tarrant Rushton
5–11–53 flying accident, repaired by Glosters
12–1–54 to 210 AFS, RAF Tarrant Rushton
13–4–54 to 211 AFS, RAF Worksop
6–12–54 Cat 4 flying accident, to 20 MU, RAF Aston Down
3–3–55 to Flight Refuelling Ltd at Tarrant Rushton for trials
4–4–57 to 20 MU, RAF Aston Down
23–5–57 to RAF Wattisham Station Flight, on charge of 56 Sqn
1–4–59 to 1 Sqn, RAF West Raynham as a hack
17–12–59 to 229 OCU, RAF Chivenor, coded 'G'
13–9–66 struck off charge (3,017 hours)

13–9–66 to 1 Radio School, RAF Locking as gate guard
30–11–89 up for disposal.

METEOR NF(T)14 WS788

Built at Baginton as part of Contract 6/Acft/16412 CB5(b).

26–2–54 ready for collection
3–3–54 to 8 MU, RAF Little Rissington
6–7–54 to 152 Sqn, RAF Wattisham, coded 'Z'
15–8–57 to 12 MU, RAF Kirkbride for storage and conversion to NF(T)14
15–5–59 to 2 ANS, RAF Thorney Island, coded 'C'
17–1–62 to 1 ANS, RAF Stradishall, coded 'C'
17–2–64 Cat 3 accident
18–2–64 for repair by 71 MU on site
25–2–64 work complete
26–2–64 to 1 ANS, coded 'C'
6–1–66 to 5 MU, RAF Kemble
8–3–66 non-effective stock
5–6–67 to RAF Patrington for display, 7967M
9–67 RAF Patrington gate guard, coded 'JHW'
74 to RAF Leeming as gate guard, in 68 Sqn colours, coded 'P'
82 refurbished on site, became 'WS844:JCF' of 264 Sqn
3–88 moved by Chinook onto airfield and put up for disposal
10–89 to Yorkshire Air Museum for permanent display.

SPITFIRE LFXVIe SL674

Built at Castle Bromwich as part of Contract B1981687/39; dated 1 Feb 1944.

26–7–45 ready for collection
26–7–45 to 29 MU, RAF High Ercall
1–4–46 to 17 OTU, RAF Silverstone, coded 'AY-A'
23–10–46 to 6 MU, RAF Brize Norton
7–8–47 to 501 Sqn, RAF Filton, coded 'RAB-R'
4–9–48 Cat C flying accident
29–9–48 to 34 MU, Mountford Bridge (Stoke Heath) for repair
8–11–48 to 501 Sqn
29–4–49 to 612 Sqn, RAF Dyce, coded 'RAS-H', later '8W-H'
17–7–51 to 9 MU, RAF Cosford as station hack
13–9–54 to RAF Biggin Hill as gate guard, 8391M
21–4–70 RAF St Athan for refurbishment
8–6–70 to Biggin Hill gate
86 to RAF Abingdon for refurbishment
87 to Biggin Hill gate
3–89 to RAF St Athan for storage (replaced by plastic replica).

SPITFIRE F21 LA226

Built at South Marston.

9–1–45	first flight at South Marston
21–2–45	ready for collection
22–2–45	to 33 MU, RAF Lyneham
7–3–45	to 91 (Nigeria) Sqn, RAF Manston, coded 'DL-E'
13–4–45	first Operational sortie
3–8–45	emergency landing at RAF Fairwood Common
17–1–46	to 122 Sqn, RAF Dalcross, coded 'EB-F'
1–4–46	122 Sqn renumbered 41 Sqn, RAF Wittering
4–12–47	to 43 Group
15–12–47	to 9 MU, RAF Cosford as non-effective stock
13–10–48	Cat B damage
3–3–49	to South Marston for repair
1–12–49	to 33 MU, RAF Lyneham for store
30–9–51	to 3 CAACU, Exeter, coded 'E'
18–1–54	to 2224 ATC Sqn, Albrighton, 7119M
?	to 9 MU, RAF Cosford
9–2–58	to RAF Little Rissington for display by CFS
67	to RAF Henlow for the Battle of Britain film, used for spares
19–11–68	to Vickers Ltd at South Marston for display
1–6–72	on display at South Marston
13–7–76	on display at Vickers House, London
6–10–77	to South Marston
84	to RAF Biggin Hill as gate guard, replaced Hurricane II LF738
4–88	to 27 MU, RAF Shawbury for storage.

SPITFIRE F22 PK664

Built at South Marston as part of 11th production order for MkIXs.

17–11–45	first flight at South Marston by P. Ayerst
5–12–45	to 39 MU, RAF Colerne
14–3–47	to South Marston for mods
21–3–47	mods complete
25–6–47	to 33 MU, RAF Lyneham
11–5–49	to 615 Sqn, RAF Biggin Hill
16–5–49	to RCMSU
29–8–49	Cat C accident at RAF Sylt, repaired on site
14–12–50	to 33 MU, RAF Lyneham (officially retired)
2–2–51	to Airwork General Trading at Gatwick for refurbishment
29–6–51	work complete
2–7–51	to 9 MU, RAF Cosford
16–6–53	to 33 MU, RAF Lyneham, non-effective airframe
4–2–54	to Vickers for trials with Griffon 85 and Contra-Rotating props

8–54 to RAF Waterbeach as gate guard
9–61 to RAF West Raynham as gate guard; replaced PS853
62 to RAF Binbrook as gate guard in 615 Sqn colours coded 'VG-B' then later in 1969 'V6-B'
89 to 19 MU, RAF St Athan store.

SPITFIRE F22 PK624

Built at South Marston as part of Contract B981687/39, dated 2 June 1943.

22–11–45 first flight at South Marston
21–12–45 to 33 MU, RAF Lyneham for storage
5–12–46 to Vickers at Eastleigh for mods
6–47 to 6 MU, RAF Brize Norton
26–8–48 to No.614 (Co. of Glamorgan) Sqn R AuxAF, RAF Llandow, coded 'RAU-A'
4–9–50 downgraded to sqn hack
31–10–50 to 6 MU, RAF Brize Norton for store
17–1–51 to Airwork General Trading at Gatwick for refurbishment
25–3–51 noted coded 'WY-A' (541 Sqn), at Gatwick, reason unknown
24–7–52 to 9 MU, RAF Cosford, for storage
4–2–54 to Vickers for resale
57 return to RAF charge, to North Weald Station Flt, used by 604 (Co. of Warwick) Sqn as hack
11–57 grounded, became North Weald gate guard
9–62 to RAF Uxbridge as gate guard (Hillingdon gate) serialled 'WP916'
63 to RAF Northolt as gate guard, in correct serial
68 underwent restoration by 71 MU, 8072M
23–7–70 to RAF Abingdon as gate guard, put into 614 Sqn markings as 'RAU-T'
16–3–89 removed from gate, put into store at Abingdon, moved to RAF St Athan, future uncertain.

SPITFIRE LFXVIe SL542

Built at Castle Bromwich as part of Contract B1981687/3, dated 1 Feb 1944.

18–7–45 to 9 MU, RAF Cosford
30–8–45 to 595 Sqn, RAF Fairwood Common
3–7–47 Cat 3 accident
24–11–47 repaired by 34 MU, RAF Stoke Heath
27–11–47 to 595 Sqn, RAF Pembrey
28–7–48 to 695 Sqn, RAF Horsham St Faith, coded '4M-N'
11–2–49 695 Sqn renumbered 34 Sqn, coded '8Q-Z'
7–12–50 to 1 CAACU, RAF Hornchurch
11–6–51 to 29 MU, RAF High Ercall
1–3–54 to 2 CAACU, RAF Little Snoring

1–4–55 to RAF Duxford Station Flight
31–1–57 Cat 3 accident
31–5–57 to 5 MU, RAF Kemble, reclassed Cat 5
58 noted RAF Duxford as gate guard (silver c/s)
? to RAF Horsham St Faith as gate guard
? to RAF Coltishall as gate guard on closure of Horsham
85 refurbished at Coltishall as '4M-N', 8390M
12–88 to 19 MU, RAF St Athan for storage, eventually replaced in 1989 by plastic replica Hurricane.

SPITFIRE LFXVIe TE476

Built at Castle Bromwich, was fifth last LFXVI built.

30–6–45 to 39 MU, RAF Colerne, for storage
19–10–49 to 33 MU, RAF Lyneham, for storage
4–7–51 to 1 CAACU, RAF Hornchurch, coded 'D'
30–9–56 to 5 MU, RAF Kemble, non-effective airframe 7451M
17–1–57 to 32 MU, RAF St Athan, prepared for Royal Tournament
7–57 Royal Tournament
18–12–57 restored to flying status
1–3–58 to both North Weald Station Flight and Biggin Hill Station Flight. This was start of BBMF
16–5–58 to Martlesham Heath Station Flight
10–9–59 minor flying accident
14–9–59 to 11 Group Comms Flt, Martlesham Heath, Battle of Britain Flight
5–1–60 struck off charge
31–1–60 Cat 5 (Exhibition) to RAF Neatishead as gate guard
6–2–67 to RAF Henlow for the Battle of Britain film, restored to taxiable aircraft and became N3311 'AI-B'
24–4–70 to 5 MU, RAF Kemble for refurbishment
2–6–70 to RAF Northolt as gate guard, 8071M
76/77 refurbished
89 allocated for rebuild to flying condition.

SPITFIRE LFXVI TB252

Built at Castle Bromwich as part of Contract D981687/39, dated 19 April 1944.

6–1–45 to 9 MU, RAF Cosford
2–45 to 84 GSU, RAF Thruxton
1–3–45 to 329 (Free French) Sqn, B.85 Schijndel, coded '5A- '
8–3–45 to 411 RSU for repair
15–3–45 to 341 (French) Sqn, B.85 Schijndel, coded 'NL- '
29–11–45 to 135 Wing
15–1–46 to 350 (Belgian) Sqn, 145 Wing, B.152 Fassberg coded 'MN- '

15–10–46 to 151 RSU for repair
29–5–47 to 61 OTU
18–1–49 to RAF Old Sarum
27–2–53 to 33 MU, RAF Lyneham for disposal, 7257M
13–8–55 to RAF Odiham for ground instructional, 7281M (ntu)
21–9–59 to RAF Acklington as gate guard coded 'RR-M'
14–7–69 to RAF Boulmer as gate guard, 8073M
5–12–69 to RAF Leuchars as gate guard coded 'GW-H, Lucky Nine' 340 Sqn
4–86 to RAF Bentley Priory as gate guard, replaced SL574
9–11–88 to Tim Routsis for restoration to fly.

SPITFIRE PR XIX PM651

Vickers built at Eastleigh to Contract AIR/1877/C23(c), dated 2 June 1943.

27–11–45 to Civilian Repair Depot, RAF White Waltham for long store
31–7–47 to M.L. Aviation
30–9–47 to 6 MU, RAF Brize Norton
15–1–51 to Airwork General Trading, Gatwick, for refurbishment
23–5–51 work complete
25–5–51 to 6 MU, RAF Brize Norton
15–3–54 to Temperature and Humidity Flt (THUM), RAF Woodvale
14–4–54 Cat 3 accident at Woodvale
15–4–54 to Home Command as a display aircraft
16–7–54 struck off charge at RAF Benson; 7758M
7–54 to RAF Hucknall as gate guard
6–69 to RAF Andover as gate guard (probably not taken up)
69 static extra in Battle of Britain film as N3329 AI-S N3317, N3320 DO-N
71 travelling exhibit with 71 MU, RAF Bicester
71 to RAF Benson as gate guard
12–89 allocated to RAF Museum.

SPITFIRE LFXVIe RW382

Built at Castle Bromwich as part of Contract B1981687/39, dated 20 Jan 1944, 15th order for FXVI.

20–7–45 to 6 MU, RAF Brize Norton for storage
1–4–47 to 604 (Co. of Middx) Sqn R AuxAF, RAF Hendon, coded 'NG-C'
28–3–49 604 Sqn to RAF North Weald
14–4–50 to 33 MU, RAF Lyneham, for storage
12–6–51 to 3 CAACU, Exeter Airport, coded 'A'

17–10–51 to Control and Reporting School, RAF Middle Wallop, coded 3L8-?
14–7–53 to 45 MU, RAF Kinloss
28–7–53 to 29 MU, RAF High Ercall
14–12–54 declared non-effective stock
28–11–55 to 609 (Co. of W. Riding) Sqn R AuxAF, RAF Church Fenton, as ground instructional airframe, 7245M sometime displayed as gate guard, 'M7245'
59 to RAF Leconfield as gate guard, initially as M7245 then as RW729:DW-X (610 Sqn colours)
67 to RAF Henlow for Battle of Britain film wore N3314, N3316, N3320, 'AI-G', 'DO-L', 'DO-M', 'EI-G'
5–12–69 to RAF Leconfield as gate guard
19–5–70 to 5 MU, RAF Kemble, for refurbishment
6–7–70 to Leconfield
4–4–73 to RAF Uxbridge as gate guard, returned to RW382: Q-31 8075M
4–88 as 'NG-C' of 604 Sqn
26–8–88 to Vintage Fabrics for restoration to flying condition.

VAMPIRE T11 XD382

Built at Christchurch as part of Contract 6/Acft/8981; construction number 15229.

11–10–53 ready for collection
11–10–53 to 10 MU, RAF Hullavington
11–11–53 to 208 AFS, RAF Merryfield
5–12–53 to 206 AFS, RAF Oakington
1–6–54 206 AFS became 5 FTS
14–12–56 Cat 3
21–12–56 repairs started by De Havilland
30–1–57 work complete
31–1–57 to 5 FTS
6–2–57 to Marshalls for mods
12–6–57 to 10 MU, RAF Hullavington for storage
29–7–59 to 5 MU, RAF Kemble for storage
24–9–59 to RAFC Cranwell, coded '38'
6–12–61 to CNCS, RAF Shawbury, coded 'L'
17–8–62 to De Havilland for mods
15–10–62 to CNCS (later became CATCS)
15–7–68 to 27 MU, RAF Shawbury, non-effective stock
13–8–68 struck off charge Cat 5 (GI), 8033M
68 to RAF Syerston for fire practice
69 to Shawbury for display
30–5–69 Shawbury gate guard in all-red colour scheme
75 refurbished into standard Training Command colours
21–9–89 auctioned for £6,500, now in Yorkshire.

BIBLIOGRAPHY

A book of this nature requires a vast amount of cross-referencing of information and research, therefore many other publications and books were read to try to achieve total accuracy.

RAF Squadrons, C. G. Jefford. Airlife, 1987.
The Squadrons of the RAF, James J. Halley. Air Britain, 1980.
Hawker Hunter, R. Jackson. Ian Allan, 1982.
Hawker Hunter: the Operational Record, R. Jackson. Airlife, 1989.
Hunter Squadrons, R. L. Ward. Linewrights, 1985.
Hawker Hunter: Biography of a Thoroughbred, F. K. Mason. Stephens, 1981
Harrier, F. K. Mason. Stephens, 1983
The Squadrons of the FAA, R. Sturtivant. Air Britain, 1984.
Wrecks and Relics Vol. 9, 10, 11, K. Ellis. MCP, 1984, 1986, 1988.
Fighting Colours, M. J. F. Bowyer. PSL, 1969.
Military Aircraft Markings, P. R. March. Ian Allan (Various).
British Military Aircraft Serials 1878–1987, B. Robertson. MCP, 1987.
USAF Serials 1946–1977, Merseyside Aviation Society, 1977.
Euromil, SeeFive Publications, 1984.
Italian Military Aviation, F. Mcmeiken. MCP, 1984.
Warbirds 33 V Bombers, Bob Downey. A&AP, 1985.
BAC Lightning, Arthur Reed. Ian Allan, 1980.
EE/BAC Lightning, B. Philpott. Stephens, 1984.
Military Airfields of Oxfordshire, M. J. F. Bowyer. PSL, 1988.
Action Stations 1, M. J. F. Bowyer. PSL, 1979.
Action Stations 5, C. Ashworth. PSL, 1982.
Action Stations 8, B. B. Halfpenny. PSL, 1984.
Action Stations 10, Bruce Quarrie. PSL, 1987.
V Bombers, R. Jackson. Ian Allan, 1982.
Shackleton, John Chartres. Ian Allan, 1985.
Avro Vulcan, Andrew Brookes. Ian Allan, 1985.
Gloster Meteor, C. Bowyer. Ian Allan, 1985.
British Fighters since 1912, Peter Lewis. Putnam, 1979.
Fighters of the 50s, Bill Gunston. PSL, 1981.
Beverley, C. Hobson. A. W. Hall Publications.
Meteor, B. Philpot. PSL, 1986.
Meteor — Glosters First Jet Fighter, S. J. Bond. MCP, 1985.

Ely's Night Fighter, Paul Smooker.
Gloster Meteor NF11-14, Derek James.
Falklands — The Air War, Various. A&AP, 1988.
Aircraft of the RAF since 1918, Owen Thetford. Putnam, 1979.
Avro Vulcan, R. Jackson. PSL, 1984.
V Force, Andrew Brookes. A&AP, 1982.
Gloster Javelin, M. Allward. Ian Allan, 1983.
Buccaneer, M. Allward. Ian Allan, 1982.
British Service Helicopters, Gardner/Longstaff. Hale, 1985.
Canberra, Beaumont/Reed. Ian Allan, 1984.
Canberra, R. Jackson. Airlife, 1988.
The Typhoon/Tempest Story, Thomas/Shores. A&AP, 1988
British Military Training Aircraft, R. C. Sturtivant. Haynes, 1987.
The Spitfire Story, Alfred Price. A&AP, 1982.
Spitfire Survivors Around the World, Riley/Trout. Aston, 1986.
Tempest and Seafury, R. Jackson. Blandford, 1989.
Aircraft Markings of the World 1919–1967, B. Robertson. Harleyford, 1967.
Lancaster: Story of a Famous Bomber, B. Robertson. Harleyford, 1967.
Spitfire: the History, Morgan/Shackleton. Key Publications, 1987.
Spitfire: Story of a Famous Fighter, B. Robertson. Harleyford, 1973.
RAF Aircraft Serials WA100–WZ999, Air Britain, 1983.
RAF Aircraft Serials SA100–VZ999, Air Britain, 1985.
British Military Aircraft Serials:
XA100–XA999, P. Jackson. A. W. Hall.
XB100–XB999, P. Jackson. A. W. Hall.
XD100–XD999, P. Jackson. A. W. Hall.
On Guard, Ken Ellis. Merseyside Aviation Society, 1978.
Squadron Histories, Peter Lewis. Putnam, 1968.
Aircraft Profile No. 208 F4 Phantom, P. St John Turner, Profile Publications, 1972.
Aircraft Camouflage and Markings 1907–1954, B. Robertson. Harleyford, 1966.
British Military Aircraft Serials and Markings, BARG, 1980
De Havilland Vampire, Venom, Sea Vixen, Philip Birtles. Ian Allan, 1986.
Sepecat Jaguar, Arthur Reed. Ian Allan, 1982.
British Museum Aircraft, Ellis/Butler, Merseyside Aviation Society, 1977.

PUBLICATIONS

Aviation News. A. W. Hall.
Scale Aircraft Modelling. A. W. Hall.
Airfix Magazine. PSL.
Flypast. Key Publications.
Aeroplane Monthly.
Air Pictorial.
Aircraft Illustrated.
Air International.
Air Enthusiast.
Aero Militaria.
Military Aviation Review.
Scale Models International.
Wing Span.
RAFAS Quarterly.
Intercom.
Airmail.
Navy News.
RAF News.
Warbirds Worldwide.
Wings.
Air Strip.